FIELDS OF PLAY

FIELDS OF PLAY

(CONSTRUCTING AN ACADEMIC LIFE)

LAUREL RICHARDSON

RUTGERS UNIVERSITY PRESS

NEW BRUNSWICK, NEW JERSEY

Library of Congress Cataloging-in-Publication Data

Richardson, Laurel.

Fields of play : constructing an academic life / Laurel Richardson.

p. cm.

Includes bibliographical references and index.

ISBN 0 – 8135 – 2378 – 8 (cloth : alk. paper).—

ISBN 0 – 8135 – 2379 – 6 (pbk. : alk. paper)

1. Sociology—Authorship. 2. Authorship. 3. Feminist theory.

4. Feminist criticism. 5. Richardson, Laurel. 6. Women

sociologists—United States—Biography. I. Title.

HM73.R53 1997

808'.066301—dc20   96 – 16174

CIP

British Cataloging-in-Publication information available

Manufactured in the United States of America

To Ernest Lockridge

Contents

Part 3: Fielding Ethics

Part 4: Writing Legitimacy

Part 5: Remapping Fields

Part 6: Arriving Where We Started

ACKNOWLEDGMENTS

WITHOUT the support for this project from my husband, Ernest Lockridge, it would not have been completed. He has been a true "helpmeet," and my gratitude is deep and abiding. He has read every chapter many times, discussed issues with me, and been an unfailing and loving companion through the process of "undisciplining" my academic life.

My dearest friend, Betty Frankle Kirschner, I thank for two decades of unflinching support for my ventures and for two decades of affection, laughter, and common sense. Gratitude, too, for the wealth of experiences provided me and the genuine kindness I felt from the family in which I grew up: my parents, Rose Foreman Richardson and Tyrrell Alexander Richardson; my brother, Barrie Richardson; my sister, Jessica Richardson Phillips; and my brother-in-law, John F. Phillips.

When my sons, Ben Walum and Josh Walum, were young, they never complained about the time I spent on academic work. Now, as adults and my friends, they never fail to ask me how my writing and my life are going. I am genuinely appreciative of the love they shower on me and on their families, which have graced and expanded my life: Tami Walum, Shana West, Suzanne Roberts, Adam Roberts, Aaron Roberts, and Akiva Walum-Roberts. Other family members have helped in different ways. I thank them, too: Ellen Lockridge, Sarah Lockridge, Vernice Lockridge Noyes, Ben Phillipps, Laurel Lockridge Woods, and Michael Woods.

Two colleagues, now friends, have been especially generous with their expertise, time, and support. Carolyn Ellis has read many drafts of my work, commented on them readily, and provided me with a trusty confidante. Norman K. Denzin has encouraged my work through invitations to conferences and symposia, through valuable critiques, and through his ready kindness. Both of them have spent considerable time doing the work of editing journals and collections that make possible a remapping of sociological inquiry. I cannot thank these "colleague-friends" enough for their roles, generally, in marshaling resources for building alternate community and, specifically, in encouraging my writing explorations.

The beneficent critiques of members of the Women's Poetry Workshop—Ellin Carter (facilitator), Molly Davis, Gay Hadley, Margaret Honton, Meg Hoskins, Liz James, Micki Seltzer, Kezia Sproat, Anne Sostrom, Cathy Tucker, and Kay Wolf—have been most helpful. I especially thank Ellin Carter for her more than two decades of leadership of the workshop and Molly Davis for special support and critical readings. The members of my Feminist Post-Modern Studies (PMS) reading group—Eloise Buker, Suzanne Damarin, Gisela Hinkle, Nancy Johnson, Marilyn Johnstone, Kaybee Jones, Patti Lather, Mary Leach, Linda Meadows, Amy Shuman, Jane Snyder, Patricia Stuhr, Amy Zaharlich—have been a continuing source of inspiration and growth. I am grateful to them all. Special gratitude to Eloise Bucher, Gisela Hinkle, Patti Lather, Mary Leach, and Amy Shuman for discussions and critiques of parts of this book; to Nancy Johnson for rhetorical advice; and to Jane Snyder for providing the Greek transliteration and English translation of the Heraclitus fragment. I also thank my Cakes for the Queen of Heaven group and Sociologists for Women in Society (SWS) for their nurturance.

Over the years, I have been fortunate in having smart, nice, and creative graduate students with whom to work. I thank all of them for their contributions to my academic life. For this book, I especially thank Mary Margaret Fonow and Judith A. Cook, who have read and commented on this manuscript; Amber Ault, who has carefully critiqued earlier chapter versions; Carla Corroto, who has lent her skills to cover design; and Elizabeth St. Pierre, who has written an extensive analysis of this book and has been a invaluable aid in the rewriting process. Institutional and collegial support from a variety of sources has been invaluable to my work over the years. I thank the Ford Foundation; The University of Chicago; National Science Foundation; National Institute of Health; National Institute of Education; Ohio Department of Health; Project on Rhetoric of Inquiry, University of Iowa; Denison University; California State University–Los Angeles; University of Colorado; and New Mexico State University. In addition, within the aid of various academic units within The Ohio State University this book could not have been written.

These include the College of Humanities, the College of Social and Behavioral Sciences (for research leave support), the Department of Sociology, the Cultural Studies Program–School of Educational Policy and Leadership in the College of Education, and the Department of Women's Studies.

Many others have provided guidance, help, or support along the way. My Ph.D. adviser, Edward Rose, modeled a life of academic independence and creativity. David Citino and Deena Metzger provided writing opportunities and professional criticism. Many were there at just the right time, even if they may not have known it: Patti and Peter Adler, Ben Agger, Joan Albrecht, Mitch Allen, Elizabeth Bell, Blue, Arthur Bochner, Richard Brown, Patricia Ticento Clough, Arlene Kaplan Daniels, Bronwyn Davies, Deanna Dennis, Marilyn Faulconer, Michael Flaherty, Andrea Fontana, Clifford Geertz, Shelia Harnett, Susan Krieger, Patricia Lynch, Maxwell, Susan Ritchie, Frank Rivas, Larry Reynolds, John Stewart, Barrie Thorne, and John Van Maanen. I am appreciative of and grateful to them all.

Three years before I had written this book, I put a note in the "Projects" section of my Daytimer. I said I wanted to write a book that put my academic writing in contexts and that I wanted to publish it with Rutgers University Press. I liked and respected Marlie Wasserman, at the time editor in chief. I knew then that I liked the books in the Rutgers line and wanted mine to be one of them. But I didn't know how easy, professional, and gracious the actual process would be. I am, therefore, more than grateful to my editor, Leslie Mitchner, for so quickly giving me a positive reading and so ably shepherding the book through the press. All the staff have been unfailingly helpful and generous: managing editor Marilyn Campbell; marketing director Steve Maikowski; designer Karolina Harris; copy editor Grace Buonocore. I thank all of them.

Some of the writing in this book I have published in different forms in other venues. Grateful acknowledgment is made to those journals and presses: *Sociological Focus*, *Journal of Contemporary Ethnography*, *Current Perspectives in Social Theory*, *Studies in Symbolic Interaction*, *Symbolic Interaction*, *Sociological Theory*, *The Sociological Quarterly*, *Qualitative Inquiry*, *Chicago Review*, and Sage Press for *Investigating Subjectivity: Research on Lived Experience* (edited by Carolyn Ellis and Michael Flaherty) and *The Handbook of Qualitative Research* (edited by Norman Denzin and Yvonna S. Lincoln). (See References for complete citations.)

I would also like to thank the following for permission to reproduce materials for which they hold copyrights: Ernest Lockridge, for coauthoring "The Sea Monster: An Ethnographic Drama and Comment on Ethnographic Fiction," *Symbolic Interaction* (1991): 335 – 341; T. S. Eliot, "Little Gidding" (four lines) from *Four Quartets*, p. 145 in *Collected Poems and Plays* (Harcourt Brace, 1950), used by permission from Harcourt Brace for U.S.A. rights and by permission from Faber & Faber for worldwide rights.

Finally, I acknowledge the importance of places and landscapes to my work and my life. My backyard, Shenandoah, Sedona, Lake Michigan, the Park of Roses, Las Cruces. I thank the many who have planted trees, wildflowers, and roses; built trails and preserved open fields; conserved the past for new beginnings.

AUTUMN EQUINOX   LAUREL RICHARDSON
September 21, 1996   *Worthington, Ohio*

FIELDS OF PLAY

INTRODUCTION

We shall not cease from exploration
and the end of all our exploring
will be to arrive where we started
and know the place for the first time.
                                    T. S. ELIOT

Fields of Play: Constructing an Academic Life applies the sociological imagination to the act of writing. How do the specific circumstances in which
we write affect what we write? How does what we write affect who we become? These are timeless and timely questions. The culmination of ten years
of works in progress, *Fields of Play* pursues these questions, theoretically and
concretely.

The text is pleated, an interplay of essays and papers, written over a ten-
year period, accompanied by "writing-stories" about their production, written
now, from a fixed point in time. Exploring time, I write about the contexts and
pretexts of "texts." I contextualize my claims to knowledge and my changing
sense of self within disciplinary politics, academic departmental constraints,
social movements, community structures, and personal history and longings.

The sociological rests in the intersection between the biographical and the
historical. Sociologists routinely turn their gaze to the lives and times of others; they are less prone to see themselves as social and cultural products, producing social and cultural products. Like the Alpha-Pluses in Aldous Huxley's
Brave New World, at least in attitude, many act as if they are suspended over
their own field, above it all.

My work in sociology has cut against the grain. My 1963 dissertation
showed how the putatively "purest" of knowledge systems, "pure" mathemat-

ics, depends on an "impure" matrix of social organization and political patronage. Work in the 1970s challenged androcentric assumptions and sexist work practices in social science. Feminist-poststructuralist work in the 1980s ruffled ethnography, interpretive sociology, and feminist theory. Now, I bring a critical sociological gaze to my own work and my life. I write critical ethnographies of the self. I do unto self as I have done unto others.

We are restrained and limited by the kinds of cultural stories available to us. Academics are given the "story line" that the "I" should be suppressed in their writing, that they should accept homogenization and adopt the all-knowing, all-powerful voice of the academy. But contemporary philosophical thought raises problems that exceed and undermine that academic story line. We are always present in our texts, no matter how we try to suppress ourselves. Powerfully entrenched academics, threatened by this poststructuralist turn, pressure those "beneath them" to conform to nineteenth-century notions of academic writing. Thus, we work in a highly complex period: On the one hand poststructuralism calls us to greater play, reflexivity, and ethical responsibility about our writing. On the other, the institutions that hire us may adhere to older canons of writing practices. How, then, do we write ourselves into our texts with intellectual and spiritual integrity? How do we nurture our own voices, our own individualities, and at the same time lay claim to "knowing" something? My hope is that hearing about my intellectual and emotional struggles with "authority" and with "my place" in my texts, academic department, discipline—my life—will be of value to others who are struggling with their "place."

Standing back from my life/work I see myself more objectively, more as an object, yet I write more subjectively, more personally. I am more aware of myself as both product and producer, object and subject. Although I view writing as a process of discovery, and although I believe that feminist research must change the researcher, I am startled by what I discover about this feminist researcher. The process of writing this book has transformed my identity: The "sociologist" has become a "writer."

What were the practices that enabled this transformation? My engagement with the theoretical concepts of feminist poststructuralism—reflexivity, authority, authorship, subjectivity, power, language, ethics, representation—led me to question the grounds of my own authority and the ethics of my own practices as a sociologist. I could no longer write in science's omniscient "voice from nowhere." I was mute, but I knew I was "somewhere."

Experimenting with textual form, I wrote sociology as drama, responsive readings, narrative poetry, pagan ritual, lyrical poetry, prose poems, and autobiography. Experimenting with voice, I coauthored with a fiction writer, played second theorist to a junior scholar, turned colleagues' words into dramas. Experimenting with frame, I invited others into my texts, eliding the oral and the written, constructing performance pieces, creating theater. Troubled with the ethical issues of doing research "on" others, I wrote about my own life. And, troubled by academic institutions, I began to discover more agreeable pedagogical, writing, and communal practices, and multiple sites and alternative spaces.

In the beginning the experiments were less volatile, less personal, more content oriented. I write about narrative, science writing, literary devices, fact/fiction, ethics. But after so much "telling," I wanted to "show." I used alternative forms of representation: drama, performance pieces, poetry, and finally, alighting on an old form (dating from Seneca in the West to Sei Shonogan in the East), the personal essay, but making it my own, writing both against and within its conventions.

"Vespers," the last essay in this book, is a deeply felt personal essay, a narrative about my life that grew out of the ethical resolution to "study" myself. Although it is profoundly sociological—and I could not have written it had I not been a sociologist—sociology concepts are nowhere to be read. "Vespers" was "literature," and I submitted it to my alma mater's literary journal, *Chicago Review*. The journal accepted it; the editor called me a "writer."

What I learned about writing methods and about myself I have recently applied to my earlier writings, contextualizing and personalizing them, making it all new for the first time, re-visioning my life and work. The reframing process displaced the boundaries between two genres: "selected writings" and "autobiography." *Fields of Play* repositions them as convergent genres that, when intertwined, create new ways of reading/writing that are more congruent with poststructural understandings of the situated nature of knowledge making. In the new convergence, we become writers, tellers of stories about our work—local, partial, prismatic stories. Writing is demystified, writing strategies are shared, and the field is unbounded.

The book's title—*Fields of Play*—found me. A name must bear, as Coleridge said, all its connotations. *Fields of Play* has multiple connotations topologically embedded in parallel and intersecting discourses. The "fields" are sociology and ethnography and theory and gender, and the settings in which those are done. "Fields" are where ethnographers go; and I am the "field," which I never leave. The "field" is also a battleground, a minefield, a war zone, as well as an open, inviting expanse, as well as a place where "energy" converts to "matter." In this book, I "play" as a child plays; "play" is my work. I enjoy the process. I am also a "player," in three other senses: a participant in the ongoing academic debates, a performer, and a writer of dramas.

Sometimes I invert (subvert?) the book's title and call it "playing the field." I "play the field" in multiple ways. Like a horse-race tout who isn't committed to a winner, I bet on a lot of less well known ponies. But I also "play the field" in a teasing, happy sort of way—messing with its boundaries, planting roses here and there, pulling up turf, defusing mines, setting up picnic tables, taking them down, feeding the birds, making trails between gardens and the pits.

When I grew up, most "boy play" was rule bound, teamed, competitive, while most "girl play" was flexible, solo or cooperative, grounded in (real or imagined) everyday life, like playing with dolls. If a man was "playing the field," the image might be of an outfielder putting another guy out or, missing a catch, losing the game. Either way, the fielder would be a member of a team in competition with another team. But if a woman was "playing the field," she'd be "playing the boys," unwilling to settle down, pick, choose permanency.

I am a woman writing. I have struggled with my relations to my university and my discipline. (Is there an academic woman who hasn't?) Joining the men's team, competing on their playing field, playing against other teams, following demeaning, mean, penny-licking rules—all of these—do not enhance my work or my life. Poststructuralist thinking, though, has helped me, now— as feminism did two decades ago—by offering a more level playing field and more of them, where everyone can pick or plant roses today, play with dolls or play outfielder tomorrow, create new games, new convergences, new "fields of play."

Constructing this book was simultaneously intuitive and systematic. As I work, I put my papers and essays in the chronological order in which they were conceptualized. I read them, sorting them into "keeper" and "reject."

Then, I reread my first keeper, "The Collective Story." After reading it, I write a writing-story about the disjunction between my departmental life and my disciplinary reputation. From there, I work systematically, chronologically through the keeper pile. Rereading and then writing the writing-story evoked by the rereading. Different facets, different contexts. Some stories require me to check my journals and files, but most don't. Some stories are painful and take an interminable length of time to write, but writing loosens their shadow hold on me.

Carolyn Heilbrun suggests that we don't imitate lives, we live "story lines." The process of rereading one's work and situating it in historical and biographical contexts reveals old story lines, many of which may not have been articulated. Voicing them offers the opportunity to rewrite them, to renarrativize one's life. Writing stories about our "texts" is thus a way of making sense of and changing our lives.

The questions *Fields of Play* poses—how context affects our writing and how our writing affects our selves—are complex and multilayered. It raises questions about finding or creating spaces that support our writing so we can keep writing, developing a care for the self, despite conflict and marginalization. It engages in a conversation about the ethical subject's relation to research practices. It talks about the integration of academic interests, social concerns, emotional needs, and spiritual connectedness.

I like the form of my writing to "tell," "signal," "display," "be" what it claims to talk about, but I also believe texts should be accessible. Thus, *Fields of Play's* structure displays the complex, multilayered nature of the issues (it "shows" what it "tells"), while making that complexity less dense, abstract, and neutral. Writing-stories prove of major use. Each writing-story illuminates a different facet of the complexity of a writing-life—departmental politics, teaching, feminism, communities, disciplines, friends, family, husband. Like a crystal, the refraction on the article depends upon the angle of repose.

Selections and writing-stories are intertwined. Sometimes the writing-story precedes and sometimes it follows a selection, depending on whether knowing the context (e.g., a symposium) would help, rather than restrict, the reading. Sometimes stories both precede and follow an essay. I call the "writing-stories," then, either "Forewords" or "Afterwords." Writing-stories and selections stand independently of each other and can be read selectively or in any sequence. Most important to me in the construction of this book, though, has been my desire that the writing form a narrative that reaches — for now — toward resolution in "Vespers."

The story of a life is less than the actual life, because the story told is selective, partial, contextually constructed and because the life is not yet over. But the story of a life is also more than the life, the contours and meanings allegorically extending to others, others seeing themselves, knowing themselves through another's life story, re-visioning their own, arriving where they started and knowing "the place for the first time."

PART 1 TROUBLING THEORY

.
.
.
.
.
.
.
.

FOREWORDS: AUTHORITY

I BEGIN this collection, and my reflections on it, at the time when I found a different way of "playing the field," of exploring its boundaries and possibilities, and my life within it. This was the mid-1980s. No more children living at home; no major medical or family crises; a husband who liked to cook; friends; completion of a major research project and book tour; academic sinecure; and severe marginalization within my sociology department, which relieved me of committee work and of caring about outcomes. For the first time in my adult life, I had free time, playtime, time I could ethically and practically call "mine."

Like a medieval warlord who executes or banishes all who might pose a threat to his absolute authority, my newly appointed department chair deposed the three other contenders for the position, all men, from their "fiefdoms," their committee chairships. He stonewalled written complaints or queries. He prohibited public disagreement by eliminating discussion at faculty meetings. He abolished one of the two committees I chaired, the "Planning Committee," a site of open dialogue. He restricted the departmental Affirmative Action Committee's province, which I also chaired, to undergraduate enrollments. I publicly disagreed with him on his new affirmative action policy. Then, at the first university Affirmative Action Awards dinner, where I was being honored, surrounded by top university administration, my face making a face, repulsed, I shrugged his arm off from around my shoulder.

The chair hired a consultant, a well-known functionalist, to review faculty vitae. The consultant declared me "promising"— the chair told me as one might tell a student, not the full professor I was—but the consultant had also declared "gender research" a "fad." The chair advised me to return to medical sociology, a field I was "in" during a one-year postdoctorate, ten years earlier. Research it, teach it, he advised, teach it now, at the graduate level. He may have already had me down to do it. He discarded ten years of my research, teaching, and service, it seemed. I told him I strongly disagreed with his plans for my academic future. Perhaps it was only coincidental that sometime later that same year at the annual departmental banquet, hitherto a lighthearted gathering of colleagues and friends, the visiting consultant, now hired as an after-dinner speaker, lectured for an hour about why people, in the interests of smooth institutional functioning, should yield to authority.

I was on quarter break, out of town, when the department chair's secretary called to tell me that the chair had added an extra undergraduate course to my teaching schedule for the next quarter, a week away. My stomach cramped in severe pain. No, I said, I absolutely will not accept this assignment. I was adamant, unyielding. I telephoned the new dean, a sociologist and putative feminist, who would soon be elevated to provost. Her "best advice" to me — on this and subsequent matters — was to "roll over." I refused. She then taught the course herself, in my place. Rather than pull rank on the chair, a man, she modeled "rolling over." It was a course on the sociology of women.

I felt no gratitude to her. I had wanted protection, for my colleagues as well as for myself, from a chair's punitive and arbitrary actions. Instead, she presented herself in my place, as the sacrificial lamb. The clear message, it seemed to me, was that if she, the dean of the college, was willing to sacrifice herself, so should we all. Her action legitimated the chair's right to do anything he wanted.

My new chair was empowered to micromanage all aspects of "his" department's life, even to the point of dictating a senior colleague's intellectual life. Any refusal to "roll over" precipitated punitive action in salary, in what one could teach and when, in virtual exile to Coventry. Thus in the mid-1980s, I experienced what has, by the mid-1990s, become an experience common to faculty members of American colleges and universities: "Total Quality Management" in pursuit of "Excellence."

Many departmental colleagues understood that, like the chair's previously conquered opponents, I had become dangerous to associate with, dangerous even to know. In their minds I had brought it upon myself, which of course I had.

As I write these paragraphs, my stomach swells and hurts just as it did then.

Terminally bored with standard sociology, and particularly with the subspeciality of gender's capture by the "sex is a variable in a log-linear equation" crowd, I was also going through a major intellectual crisis. I was questioning the entire sociological enterprise—its paradigms, desires, culture, methods, institutional arrangements, customs, and forms of writing. I was questioning the grounds on which sociology claimed authority. My feelings of alienation manifested themselves in writing paralysis. I didn't know what to write about, how to write it, or for whom. I feared I would never be able to write again.

In 1987, I was elected president of the North Central Sociological Association. Propitiously, my main duty would be to give a presidential speech in 1988. I would have to say "something"; and I wanted to say "something" *important*. Typically, a presidential speech reviews the speaker's career; I wanted to make sense of my career history and shaky future. Working on the speech propelled me out of my departmental woes and intellectual crisis. It solidified my concerns with politics, ethics, and writing practices. It plunged me headfirst—the heart was to follow—into an intellectual community of like-minded scholars, who were troubling the holds of paradigmatic authority on their disciplines. I learned that there were academics everywhere questioning the grounds of their own authority, their representational practices, the boundaries of their disciplines, and the social practices within departments that reproduced unyielding authority structures. These people— authors I had never met and probably never would—were my "real" colleagues. I no longer felt quite so alienated.

I had no idea, then, that the writing/presenting of my presidential speech, "The Collective Story: Writing a Postmodernist Sociology," would launch me on the career-altering, life-transforming venture embodied in this collection. I only knew that I gave the speech I needed to hear. Rereading the speech and thinking about it now confirm my faith in the transforming possibilities of writing of and for one's life. I wonder, as I write this first "Forewords"—a "writing-story"—how the writing of this book will transform me yet again.

THE COLLECTIVE STORY

PRESIDENTIAL ADDRESS,
NORTH CENTRAL SOCIOLOGICAL ASSOCIATION

At the 1987 American Sociological Association Meetings in Chicago, colleagues asked me the conventional convention question — our functional equivalent to "How are you?"—namely, "What are you working on?" Instead of responding ("Fine") by enumerating my projects in progress, I heard myself saying, "I don't know *what* I want to write about, *how* I want to write it, or *who* I want to write it for." The heresy just popped out. Nevertheless, my answer did not reflect only a temporary lapse of sensibility, a moment of unorthodoxy that would soon pass. Rather, these concerns with the writing of sociology are issues I have struggled with throughout my professional career. I embrace them now as priorities for myself and for the future of sociology: *What* do we write about? *How* do we write it? And for *whom* do we write?

My speech this afternoon will reflect my penchant for mingling the personal, the political, and the intellectual. I will first talk about "what to write about" and "how to write it" as postmodernist problems. I will defer the question of "for whom do we write" until the latter part of my speech, where I reflect upon my own writing decisions and processes.

We ply our sociological craft within — not above — broader historical, social, and intellectual contexts. Today, the dominant intellectual context challenges all "grand theory" and all claims for a singular, correct style for organizing and presenting knowledge. Lacking a totalizing vision, the contemporary intellectual context lacks a name of its own. The period is defined not by what it is but by what it comes *after*. It is variously called post-paradigmatic — postmodernism, post-Marxism, poststructuralism, postpositivism — some even say, postfeminism. Characteristic of this period is the loss of authority of "a general paradigmatic style of organizing research" (Marcus and Fisher 1986, 8). Ideas and methods are freely borrowed from one discipline to another, leading to a "blurring of genres" (Geertz 1980). A totalizing vision is replaced by concerns with contextuality, exceptions, indeterminants, and the meanings to participants. Even the totalizing vision that feminism created is now being reassessed by feminists as we critique that vision as being, itself, contextually created, a product primarily of privileged women in a social movement which has glossed over meaningful differences in the experiences of differently situated women.

The loss of grand theory has affected all disciplines, although their responses have differed. In literary criticism, literature is aesthetically equivalenced. All texts can be "deconstructed" so that Dickens and Tolstoi, for example, are no better writers than their deconstructors. In law, the Critical Legal Studies Movement abrogates the legal reasoning model (Livingston 1982). In philosophy, the principles of uncertainty and contextuality undermine the possibility of universal systems of thought (Rorty 1979). In physics and mathematics, the focus is on the inelegant, the disorderly, indeed, even "chaos" (Gleick 1984). In sociology and the other social sciences, the critiques of grand theories have dislodged their hegemony; sociological production, like other human productions, is seen as socially produced (cf. Fiske and Shweder 1986).

When there is no dominant paradigm, indeed, when the very grounds upon which paradigms can be considered valid are themselves subject to contextualization and indeterminacy, scholars face what Marcus and Fisher (1986, 8) refer to as a "crisis in representation": uncertainty about what constitutes adequate depiction of social reality. When scholarly conventions are themselves contested, politics and poetics become inseparable and neither science nor art stands above the historical and linguistic processes (Clifford 1986, 2). As a result, the growing edges of the intellectual-sociological enterprise have shifted. Attention is focused on epistemology (cf. Cook and Fonow 1986; Fonow and Cook 1991; Fiske and Shweder 1986), interpretive understanding (DiIorio 1989; Mischler 1986), and the discursive forms of representation themselves (cf. Becker 1986; Long 1987; Krieger 1983; Stewart 1989; Clifford and Marcus 1986; Strathern 1987). Our commonsense understanding of method is extended to include epistemological assumptions, on the one hand, and the writing process on the other.

How in the midst of this ferment and uncertainty do we prevent a paralysis of intellect and the will to work? Why do any intellectual work at all? But, conversely, "Why not?" We can be caught in the infinite regress of deconstructionism, where nothing is better than anything else, but we can also be drawn to infinite expansion. When there is a crisis of representation we are freed from the intellectual myopia of hyperdetermined research projects and their formulaic write-ups, what Thomas S. Kuhn has termed "normal science" (1962). We can turn uncertainty to our advantage; we can be more sociologically imaginative in our thinking, apprehending, and writing of the social world. We can, as C. Wright Mills (1959, 195) proposed, resist the "codification of procedures" stratagem for developing theory and methods and get on with the "exchange of information about . . . actual ways of working."

SCIENCE AND LITERATURE

At this historical point, I have chosen to think about my sociological work as telling what I term *the collective story*. A collective story tells the experience of a sociologically constructed category of people in the context of larger sociocultural and historical forces. The sociological protagonist is a collective. I think of similarly situated individuals who may or may not be aware of their life affinities as coparticipants in a collective story. My intent is to help construct a consciousness of kind in the minds of the protagonists, a concrete recognition of sociological bondedness with others, because such consciousness can break down isolation between people, empower them, and lead them to collective action on their behalf.

People make sense of their lives, for the most part, in terms of specific events, such as the birth of a child, and sequences of events, such as the life-long impact of parenting an injured child. Most people do not articulate how sociological categories such as race, gender, class, and ethnicity have shaped their lives or how the larger historical processes such as the Depression or the Women's Movement have affected them. Erik Erikson (1975) contends that only great people, people who see themselves as actors on the historical stage, tell their life stories in a larger social and historical context. Yet, as C. Wright Mills (1959, 5) cogently argued, knowledge of the social context leads people to understand their own experiences and to "gauge . . . [their] own fates"; this is the promise of the "sociological imagination." What sociologists are capable of doing is to give voice to silenced people, to present them as historical actors by telling their collective story.

The notion of sociological writing as allegorical goes contrary to received wisdom about the separation of the literary from the scientific. From the seventeenth century onward, Western science has rejected "rhetoric (in the name of 'plain' transparent signification), fiction (in the name of fact), and subjectivity (in the name of objectivity)" (Clifford 1986, 5). Rhetoric, fiction, and subjectivity were located in "literature," a new historical construction, aesthetically pleasing but scientifically ridiculed. Literature was denied truth value because it "invented" reality rather than observing it. Dependent on the evocative devices of metaphor and imagery, literature could be interpreted in different ways by different readers. Worse, "the narrating is always multi-vocal—it says one thing to illuminate something else" (De Certeau 1983, 128). Literature violates a major pretension of science: the single, unambiguous voice.

Science was to be written in "plain style," in words that did not, in John Locke's estimation, "move the Passions and thereby mislead the Judgment," unambiguous words unlike the "perfect cheats" of poetic utterances (quoted in Levine 1985, 3). The assault on poetic language intensified throughout the eighteenth century. Locke urged parents to stifle poetic tendencies in their children. David Hume depicted poets as professional liars. Jeremy Bentham proposed that the ideal language would be one without words, only unambiguous symbols. Samuel Johnson's dictionary sought to fix "univocal meanings in perpetuity, much like the univocal meanings of standard arithmetic terms" (Levine 1985, 4). The search for the unambiguous was "the triumph of the quest for certainty over the quest for wisdom" (Rorty 1979, 61).

Such was the attitude toward language when the Marquis de Condorcet introduced the term "social science" (Levine 1985, 4). Condorcet contended that with precise language about moral and social issues "knowledge of the truth" would be "easy and error almost impossible" (quoted in Levine 1985, 6). Emile Durkheim affirmed the need for sociology to resolutely cleanse itself of everyday language. Max Weber urged the construction of ideal types as a way to achieve univocity—the single voice of science. By the nineteenth century, intellectuals divided knowledge into two parts: literature and science. Literature was a bourgeois institution aligned with "art" and "culture." Given to literature were the "higher values" of taste, aesthetics, ethics, humanity, and morality as well as the privilege to be experimental, avant-garde, multivocal, transgressing (Clifford 1986, 6). Given to science was the belief that its words were objective, precise, unambiguous, noncontextual, nonmetaphoric.

This historical separation between literature and science does not imply an immutable schism. Historical implies human construction. What humans construct, they can reconstruct. And, indeed a plethora of disciplines—communications, linguistics, English criticism, anthropology, folklore, women's studies, as well the sociology of knowledge, science, and culture—has been engaged in reconstructive analyses. Their analyses show that literary devices appear in all writing, including scientific writing. All works use such rhetorical devices as metaphor, image, and narrative which affect how ideas are formed, how field notes are taken, how survey questions are phrased, how the work is written up, and how readers make sense of it. "Literary devices are inseparable from the telling of 'fact'" (Clifford 1986, 4).

Once we fully recognize this, it seems to me, we can lay claim to some of the "higher values" that were historically given to literature. We can lay claim to a *science* that is aesthetic, moral, ethical, moving, rich, and metaphoric as well as avant-garde, transgressing, and multivocal. We no longer need give up our humanity for the illusion of objective knowledge.

METAWRITING ISSUES: METAPHOR AND NARRATIVE VOICE

If we give up the ill-fitting conceit that our sociological concepts are precise, their referents clear, and our knowledge unambiguous, we are met with an interesting question: the *writing* of sociology. The final solution to the writing problem is not the extermination of jargon, redundancies, passive voice, circumlocution, and (alas) multisyllabic conceptualization referential indicators.

How we choose to write raises two metawriting issues: guiding metaphor and narrative voice. Our choices are simultaneously political, poetic, methodological, and theoretical.

Writing exists in the context of an implicit guiding metaphor that shapes the narrative. We have an implicit "story which we tell about the people we study," a story that is itself historically rooted (E. Bruner 1986, 2). Edward Bruner's analysis of the scientific discourse about Native Americans is highly instructive in this regard. In the 1930s and 1940s, the social scientific narrative of Native American social change viewed the present "as disorganization, the past as glorious, and the future as assimilation." Now, there is a new implicit narrative; "the present is viewed as a resistance movement, the past as exploitation, the future as ethnic resurgence" (4). With great rapidity, the guiding concepts of assimilation and acculturation have been replaced with the concepts of exploitation, oppression, liberation, colonialism, and resistance.

The shift in story was more than a theoretical shift; it was a shift in syntax and politics. As science is the child of metaphor, metaphor is the child of politics. For the acculturation story, the writing problem was the description of past culture. Indian life had no future, and the present was interpreted in light of this futurelessness as pathology and disintegration. The political action consistent with this metaphor was to send Native American children to Anglo boarding schools, to create urban relocation projects, to undermine tribal tradition. For the contemporary resistance narrative, however, the writing problem concerns the future: the resistance of indigenous people to exploitation in their struggle to preserve ethnic identity. The writing describes the resistance in the present to preserve the past for the future. Political action consistent with this narrative is intervention to prevent cultural genocide.

Analogous implicit narrative shifts have occurred in the collective stories of other groups of people. Within American society, certain sociologists have positioned blacks, women, gays and lesbians, the aging, and ethnics within a liberation narrative. And we have extended the liberation narrative to Third World countries, no longer conceptualizing them as "developing," a metaphor that implies their current inferiority but their eventual future as Western clonettes. Instead, the notion of ethnic nationalism is gaining ascendancy. The implicit liberation narrative is consistent with liberation movements. Indeed, the outstanding success of feminist scholarship across disciplines arises from its explicit link to the feminist movement, a continuity of purpose between research and activism, namely, the empowerment of women.

The second metawriting issue is the narrative voice. Who is telling the story? The researcher? The researched? Both? Postmodernist critique challenges the grounds for authority in the writings of positivists as well as phenomenologists, measurers as well as ethnographers, because it rejects dichotomizing the "knower" and the "known." In scientific writing, authority has been accomplished through the "effacement of the speaking and experiencing" scientists (Pratt 1986, 32). Neither "I" nor "we" are used. With no apparent narrator, an illusion of objectivity is created. The implied narrator is godlike, an all-knowing voice from afar and above, stripped of all human subjectivity and fallibility. But, in fact, science does have a human narrator, the camouflaged first person, hiding in the bramble of the passive voice. The scientist is not all-knowing. Omniscience is imaginary, possible only in fiction.

Ethnographies have depended upon two forms of authority: the personal experience of the ethnographer in the field and the presumed objective, factual report. Rather than fusing the two forms of knowledge into one, the ethnographer's first-person account is separated from the objective account. Personal experiences, anxieties, and fears are marginalized, written about in introductions, appendices, memoirs, and "reflections" sections of qualitative journals.

Contemporary concern with the narrative voice problem has led some social scientists to what is termed "experimental writing," writing social science in nontraditional ways. Experimental writing includes the use of multiple voices, split pages with the storyteller's account filling one column and the analyst's another, and the writing of "true fiction" (cf. Stewart 1989; Marcus and Fisher 1986; Clifford and Marcus 1986; Krieger 1983; Reinharz 1979). But the reasons for experimenting with literary style and genre are not simply to deal with the false dichotomization of subject and object; the writing experimentalists are raising political and ethical questions as well. Separating the researcher's story from the people's story implies that the researcher's voice is the authoritative one, a voice that stands *above* the rest. But because people have differential access to the use of the authoritative voice — and for the most part the people we study have less access than we do — we may unwittingly colonize, overgeneralize, or distort. Further, by objectifying ourselves out of existence, we void our own experiences. We separate our humanity from our work. We create the conditions of our own alienation.

REFLECTIONS

What I choose to write about, how I choose to write it, and for whom I write it say more about me than sociodemographics, personality inventories, or horoscopes. My sociological work has been the analysis of power inequalities; my activism, the challenge of those inequalities. To do my work, I have consciously chosen to use the liberation narrative. This narrative tells the collective story of the disempowered, not by judging, blaming, or advising them, but by placing their lives within the context of larger social and historical forces and by directing energy toward changing those social structures that perpetuate injustice.

In my recent work (Richardson 1985), I have told the collective story of a particular set of women, namely, single women involved in long-term relationships with married men. Sociologically, their lives had been ignored, their experiences shrouded in secrecy and stigma, and their relationships told about and judged by others, not themselves. I wanted to give voice to this muted group of women: the second sex in a secondary world. I wanted to tell their collective story.

To do this, I first listened to the personal stories of single women involved with married men. I heard how single women got involved, fell in love, and ended their relationships with married men. Although the details of the single women's stories differed, the contours of their experiences were similar. My analytical task was to place their narratives in social and historical context and to discern what in the contemporary world was disempowering them.

In a world where there were not enough eligible men, but where a woman's self-esteem was still embedded in having the love of a man, and in a world where women were urged to achieve autonomy and career success, but where they were expected to put their lover's needs above their own, the tension between achieving both an independent identity and a satisfying intimate relationship was severe. One solution to an untenable situation was a relationship with a married man. Believing that these liaisons would be temporary, single women imagined they would achieve intimacy in them without sacrificing independence. However, because of the relationship's secrecy in conjunction with overarching gender inequalities, the woman ended up caring for her lover more than she had intended. The more she cared about him, the more dependent and less powerful she became, because she carried into the relationship the normative expectations for women in love—personal sacrifice.

I struggled with what to call these women. I finally chose the term "The New Other Woman," or collectively "New Other Women." I consciously chose to claim the label "other woman," but I capitalized it, wresting it from its stigmatized context. The capitalization continually reminds me and my readers that these women are not just "others" in the "some . . . others" grammatical construction: They are a distinct social category worthy of a collective story. The "New" in the name modifying "Other Woman" metaphorically suggests the women's simultaneous embrace of contradictions, modernity and traditionalism. Allegorically, we are reminded of the tensions between the old and the new within all modern societies and within our own psyches, as well. In some ways, we are all Other Women—striving to make a life in a contradictory world, torn between our needs for belonging and independence.

The narrative voice in which to tell their collective story troubled me. I was never able to resolve—nor have I yet—the mare's nest of authorial authority, the dichotomy between the observer and the observed. But if I did not "find" a voice, I feared I would descend into the Prince Hamlet syndrome, frozen by indecision, and—Shakespeare please forgive me—eternally plagued with the question "to write or not to write."

Remembering how C. Wright Mills (1959) grounded issues of "intellectual craftsmanship" in the work process rather than in the codification of procedures, I read sociology for style and voice. I rejected the sociologicaly vérité style, the publication of the interview transcript, because—to modernize Socratic wisdom—the unanalyzed transcript is not worth reading. I rejected the paraphrasing style because it lacked credibility and was boring. I rejected the self-centered reflexive style, where the people studied are treated as garnishes and condiments, tasty only in relationship to the main course, the sociologist.

Struggling with finding my narrative voice, I first wrote a woman's story as a scene in which she and I were two "characters" engaged in dialogue. I used my mini-arsenal of literary devices. I set the scene and established the ambience. I showed the woman's feelings, rather than telling about them. I wrote in concrete detail. I quoted. I gave the women fictitious names that inscribed their "narrative essence." "Lisa Maxwell" used her liaison to get a new lease on life by changing careers, a change that was of maximal value to her. "Michelle

Mitchell" was an avant-garde architect, who used her liaison to explore and to eventually reject heterosexuality as a way of life. "Abby Goodman" was a psychologist who prided herself on her listening ability, her kindness, and her Jewish hospitality. She was duped by her lover. Each woman had her own story, her own chapter, her own analysis. I felt powerful. I felt like a "writer."

But this narrative voice did not work. The format implied that each story represented something different sociologically. Because each story was separately analyzed, I was in fact writing a collection of individual sociobiographies, rather than what I wanted to write, a *collective* story.

My final decision was to organize the research as a unified chronological narrative based on the women's narratives. I typified events and sequences of events, illustrating them through multiple voices and direct quotations. I was trying to simultaneously have the women speak of and for themselves, and for me to speak of and for them, as a sociological analyst. I was constructing a collective story.

Deciding on my narrative voice was more than a literary and theoretical problem. It was a political issue: "Sociology for Whom?"—a question I have had since graduate school. At the defense of my dissertation, *Pure Mathematics: Studies in the Sociology of Knowledge,* a defense attended by a flock of university officials as part of a university-wide evaluation of graduate programs, I was asked, "What do you plan to do now?" Being madly in love with sociology and desiring to communicate that passion to the world, I answered, probably with feeling, "I want to write for the public." A hush fell upon the examiners, and, like an errant child, I was excused from the room while they decided my fate. Despite my heretical answer, I passed. With great seriousness, my responsible, if embarrassed, Ph.D. committee publicly advised me not to "waste my intelligence on people."

Over the years, I have wrestled with identifying the audience I want to write for, temporarily solving the problem, or perhaps absolving myself of my unwitting sins, by writing, alongside abstract articles on science, mathematics, and literature (cf. Richardson [Walum] 1965; Richardson [Walum] 1968; Richardson [Walum] 1975), socially relevant sociology (cf. Richardson [Walum] 1970; Franklin and Richardson 1972; Richardson [Walum] 1974; Kirshner and Richardson [Walum] 1978), gender texts, accessible to students and their parents (cf. Richardson 1988b), and feminist teaching tools such as an anthology, syllabi, and classroom exercises.

But the more my work on single women and married men progressed, the more I found myself saying, as I did in my dissertation defense, "Sociology is for the people." I decided to write words and sentences that could meet a different standard of science and truth: accessibility to lay audiences. Because I wanted the sociological analysis widely disseminated, I chose to write a trade book, working with a publishing house noted for its sociology list (Richardson 1987).

But the writing story does not end here. Telling the collective story of these women has propelled me back into thinking and writing about very large and abstract sociological questions: questions about the sex and gender system and the social construction of intimacy (Richardson 1988a); about the complementariness of symbolic interactionism and feminist theory (Statham, Richardson, and Cook 1991); about how gender interacts with other social characteristics, such as age, race, class, sexual orientation, marital status, and ethnicity—how we are like each other, how we are different; and questions most of all about how to tell *well* the story of people. My image of sociological work now is an ever widening spiral, where I write collective stories that are more and more accessible to more people, and then I write more and more sociologically abstract work directed to professionals, each kind of writing deepening the other.

When I was a preschooler, I would daily ponder the mystery of the Morton salt box, where a little dark-haired girl held a Morton salt box with a picture of a little girl holding a Morton salt box and so on and on and on. Was there ever an ending? As infinite regress riveted my attention in childhood, infinite expansion attracts me now. I welcome the writing of collective stories. I welcome metaphor, imagery, evocative prose. In them, I see the possibility of fulfilling sociology's promise to become a sociology *of* and *for* the people.

Forewords: Palimpsest

I HAD never been to a Society for the Study of Symbolic Inter-action (SSSI) meeting, but the American Sociological Association news-letter listing for the SSSI-Stone Symposium was irresistible. It would be held in mid-March 1989 at the Arizona State University. If my paper was accepted, my family's between-quarter "vacation" would be par-tially underwritten, and I could spend a day with my best friend from fourth grade, Gloria Fenner, now an anthropologist living in Tucson. I hadn't seen her since we were nine, when I visited her in the "country" where she had moved, and where I nearly drowned in a quarry.

But I was most excited about sharing my new work. I was enthralled with the concept of "narrative knowing" as an alternative to "sociologi-cal telling." I saw narrative working in the everyday, autobiographical, biographical, cultural, and collective sense-making of people. My goals were brash: to move narrative to the center of sociology, and to position my work as the axis for "the narrative turn." I wanted my ideas to cir-culate, and I wanted to be cited. I wasn't ready, then, to displace sociol-ogy: I wanted my place within it secured.

As I read the paper now, I am surprised at how certain, imperious, and optimistic I am about narrative's role in sociology and how noncon-sciously I wrote about narrative in the omniscient voice of science. I think I wanted to write the definitive article on narrative, a justificatory summary that would guarantee me citations. I am most surprised at how I masked my feminist-poststructuralist interests and suppressed narratives of my life, my self.

Not since my first paper presentation as a second-year graduate student had I been so anxious. I had conceived that paper grandiosely, too: I thought my work would "bridge the ocean" between American and European sociology of sciences. Robert K. Merton, the discussant, said I was a "craftsman." I felt publicly embarrassed, as though I had fallen off the bridge into the sea, as my adviser feared I might. I did not try to publish the paper. It wasn't until fifteen years later—after my tenure review in which Merton played a positive part—that I discovered he categorized most sociologists as "technicians" and a few, more "talented" ones as "craftsmen."

Wanting sociological confirmation for the new direction of my work and as a balance against my increasing marginalization within my department, I felt that any hint of ridicule, or worse, apathy, would be intolerable. "Good" would be a failure, too, and I would feel shame. My father, though long dead, was—I see now—still directing my relationship to my work. Bringing home all A's on a report card had brought no favorable comment. Why, he reasoned, would you reward that which is routine, expected?

Being a visitor to SSSI—not knowing the norms and actors—intensified my anxiety. Father believed that his children's actions reflected on him. Father's income might be reduced or his political career destroyed because his daughter erred in public dress, demeanor, or deportment. An innocent man might be found guilty because judge or jury lost faith in the man's attorney, my father, and all because of me. To this day I don't wear jeans in downtown Chicago where my father practiced law.

I rehearsed the paper at home, cutting out awkward phrases, sentences that didn't speak well, underlining points of emphasis, noting pause points. I carefully chose my "professional drag." Norman Denzin presented his paper immediately before mine. He was soundly attacked by his colleague-friends for not doing sociology. He was accused of treason. What would happen to me?

But they liked it! The audience clapped loudly and spontaneously, and conferees asked about my provenance. They nodded when I told them I was a University of Chicago undergraduate and an advisee of

Edward Rose at the University of Colorado, as if these biographical details explained my conference presence and my work. My paper's point was similar to Norman's, but mine was gentler in spoken and written style. At the time, I thought that "style differences" explained the differential receipt of our work—Father speaking, again: "You can get away with murder if you polish your shoes." Soon after, I thought they applauded me because I wasn't yet a player in the SSSI field; I was a promising recruit, but maybe only good for the season.

And, I liked these SSSI people, too. There were about fifty of us from thirty universities and several countries. We talked about ideas, hiked in a mountain preserve, and ate southwestern. There was a social ease, an inclusionary attitude. To commemorate the symposium, the organizers (John Johnson and David Altheide) had T-shirts printed with a line drawing of a brain. On the frontal lobe were printed the words "Interaction Happens." Barely visible beneath "interaction" were the tops of the letters "S-H-I-T"—although I only now notice them.

I had happened upon a living, interacting, sociological community that welcomed me and my ideas; I returned to my department ecstatic. I felt triumphant, exonerated, and, most important, identified with a group of sociological practitioners. I chose to ignore that SSSI was a heterogenous organization, male centered with infighting and politics, male-only spaces, and male models of intellectual debate, science, and knowledge. And why wouldn't it be male dominated? It was, after all, a part of the larger sociological world. But my need for full acceptance by a sociological community was too great to be wary or critical. For the while, I did not want to see any "S-H-I-T."

Narrative Knowing and
Sociological Telling .
.
.
.
.
.
.

LIFE histories, informants' oral accounts, in-depth interviews, case studies, historical documents, and participant observation are the major methods used by qualitative researchers. An abundant literature discusses how to gain entrée, ask questions, listen, take field notes, and tape-record. The tapes and notes, however, do not constitute the "findings." Rather, as part of our research agenda, we fashion these accounts into a prose piece; we transform biographical interviews and field notes into a sociological text. Although this stage of the research process requires complex decision making, there is little in the literature about the issues and their resolutions (but see the literature review in Van Maanen 1988).

How should we write our research? The rhetorical, ethical, and methodological issues implicit in this question are neither few nor trivial. Rather, the question reflects a central postmodernist realization: all knowledge is socially constructed. Writing is not simply a "true" representation of an objective "reality"; instead, language creates a particular view of reality. All language has grammatical, narrative, and rhetorical structures that "create value, bestow meaning, and constitute (in the sense of imposing form upon) the subjects and objects that emerge in the process in the inquiry" (Shapiro 1985 – 86, 192).

How we choose to write, then, involves many major and minor rhetorical and ethical decisions (cf. Brown 1977; Nelson, Megill, and McCloskey 1987; Edmondson 1984; Van Maanen 1988; Fisher 1987). By what criteria should we evaluate the writing? Scientific soundness? Aesthetic resonance? Ethical rightness? What are our goals? Who is our audience?

My goal is a modest one: the provision of an argument for the presence and value of narrative within sociology. In the process, I will cover some familiar ground and touch on some new. Although narrative has been rhetorically marginalized, justified within conventional sociology during "exploratory" research or when used as human "filler" to "flesh out" statistical findings, I will argue that narrative is quintessential to the understanding and communication of the sociological. All social scientific writing depends upon narrative structure and narrative devices, although that structure and those devices are frequently masked by a "scientific" frame, which is, itself, a metanarrative (cf. Lyotard 1979). The issue is not whether sociology should use the narrative, but which narratives will be provided to the reader. Can we construct a sociology in which narrated lives replace the narrative of unseen, atemporal, abstract "social forces"?

WHAT IS NARRATIVE?

Narrative displays the goals and intentions of human actors; it makes individuals, cultures, societies, and historical epochs comprehensible as wholes; it humanizes time; and it allows us to contemplate the effects of our actions and to alter the directions of our lives. Narrative is everywhere; it is present in myth, fable, short story, epic, history, tragedy, comedy, painting, dance, stained glass windows, cinema, social histories, fairy tales, novels, science schema, comic strips, conversation, and journal articles. Children everywhere learn how to listen to and tell stories at very early ages. Roland Barthes comments, "The narratives of the world are without number. . . . [T]he narrative is present at all times, in all places, in all societies: the history of narrative begins with the history of [hu]mankind; there does not exist, and never has existed, a people without narratives" (1966, 14).

Narrative is the primary way through which humans organize their experiences into temporally meaningful episodes (Polkinghorne 1988, 1). People link events narratively. "Narrative meaning is created by noting that something is a "part" of a whole and that something is a "cause" of something else" (Polkinghorne 1988, 6). The meaning of each event is produced by its temporal position and its role in a comprehensible whole.

Narratively, to answer the question "What does something mean?" requires showing how the "something" contributed to the conclusion of the episode. To borrow E. M. Forster's classic example, "the king died and then the queen died" are events told in a temporal order, but they do not form a narrative. "The king died and then the queen died of *grief*," however, is a narrative because it relates events by causality, encapsulating a miniplot and addressing the question of "why." In a story "something" happens because of something else. The connections between the events constitute meaning.

Narrative is both a mode of reasoning and a mode of representation. People can "apprehend" the world narratively and people can "tell" about the world narratively. According to psychologist Jerome Bruner (1986), narrative reasoning is one of two basic and universal human cognition modes. The other mode is the logico-scientific. The two modes are irreducible to each other and complementary. Each mode provides a distinctive way of ordering experience and constructing reality; each has its own operating principles and criteria of "wellformedness"; and each has radically different procedures for verification (11). Causality plays a central role in both cognitive modes, but each defines it differently. The logico-scientific mode looks for universal truth conditions, whereas the narrative mode looks for particular connections between events. Explanation in the narrative mode is contextually embedded, whereas logico-scientific explanation is abstracted from spatial and temporal contexts. Both modes are "rational" ways of making meaning.

Not surprisingly, the two modes of reasoning rely primarily on different communication codes to get their messages across, although they borrow freely from each other's codes (Jakobson 1960). The narrative code "demonstrates" narrative reasoning, the type of reasoning that understands the whole by the integration of its parts, whereas the logico-scientific code demonstrates empiricist reasoning, the type of reasoning that "proves" statements. Both modes, however, are framed in metanarratives such as "science," "the enlightenment," or "religion." Narrative structures, therefore, are preoperative, regardless of whether one is writing primarily in a "narrative" or a "logico-scientific" code.

Sociology has constructed its writing practices so that the logico-scientific code is privileged and the narrative code suppressed. It acts as if it were untrammeled by narrative structure and conventions. Hiding behind the metanarrative of "science," conventional social science, however, deploys such master narratives as the impact of "social forces" or the "functional interdependence" of "complex systems." Literary devices flourish within social science, not only for adornment but to carry cognitive meaning. Even when social scientists think they are avoiding literary devices, they are using them.

Narrative is unavoidable; human values, sensibilities, and ambiguities continuously reassert themselves in "plain" social science writing. Narrative cannot be suppressed within sociology because it is ineluctably tied to the human experience; trying to suppress it undermines the very foundations of the sociological enterprise.

TIME AND NARRATIVE

Everywhere, people experience and interpret their lives in relationship to time. Time is the quintessential basis for and constraint upon the human experience. And, everywhere, humans make sense of their temporal worlds through the narrative. Ricoeur's thesis is that the coexistence of the temporal nature of the human being and the activity of narrating a story is not accidental but represents a "transcultural form of necessity" (1984 – 86, 52). Through the narrative, temporality becomes interpretable in human terms. Time is made human; narrative is a condition of temporal experience.

Unlike the clock and calendars that measure out life in moments, days, and years, people do not experience time as a succession of instants, or a linear linking of points in space, but as extended awareness of the past and the future within the present (cf. Husserl 1964). Sometimes, time is experienced as a concordant whole, such as when reading a familiar poem, where the whole piece is experienced despite the fact that some of it has already been read and more is yet to come. Other times, time is experienced as discordant, such as when regret about the past or fear of the future impinges upon the present. This discordance cannot ever be totally overcome because human knowledge includes the knowledge that one's days are numbered. The future always becomes the past. The future is always death.

Narrative, I will argue, provides powerful access to this uniquely human experience of time in five sociologically significant ways: the everyday; the autobiographical; the biographical; the cultural; and what I term the collective story. Although I present these ways as analytically separable, in practice they can overlap and intersect, as for example when an interviewee "tells" his or her autobiography, which the interviewer "writes up" as a biography but "presents" as a part of a more general cultural or collective story.

In everyday life, narrative articulates how actors go about their rounds and accomplish their tasks. The narrative of "what we did today" assumes an experience of time. We "had time to," "we took time for," "we lost time." We organize our days with temporal markers, such as "first," "then," and "after." Our experience of daily time links us to others and to the public world. We meet people at particular times, we get caught in "rush hour" traffic, we watch the "six o'clock news." Social order is sustained through these collaborative efforts of individuals "timing" the logistics of their daily activities. People routinely talk to each other by accounting for how they spent their day—what did you do in school today? What happened at work today? Ethnomethodologists and conversational analysts have been especially attuned to these quotidian accounts, and a large research literature exists based on those perspectives. Few of these researchers, however, have explicitly analyzed and articulated how the individual's narrated experiences of daily time are linked to larger social structures, linking the personal to the public.

Second, autobiographical narrative is how people articulate how the past is related to the present. Events have a beginning, a middle, and an end. The past can be retrieved and relived in the present. Narrative organizes the experience of time into personal historicity. "Autobiography is the highest and most instructive form in which the understanding of life is confronting us" (Dilthey, quoted in Kohli 1981, 63). Telling one's story gives meaning to the past from the point of view of the present and future and "deeply gives meaning to the past in order to give meaning to the present life of the person" (Bertaux-Wieme 1981).

People organize their personal biographies and understand them through the stories they create to explain and justify their life experiences. When people are asked why they do what they do, they provide narrative explanations, not logico-scientific categorical ones. It is the way individuals understand their own lives and best understand the lives of others. Experiences are connected to other experiences and are evaluated in relation to the larger whole. Something does not make sense when it does not "fit in" with the narrative. To make sense of the events in their lives, people reconstruct biographies. The experience of (re)narrativizing, like the experience of biographical time itself, is open ended and polysemous, allowing different meanings and systems of meanings to emerge.

Narrative functions at the autobiographical level to mark off one's own individual existence from all others by its finitude. One's life is separable from others; it has its own beginning and its own ending. But, because of that separation, one can be an integrated whole—a being with its own unique past, present, and future. Narrative, thus, provides the opportunity for the individual to make existential sense of mortality, and, correlatively, through the narrative, the profound experience of mortality becomes sociologically accessible.

Autobiography by historical, popular, and literary figures is a well-established genre. Anthropologists have customarily written autobiographical statements in the margins of their ethnographies or as separate books (for a review of these, see Van Maanen 1988). Although contemporary sensibilities question the purposes and veracity of these tales, especially as they inscribe the ethnographer as the "knower" and the culture of the "other" as a known, they are exemplars of the ethnographer making autobiographical sense of her or his lived experience. More recently, sociologists have begun writing autobiographies and writing narratives about sociology (cf. Ellis 1991a, 1991b; Riley 1988; Reinharz 1979; Linden 1992).

Third, because people can narrativize their own lives, the possibility of understanding other people's lives as also biographically organized arises. So-cial and generational cohesion, as well as social change, depend upon this ability to empathize with the life stories of others. Social interaction depends on actors making sense of others' actions and motivations from the point of view of the others, from their biographical perspective. Social cooperation re-lies upon this human capability, a capability grounded in narrative. But the ability to understand another's biography goes beyond creating an interactionally, presently shared world: Narrative makes possible the understanding of people who are not present. Narrative creates the possibility of history beyond the personal. Contemporaries, predecessors, and successors communicate through the narrative (Schutz 1962). Passing on the biographies of heroes and villains links the generations and shapes the disorderly and chaotic, or boring and repetitive, into a communally shared world of experience. Through the communication of the past to present listeners, contemporary worlds are enlarged and grounded. Social scientists are now adding to the bounty of biographies written by historians, journalists, literary "biographers," and "factual-fiction" writers (cf. Stewart 1989; Deegan 1988).

The cultural story is the fourth way in which narrative is sociologically significant. Participation in a culture includes participation in the narratives of that culture, a general understanding of the stock of meanings and their relationships to each other. The process of telling the story creates and supports a social world. Cultural stories provide exemplars of lives, heroes, villains, and fools as they are embedded in larger cultural and social frameworks, as well as stories about home, community, society, and humankind. Morality and cautionary tales instruct the young and control the adult. Stories of one's "people"—as chosen or enslaved, conquerors or victims—as well as stories about one's nation, social class, gender, race, or occupation affect morale, aspirations, and personal life chances. These are not "simply" stories but are narratives that have real consequences for the fates of individuals, communities, and nations (McClelland 1961).

The cultural story is told from the point of view of the ruling interests and the normative order and bears a narrative kinship to functionalism. Since, for example, the central character in a patriarchal system is the male, a cultural story of "adultery" is about the normative status "marriage" and how an "other woman" tries to "ruin a family" by "stealing a man" from his wife. The central character in this story is the husband, and the story line "blames" the minor characters, the women: the wife for her deficiencies in sex, love, and understanding; the other woman for her deficient morality. This particular cultural story, in the United States, transcends race and class lines, making it seem "true" and giving it a hold on the imaginations of men and women. Cultural stories, thus, help maintain the status quo.

There is, however, a fifth kind of narrative that gives voice to those who are silenced or marginalized in the cultural narrative. I call this narrative the "collective story." The collective story displays an individual's story by narrativizing the experiences of the social category to which the individual belongs, rather than by telling the particular individual's story or by simply retelling the cultural story (cf. Richardson 1988c). There are a multitude of such collective stories in contemporary society. Some of the collective stories arise through social movement activity, such as the civil rights movements, which resist the cultural narratives about groups of people and tell alternative stories. Other collective stories are about people who are not collectively organized. There are the "cancer survivor," "battered wife," "chronic illness," "co-dependent," and "divorce" narratives, to name but a few (cf. Denzin 1987; Maines 1989; Ferraro and Johnson 1983). Although the narrative is about a category of people, the individual response to the well-told collective story is, "That's my story. I am not alone." New narratives offer patterns for new lives. The story of the transformed life, then, becomes a part of the cultural heritage affecting future stories and future lives.

Transformative possibilities of the collective story also exist at the sociocultural level. People who belong to a particular category can develop a "consciousness of kind" and can galvanize other category members through the telling of the collective story. People do not even have to know each other for the social identification to take hold. By emotionally binding people together who have had the same experiences, whether in touch with each other or not, the collective story overcomes some of the isolation and alienation of contemporary life. It provides a sociological community, the linking of separate individuals into a shared consciousness. Once linked, the possibility for social action on behalf of the collective is present, and, therewith, the possibility of societal transformation.

COLLECTIVE STORIES, CIVIC DISCOURSE, AND SOCIETAL TRANSFORMATION

Civic discourse about societal identity, social goals, and societal transformation is largely constituted through social scientific language. The rhetorics of the social sciences identify and shape our social past, present, and future. They are nearly unavoidable in modern societies. At issue, then, is not the presence of social scientific rhetorics, but what kind(s) of social scientific representation do we foster, and with what consequences for whom. The logico-scientific paradigm has dominated public policy, but what might happen to our personal and civic discourses if narrative were valued as a way of acquiring and representing knowledge? The consequences of sociologists consciously attending to narrative structure, I contend, will empower individuals, contribute to liberating civic discourses, and support transformative social projects. Sociologists can give voice to silenced people, presenting them as historical actors by telling their collective stories.

Sociologists tell the collective stories of constituencies to which they may not even belong; this, of course, raises central postmodernist problems about the researcher's authority and privilege. Narrative explanation means that one person's voice — the writer's — speaks for others (Roth 1989, 31). But what are the alternatives? To propose the stilling of the sociologist-writer's voice not only rejects the value of sociological insight but implies that somehow "facts" exist without interpretation. This presupposes a belief in essences and authenticity, a view that carries its own metaphysical and political baggage. Accordingly, "there is no principled resolution, no alternative, to the problem of speaking for others. There is no getting it right about who or what another is; there is no essence defining what 'right' is" (Roth 1989, 31). Narrativizing, like all intentional behavior (including the writing of conventional social science), is a site of moral responsibility. Further, because power differences are always being played out in personal and civic arenas, the most relevant issue, as I see it, is a practical-ethical one: How can we use our skills and privileges to advance the case of the nonprivileged? Telling collective stories is an effective way in which we can do just that, a way in which we can use our "sociological imagination" (Mills 1959) to reveal personal problems as public issues, to make possible collective identity and collective solutions.

Rhetorically, through curricula, grants, honorees, and written exemplars of "core" sociology in "core" sociology journals, the belief that narrative is non-problematic for "practicing sociologists" is reproduced and reconstituted term after term in academic sociology. Yet, as the new rhetoric of the social sciences has made clear, and as this chapter has indicated, rhetorical decisions are constantly being made, often unconsciously, by the practitioners (cf. Nelson, Megill, and McCloskey 1987). We choose how we write. Those choices have poetic, rhetorical, ethical, and political implications.

All social science writing exists in the context of metaphors that shape the narrative. In addition to the deeply burrowed ones, such as the "thingness," "tool," and "management" metaphors of empiricism, there are more easily graspable and evocative guiding stories we tell about the people we study. Many of us work implicitly and explicitly to position Afro-Americans, women, gays and lesbians, the aging, and ethnic groups within a liberation narrative. The implicit liberation narrative is consistent with liberation movements. Social scientists thus have the opportunity consciously to stage their research within guiding narratives that empower those whom they study.

Sociologically grounded narrative, thus, can alter the shape and content of civic discourse by biographically, collectively, and politically enfranchising the previously disenfranchised. Because collective stories — including the ones written by sociologists, including this one — can become cultural stories, petrified and limiting, however, they too should be subject to future resistance and rewriting.

If we wish to understand the deepest and most universal of human experiences, if we wish our work to be faithful to the lived experiences of people, if we wish for a union between poetics and science, or if we wish to use our privileges and skills to empower the people we study, then we should value the narrative. Marginalizing narrative may serve the political interests of entrenched sociological elites, but it does not serve sociology or society.

Forewords:

Something Wonderful

Something wonderful happened on my campus during 1988 – 1989. A dozen or so feminist professors from different disciplines interested in poststructuralist theory found each other. We did not find each other through Women's Studies, which was uninterested in creating faculty-only (i.e., "elitist") reading groups, but through the attendance of some of us in a "mixed" (graduate/faculty) sociology theory group. When the graduate students chose to focus on direct political actions and dismiss the faculty as "academic," faculty decided we needed a room of our own.

Colleague told colleague. We came from education, English, philosophy, sociology, social work, art, music, history, classics, political science, and mathematics. We formed a study group, acronymed PMS (postmodern studies). We would only read theory written by women, choosing texts that nudged, jostled, and shoved us intellectually, supporting our mutual desire to learn from each other, to feed each other's projects. Oh, how glad we were to find each other!

We met for two hours each week in the sociology's dingy, windowless, basement seminar room next to the Cop-Ez center, in a building that recirculated its stale air. We were heady with ozone and with each other and the difficult readings we had assigned ourselves. Lacking a mutual political history, we were freer to learn with and from each other, an academic simulacrum of the 1970s "consciousness raising" group. We had created a feminist-poststructuralist faculty space in which women read "high theory" about and by women, an interdisciplinary space where we could be timid or bold, knowledgeable or ignorant, smart or dumb, cantankerous or sweet, loud or quiet, "for" or "against," and "both . . . and" all of the above. We struggled *both* to create practices that reflected feminist-poststructuralist theory *and* to create theory that generated feminist-poststructuralist practices. We became friends; potlucks and parties followed. Not since the 1970s feminist movement had I felt so connected, been so glad to have found others like myself, seen my identity shift through community building.

With the nudging and support of PMS, I grew bolder in my writing. The boldness played out in two ways: experimental writing forms, and oblique attacks on the entrenched culture of my department.

In a critical paper, "Value-Constituting Practices, Rhetoric, and Metaphor in Sociology," prepared for the American Sociological Association (ASA) 1989 annual meeting, I wanted to demonstrate how social science writing uses rhetoric and metaphors to grant itself authority and mask its ideology. I wanted both to criticize standard sociological texts and to "deconstruct" the text I was writing.

I had a great time experimenting with writing form. I wrote two different conclusions, one applying to "them" and one to me: The conclusions were substantially the same, but the narrator's voice (mine) shifted from omniscience to first person, the tone from scorn to irony. Having a grand time, I added a "Theoretical Appendix," where I joined poststructuralist jargon and sociological concepts, neatly interlinking them like well-fitting Lego pieces: language, subjectivity, social control, social organization, political practices. I needed to show that I was as smart as those playing the game according to the old rules—smarter, because my theory was parsimonious, self-aware, and principled. My writing was a toy of war launched onto their little battlefield.

To win the war, though, I needed a fresh target to show precisely how modernist sociology, with its claims of scientific purity, relies nonconsciously on metaphor as its message bearer and security blanket. Lucking out, I found a veritable bull's-eye written by a colleague in my own department and newly published in the *American Sociological*

Review (ASR), also housed in my department. I had great fun teasing out the article's naive metaphoric tangle: thirteen distinct metaphors, for instance, in two sentences. What a hoot!

But I was dead serious. I was on a mission. I wanted sociology to fulfill its possibilities, and I wanted my department to reward my contributions. Suddenly, my colleague was appointed the new chair by the dean. At a faculty promotion committee meeting, the new chair decreed that "postmodernism" was not sociology; no, sociology was "relations in vector space." Somehow, I had neglected to apply my analyses of power and knowledge to my own playpen. Smart.

Perhaps diplomacy would help. I tried catching the chair to discuss postmodernism, his paper, my paper. I did catch him once as he marched down the steps, which was the only way I saw him, since he was a morning chair (6:00 A.M. to 8:00 A.M.), and I was an afternoon/evening kind of professor, but I couldn't capture his attention.

Since legitimation (translated into salary and teaching assignments) could be conferred by publishing in the *ASR*, I sent the paper to its "Problems of the Discipline" section. The paper was quickly and summarily rejected. According to the reviewer the issues were (a) not problems and (b) not new.

Writing about this, now, I am experiencing mild post-traumatic stress syndrome. I remember the first paper I had ever submitted to an academic journal. It was 1963. I was nearly a Ph.D. The paper? "Women in Science: Why So Few?" The journal? *ASR*. The sole reviewer penned a one-line rejection: "This paper was obviously written by a woman because no one but a woman would be interested."

VALUE-CONSTITUTING PRACTICES, RHETORIC, AND METAPHOR .
· · · · ·

> *It's an odd feeling . . . writing against the current: difficult entirely to disregard the current.*
>
> VIRGINIA WOOLF

My goal is to apply theory to my writing practices in order to engage others in a conversation about sociology's writing practices. Although sociologists tend to be cognizant of the use of language by the people they study, they are less sensitive to their own linguistic practices and how their writing has value-constituting effects. They are unlikely to see their language/writing as conduct that imposes and orders reality, and are more likely to believe that their writing is objective.

Only since the nineteenth century have kinds of writing been located in two separate domains, "literary writing" and "science writing." Literary writing has been aligned with the evocative, emotional, nonrational, subjective, metaphoric, aesthetics and ethics; science writing has been undertaken with the belief that its words were nonevocative, rational, objective, unambiguous, accurate, and correct. This is the Faustian bargain that has birthed modern, core sociology and its homunculus, "midwestern empiricism" (Agger 1989a).

THE RHETORIC OF SCIENCE

Recognizing the historicity of writing practices, scholars in a host of disciplines are concretely analyzing both literary and scientific writing. Some of the most powerful analyses are coming from the "new rhetoric," also known as the "rhetoric of inquiry" (cf. Nelson, Megill, and McCloskey, 1987). The new rhetoric makes two assumptions: first, that all writing shares common rhetorical devices such as metaphor, imagery, invocations to authority, and appeals to audience; and second, that each field has its own set of literary devices and rhetorical appeals such as theorems, invisible hands, probability tables, archival records, and firsthand experience, which are themselves rhetorically constructed. Rhetorical devices are not ornamental but instrumental in the "persuasive discourse" of science. Any time words are used, technical writing problems are involved, including the use of rhetoric. "The only road from grammar to logic . . . runs through the intermediate territory of rhetoric" (Frye 1957, 331). Science does not stand in opposition to rhetoric; it uses it. And, conversely, the use of rhetoric is not irrational.

Resistance to the idea of rhetoric in science is strong and is based on two major contentions: (1) rhetoric is not rational, and (2) language is not relevant to scientific truth. The first contention views rhetoric as an endorsement of radical relativism, if not nihilism, while seeing science as quintessentially rational. The second ignores the history and sociology of the actual practices of scientists.

Social scientists are encultured as members of both a popular and a social scientific culture with the belief that science, truth, rationality, and objectivity are inseparable. We are professionally socialized into the "logic of inquiry" model of science, which views science as an objective and impersonal system of observation and inference governed by a set of universal rules. Regardless of the substantive problem, logic of inquiry holds that all sciences follow the same set of procedures. "Rational," consequently, has become identified with being "methodical," following preestablished rules of procedure and having preestablished criteria for success, such as the prediction of outcomes.

However, if this definition of rational is adhered to, then the social sciences will be found soundly lacking in rationality. It is impossible in research to specify all the rules and procedures in advance. Researchers typically create new rules and change the old ones as they go about the doing of their research. Members of carefully chosen representative samples do not respond; key informants lie; data get lost and mishandled. Each of these require contextual research decisions. Coders typically "ad hoc" their coding, making up new rules as they go along because their coding books, the "preestablished rules of procedure," do not cover the actual cases. With the advent of high-speed computers, researchers can run all the variables against each other. Only one hundred runs give them the likelihood of at least one "significant" finding, which they can explain "post hoc." Qualitative researchers routinely expect to alter their procedures as they "proceed." In brief, the logic of inquiry model is a "seriously misleading conception of research" (Nelson 1987, 204).

But the fact that social science research does not meet the logic of inquiry model of research does not mean that the research is irrational. The problem is not with social science, but with the inappropriate narrowing of the meaning of "rational." There is another possibility. We could simply appropriate for the social sciences another commonsense meaning of rational: sane and reasonable. This meaning "names a set of moral virtues: tolerance, respect for the opinions of those around one, willingness to listen, reliance on persuasion rather than force" (Rorty 1987, 40). Rationality construed this way does not divide the arts from the sciences nor qualitative from quantitative research. Rather, to be rational is to look at a topic in a reasoned, open, nondefensive way.

The second source of resistance to the idea of rhetoric in science is a legacy from the seventeenth century. Intellectual heirs insist that language is intrinsically irrelevant to the scientific enterprise and that science writing is neutral and transparent. Like a clear pane of glass, science writing presumably neither distorts nor smudges reality but aims to let the "audience see the external world as it is" (Gusfield 1976, 17). Reality is conceived of as standing outside and independent of any observation of or writing about it. The "conduit" between "thing" and "thought" is unobstructed. This modernist belief in the externality of "facts" and the neutrality of language, however, is out of step with contemporary *scientific* thought about science and its construction. Werner Heisenberg, the author of the "uncertainty principle," for example, states, "Science no longer confronts nature as an objective observer, but sees itself as an actor in this interplay between man and nature" (1965, 446).

The modernist vision of science writing as "transparent" is blind to the actual practices of science—rhetorical practices that exist in all the sciences but vary throughout the centuries (cf. Nelson, Megill, and McCloskey, 1987). The universality of rhetorical techniques testifies to the dependence of science on rhetoric, whereas the historical variability of rhetorical devices testifies to the social construction of science and science writing. Sociologists might be expected to be especially attuned to these because they reflect how science is a social institution in particular historical contexts.

A particularly valuable example of the rhetorical construction of science is Charles Darwin's *On the Origin of Species*. Darwin, unlike many modernists, recognized the rhetorical nature of science writing and kept writer's notebooks. The notebooks reveal Darwin, the rhetorician. Darwin consciously wrote *Origin* according to the scientific conventions of his time, "Baconian induction and quasi-positivistic standards of proof" (Campbell 1987, 72–73). He purposefully insisted "that his ideas were the results of 'facts' and his metaphors mere expressions of convenience" (72). Darwin's insistence that he was simply a naturalist gathering facts and working inductively, however, is belied by his notebooks. He had a theory and wanted to solve a theoretical problem — not marshal facts; and disclaimers that his language was merely "convenient" are contravened by his own nonpositivistic theories of language. He suppressed how he did his work and why he wrote as he did because he knew these aberrations would impugn his credibility. He chose to report his work within the methodological conventions important to his colleagues. The protective coloration of scientific conventions disguised Darwin's heretical ideas and contributed to the survival of his thesis.

Styles of writing science are not fixed or neutral but reflect the historically shifting domination of particular schools or paradigms. Darwin's style, today, would doom his writing to extinction because the sciences have adopted different rhetorical conventions. This is quite evident in the American Psychological Association's *Publication Manual*, two hundred oversized pages of rules ranging from punctuation to content and organization. The currently prescribed style gained ascendancy simultaneously with the ascendancy of behaviorist psychology. The articles have become increasingly narrow in scope and focused on a little bit of knowledge — as though knowledge really were a bin of bits. The main unifying theme is the hypothesis, which might be repeated up to four times. The repetition elicits a response. The official style institutionalizes behavioristic assumptions about writers, readers, subjects, and knowledge itself. "The prescribed style grants all the participants exactly the role they have in a behavioristic universe" (Bazerman 1987, 126).

All the social sciences have prescribed writing formats — none of them neutral, all of them value constituting. *How* we are expected to write affects what we can write about. The referencing system in sociology (and most of the other social sciences) discourages the use of footnotes, a place for secondary arguments, novel conjectures, and related ideas. Incorporated into the text, albeit in parentheses, are the publication dates for citations, as though this information counts the most. Knowledge is constituted as "focused," "problem" (hypothesis) centered, "linear," straightforward. Other "thoughts" are "extraneous." Further, research that may have been done inductively is to be reported deductively; the argument is to be "abstractable" in 150 words or less; and researchers are to explicitly identify with a "theoretical-methodological" label. Each of these conventions favors — creates and sustains — a particular vision of what constitutes sociological knowledge. Recognizable discourses cluster together by virtue of themes, strategies, and styles; we can identify a piece of writing, with some degree of assurance, as belonging to a particular discipline, school, intellectual tradition. The explication of these differences alerts us to the linkages between writing and ideology, tradition, stereotype, and theoretical hegemony.

METAPHOR IN THE SOCIAL SCIENCES

Arguably, the most important literary and rhetorical device deployed in the social sciences is metaphor. Metaphor is not merely an ornamentation or grace note: It conveys cognitive content. Social science — like all writing — depends upon metaphor for articulating its ideas. Metaphor is unavoidable. The essence of metaphor is "understanding and experiencing one kind of thing in terms of another" (Lakoff and Johnson 1980, 5). This is accomplished through comparison or analogy, for example, "my love is like a red, red rose." More subtly and more relevant to conventional social science writing, the metaphor can be carried implicitly in everyday "plain" language. Consider the following statements about theory (examples based on Lakoff and Johnson 1980, 46): "What is the *foundation* of your theory?" "Your theory needs more *support*." "Your position is *shaky*." "Let's *construct* an argument." "The *form* of the argument needs *buttressing*." "Given your *framework*, no wonder your argument *fell apart*."

The italicized words in the preceding paragraph are expressions that convey the metaphor "theory is a building." This customary way of talking about theory presupposes a metaphor that we are usually unconscious of using. Moreover, the metaphor structures the actions we take in theorizing and what we believe constitutes theory. We try to *build a theoretical structure* that we then experience as a *structure*, which has a *form* and *foundation*, which we then experience as an *edifice*, sometimes quite *grand*, sometimes in need of *shoring up*, and sometimes in need of *dismantling* or, more recently, *deconstructing*. Consider how differently we would experience theory if the metaphor were "theory is a feather." Or, who might be considered capable of theorizing if theory were metaphored as "like life."

Metaphors exist at the conceptual level and prefigure judgments about the truth value of a text. The truth value of social science writing partially depends upon a deep epistemic code regarding "the way that knowledge and understanding *in general are figured*" (Shapiro 1985 – 1986, 198). Figures of speech and metaphors external to the particular piece of research prefigure the analysis with a code belonging to another domain (Jameson 1981). For example, the use of "enlighten" or "idea" for knowledge is a light-based metaphor, what Derrida refers to as the heliocentric view of knowledge, the passive receipt of rays (1982). Immanent in these metaphors, Derrida argues, are philosophical and value commitments so entrenched and familiar that they can do their partisan work in the guise of neutrality, passing as literal.

Implicit metaphors orient and prefigure knowledge. Positivist empiricism, the "guiding light" of the social sciences, uses three metaphors, which remove the "datum" from the temporal and human practices that produced it (Shapiro 1985 – 1986). First is the grammatical split between subject and object, a wholly unnoticed metaphor for the separation between "real" subjects and objects. The metaphor is particularly powerful because it is a part of our language structure. Second, empiricism views language as a *tool*. The empiricist world is fixed and available for viewing through the instrumentality of language, downplaying that *what* we speak about is partly a function of *how* we speak. Third, empiricism uses a *management* metaphor. Data are "managed," variables are "manipulated," research is "designed," time is "flow-charted," "tables" are "produced," and "models" (like toothpaste and cars) are "tested." The three metaphors work together to reify a radical separation between subject and object and to create a static world, fixed in time and space. In this world, the "knower" is estranged from the "known"; intellectual inquiry becomes a matter of precise observation and measurement of what is "objectively" out there.

Metaphor does not stop at the philosophical level but enters each stage of social scientific reasoning. The social scientific world is thought to be "like" a "complex model" whose measurements are "like" the "proxy variables" at hand. "The complex model is said to be like a simpler model for actual thinking, which is in turn like an even simpler model for calculation" (McCloskey 1985, 75). The analogic structure is aided by the use of other rhetorical devices such as the ordering of material, the use of examples to "prove" the general case, the construction of "ideal" or "test" "cases," repetition (e.g., of the hypothesis), appeals to authorities (citations), and so on (cf. Edmondson 1984).

Within sociology itself, metaphors are everywhere. "Functionalism," "role" theory, "game" theory, "dramaturgical analogy," "organicism," "social evolutionism," the social "system," social "structure," "ecology," "labeling" theory are obviously metaphoric. Conceptually, we talk about "equilibrium," "human capital," the "power elite," "resource mobilization," ethnic "insurgency," "developing" countries, "stratification," and so on. Methodologically, we talk about the "power" of a test and statistical "significance" (as distinct from sociological significance); we "sample" a "target" population that we "survey" and "probe." Some areas of the discipline are thought to be "core" or "mainstream." Metaphors are everywhere. They organize sociological work and affect the interpretations of the "facts"; indeed, facts are interpretable ("make sense") only in terms of their place within a metaphoric structure. The "sense-making" is always value constituting—making sense in a particular way, privileging one ordering of the "facts" over others.

As sociology is written in its "flagship" journals, metaphors work together to create an image of a particular kind of sociology as the presumptively standard and correct one. A "systematic" approach is consistent with the metaphor of the "social system." There is a common "core" (a heart¿) that can be "treated" and "handled" and "kept an eye on." Sociological growth takes place through "partnerships" at the "core" (not by "divorces" at the "boundaries"). "Paradigms" (like managers¿) are judged by their "power" at "handling" problems. And like managers, the paradigms decide which problems are "real" ones. In the ecological-demographic world, the family is a "cluster" of persons in relationship to a "marker"; populations are a "set" of individuals in an "interdependent system" of "functions." "Production" of "outputs" is based on "ingredients" called "inputs." Human beings are metaphored out of this world. Metaphored in are rather reassuring values—such as *the social world is controllable* and *sociology can do the controlling.*

CONCLUSION I

What sociological writing has tried unsuccessfully to keep out of its writing may very well be the proper approach to and subject matter of the discipline. No matter how plainspoken sociologists try to be, the unavoidable human content keeps invading their thinking and shaping their writing. The "marker," the "handler," "the controller," the human body is present in every sentence sociologists write and appears whenever they break out in prose.

REFLEXIVE ANALYSIS OF "VALUE-CONSTITUTING PRACTICES . . ."

Social science writing is sociohistorically constructed. The writing uses rhetorical and literary devices to create and sustain values and to convey cognitive content. To ignore the ubiquitousness and power of these practices is perverse and short sighted — not to mention unscientific. Let me then, now, look at (some) of my own writing practices in the construction of this article. I recognize that I am a privileged reader of my own text, because I wrote it, and a biased reader, in a particular way, because I wrote it. My intention here is to view this article as an example of how writers, interested in challenging the hegemony of disciplinary discourse, manage to reinscribe as well as challenge that discourse.

My analysis will look briefly at the "text" — the written article, "Value-Constituting . . ." — and my subjective feelings about what I have "textualized." By making this declaration, I have constructed a "self," reifed a "text," and, in fine Cartesian and positivist-empiricist fashion, separated my "self" from its "products." In postmodernist signage, I have created a bipolar opposition between "subject" and "object" and then claimed that I exist, and exist as an author, and that my authorial understanding of my own authorial labor has some authority and deserves valorization in this text. Even as I frame the discourse, I reinscribe hegemonies — that of positivist empiricism or that of emergent postmodernism. The very writing of this article — the content, its shape, its form, its questions, its reflexivity — places it as a writing positioned within postmodernist discourse; it is unabashedly a product of its time.

I also recognize that I have placed this reflexive analysis at the end of the text, rather than integrating it throughout, and that I have marginalized my "subjective" state by positioning it as a "reactant" to the "text." I do this, self-consciously, as a power move: I shall give my "self" the last word.

No textual staging is without responsibility. All texts are power moves. As I construct the "Value-Constituting . . ." text, I mask my position as a player in a power game. I do this through the deployment of some standard rhetorical devices, devices that ostensibly position my work within regular sociology. "On purpose," I write "enough" like a sociologist to "pass" into that world; if I am rhetorically skillful enough, my buried subtext can help reshape that world. My text both reinscribes and challenges.

Rhetorical devices that position this paper as a "sociology" paper are abundant. First, the text is preencoded as social science writing by its format, its publication in a social science journal, having a title, a named author with departmental and university affiliation, a stated goal, demarcated sections with titles, appeals to social scientific authorities and authoritative styles of argument, the use of scientific research/theory to rewrite science, choice of examples (e.g., using the American Psychological Association style manual), use of the grammatical split of subject/object, language as a tool and problem-focused metaphors, citations, references, a particular referencing format, the deployment of established grammatical forms, punctuation, spelling, and a linear and orderly presentation of arguments.

The title signals the encoding of the paper as typical "sociology" with key words—"constituting," "reflexive," and (yes) "sociology." Scattered throughout the text are names of sociological authority figures and jargon such as "professional socialization" and "sociohistorical." At crucial junctures, such as at the end of the first paragraph and the beginning of sections that might have resistant readers, I deploy (the engaging) "we sociologists." I speak as an insider. I write from a shared sociological discourse about the social construction of knowledge, about sociohistorical contexts, about the social production of "things." I take these as axiomatic, (power) "tools" in my argument chest—not socially constructed beliefs amenable to deconstructive analysis.

But, even though I use many standard writing conventions, I write against others. "Value-Constituting . . ." challenges conventions, primarily through its reliance on literary codes. Beginning with the title, key literary words, "metaphor" and "rhetoric," have equal billing with the sociological signifier, "value-constituting." I link all three concepts to "sociology." An aphorism, a literary device, begins the paper, and that aphorism is by a well-known literary figure, Virginia Woolf. I give neither myself nor the paper a methodological or theoretical label, but there is a point-of-view character—me—present from the first word—"my." Images, alliterations, foreshadowing, oral speech rhythms, and language play enter the text at crucial points, to clinch "rational" arguments by (hopefully) eliciting a "bodily" response, a smile or a head nod, in the reader.

Any writing project imposes and orders reality, in part, accomplished by submerged subtexts (Lockridge 1988) and masked authorial agendas. Masked, for example, is my feminist agenda, according to which all texts—not only those by or about women—are analyzed, asking what social, sexual, and power relationships are being reproduced. Masked is how the deeper feminist agenda of rewriting texts drives this text. "Power" as a concept/issue is stated explicitly at the outset but then is treated obliquely, an issue of interest, in passing, to Derrida—the paper masking how it is itself a power move that privileges a particular kind of writing—narrative, literary, ethnographic—which just happens to be the kind of writing I (now) do (most of the time).

I use strong metaphoric language to decenter the reigning orthodoxy, "sociology is a science." I speak of social science's production as equivalent to "toothpaste and cars," evoking imagery of the assembly line, waste, obsolescence, capitalism, hype, and consumerism. I speak of science writing as a "Faustian" bargain, the selling of one's soul to the devil for earthly gains, evoking the familiar feeling of exchanging one's labor/interests/time for National Science Foundation grants. I speak of contemporary "mainstream" sociology as an homunculus.

Masked, also, are the processes that produced this paper: the material ones of academic sinecure, libraries, photocopy machines, secretarial help, and computers; my social and power relationship(s) to my particular site of production (my university and department); my subjective state, as an ideological site in contestation by colliding and conflicting discourses; and my embodiment. In writing "Value-Constituting . . . ," I have, then, written a literary narrative of the writing of science, social science, and sociology, articulated as an "objective" and true one, but which is driven by my own subordinated material and subjective positions within the discourses of power. I have been writing for and of my life.

Conclusion II

What sociological precepts I have tried unsuccessfully to keep out of my writing may very well be the proper approach to my subject matter. Unavoidable human content keeps invading my thinking and shaping my writing. My human body is present in every sentence I write and appears every time I break out in prose. Thankfully, there is no antidote.

THEORETICAL APPENDIX

A viable feminist-postmodernist theory would address the relationship between language, subjectivity, social organization, and power, linking social processes to individual subjectivities, and both of these to political praxis. Such a theory would show how particular discursive practices both subordinate the theorist's interests and further them. Language is central to such theorizing because it is a way of defining, and thus constituting, the social world and the subjective world. Wherever worlds are being constituted, political struggles exist. The political struggle is over both how the society will be organized and how individuals will experience that society. Subjectivity, consequently—like the social world—is fluid, often contradictory and ambiguous, rather than fixed and unified, and subjectivity, like the social world, is a site where discourses compete. Just as theorizing reinscribes and transforms the external world, the theorist's internal world is reinscribed and transformed by her or his words. Some theoretical stances inscribe protagonists as conscious actors in their own stories, capable of transformation; some metaphor out, not only human agency, but humans. How one writes one's theory is not simply a theoretical matter. The theoretical inscribes a social order, power relationships, and the subjective state of the theorist.

FOREWORDS: ERASURE FIGHTS

W HEN I was a little girl, I liked beating up the boys. When their parents complained, my father instituted fight rules. I had to measure myself against the boy. If he was bigger, I could fight him; smaller or the same size, I had to retreat, lose by default.

In my last street fight, when I was seven, I was publicly humiliated, thrown down our cement stairs by a new boy on our new block, who fought differently than the others, more fiercely and cleverly. He had accused me of "killing Jesus." My older brother watched me hit the sidewalk; Mother was upstairs in the kitchen, when I came to her, unaided, scraped, bleeding, and crying. She chastised me for fighting.

When Norman Denzin asked me to take part in a symposium on postmodernism that had as its centerpiece Peter Manning's article "Strands in the Postmodernist Rope: Ethnographic Themes," I was pleased, because I saw the symposium as a historically momentous occasion: Whose work would be inscribed, valorized, canonized? Whose work erased?

Manning's article made me mad. His review of the "strands" of postmodernism omitted — except for the tiniest curl of frayed thread — feminism and feminist postmodernism within sociology. I was fighting mad. I took Manning's measure, judged him "bigger" (more prestigious) than I, and prepared myself for battle. My fight would be not just to reinscribe feminist writers into the emerging sociological postmodern canon but to move feminist postmodernism into the center of a future sociology. I was the sole woman speaker. Would there be a "mother" there to patch me up, if I needed patching? Chastise me?

Erasure of feminist scholars from the new academic blackboard was infuriating. And tiring. Being invited to share the stage as a feminist speaker, to box in the ring, is ephemeral, unlike inviting women into the textual history through which a discipline socializes its young, rewards its old. Exclusion is multitiered. Feminist thought had already been minimized within sociology—worse, depoliticized, stripped of its radical implications, sanitized into "sex roles" or "sex and gender," or "gender/family/work." Should Manning's analysis and citation practices prevail, postmodernism in sociology would become yet another male preserve, "older brothers" ignoring their "sisters'" wounds.

Rereading now "Speakers Whose Voices Matter," I see myself straining, splitting, moving in two directions at once, cleaving—simultaneously in both senses of the word. I align myself with feminist writers outside social science—literary critics and philosophers. It is their work I use to justify my feminist speaking position. Yet, I still want to "save sociology" by moving feminist speakers to its center. I was still thinking, writing, and feeling in terms of cultural dualisms: center/margin; inclusion/exclusion; sociology/not sociology. Rather than "give up" on sociology, I would breach its walls with the irresistible logic, passion, and moral fortitude of feminist-poststructuralist theory.

The live conference audience liked the piece. There were many feminists present. I wasn't bloodied or chastised. The symposium got published "as was." Manning's male-centered postmodernist sociology continues to prevail.

SPEAKERS WHOSE
VOICES MATTER.
.
.
.
.
.

M Y intention is to present a femi-
nist speaking position through which postmodernist issues within sociology
can be framed, debated, transformed, or abandoned. My desire is to write a
progressive future for sociology, but I begin by addressing Peter Manning's
(1991) paper "Strands in the Postmodernist Rope: Ethnographic Themes," because at the 1989 Symbolic Interaction meetings it was "centerpieced" as
"background"—both the figure and the ground—of postmodernist issues
within sociology. His paper is symptomatic of "what's happening now."

Using Baudrillard's *America* (1989) as an exemplar of postmodernist imagery, and postmodernism as a symbol that is speaking, Manning sets himself
the task of considering how postmodernism might shape the ethnographic enterprise. He concludes that the "intellectual roots of significance of postmodernism are rather far removed from American pragmatism and positivism, and
we are viewing the light cast by postmodernism in the same way one views
the light of distant stars: long after the beams were emitted" (12).

In Manning's account, women are left out, have nothing to say, no place
from which to speak. The word "feminism" does appear once—in the Appendix on "Sources and Genres in Postmodernism," in a list of five forms of postmodernist writing, in parentheses, after "deconstructive" (1991, 29). Feminism
is inscribed as parenthetical, a subset of the French male-driven deconstructionism popular five years ago in literary studies, without an independent existence (shades of the generic "he"), narrowly focused, containable, "outside

of" again, the "other," and like other (good and charitable) works of women, not requiring serious consideration beyond a polite acknowledgment, a gratuitous mention, a tip of the Stetson.

The egregious subsuming of feminism under deconstructionism is neither intellectually accurate nor politically benign. Writing "deconstructive (feminism)," as Manning does, is as odd a distillation/encapsulation as writing "Catholicism (feminism)," "liberalism (feminism)," "feminism (deconstructionism)," "radicalism (feminism)," or "role theory (feminism)"—as perverse as writing "positivism (symbolic interactionism)." Some feminists are deconstructive just as some deconstructionists are feminists, but not all feminists are deconstructionists and not all deconstructionists are feminists. This is not, unfortunately, just a "logical" matter: bedfellowing feminism and deconstructionism (in missionary position no less!) subverts the essence of feminism, which is political.

Intellectual labor is accomplished in social institutions and through particular social relationships. Gatekeepers "man" gates. Trendsetters set trends. Deconstructionism is now being variously deconstructed, by adherents and enemies, as "faddish," "trendy," "negative," "on its way out," "reactionary," "intellectually sterile," and/or "destructive of civilized values." To associate feminism with—and only with—deconstructionism makes feminism "trendy" by association, worn out and addled, destructive. It makes it easy to rationalize "skipping" articles written by/about feminists/feminism, and downright effortless to bypass the question "Destructive for whom?" (For feminist readings of deconstructionism/feminism, see Flax 1987; Scott 1988).

Other genres identified by Manning as "technique driven," "Eco," and "descriptive and ethnographic in bigger context and reflective in style," accordingly, have no feminist contributors. Pauline Bart, Sucheng Chen, Patricia Hill Collins, Tim Diamond, Arlene Kaplan Daniels, Bronwyn Davies, Judith DiIorio, Bonnie Thornton Dill, Carolyn Ellis, Cheryl Townsend Gilkes, Evelyn Nakano Glenn, Elizabeth Higgenbottom, Arlie Hochschild, Rosabeth Kanter, Sharon Kaufman, Susan Krieger, Cherríe Moraga, Shulamit Reinharz, Judith Rollins, Barbara Katz Rothman, Melba Sanchéz-Ayéndez, Beth Schneider, Judith Stacey, Gaye Tuchman, Barrie Thorne, Carol Warren, Maxine Baca Zinn—to name but a few feminist ethnographers—apparently do not exist. Nor do feminists who write in the (epitomic?) genre Manning calls "seeking moralities of truth" (as do Habermas, Lyotard, Jameson, and Derrida).

Manning only thus excludes the entire corpus of contemporary feminist theory and ethnography (cf. Harding 1986)! In braiding his postmodernist rope, Manning joins the priesthood at the altar of postmodernism, resubstantiated as an "overwhelming male pantheon of proper names" serving "as ritual objects of academic exegesis and commentary" (Morris 1988, 12).

Nevertheless, feminist-postmodernist writing is burgeoning. Journals have highlighted the dialogue (*Feminist Studies* 14 [Spring 1988]; also, *Critical Critique* 1987–1989, *Signs* 1987–1989, and *Studies in Symbolic Interaction* 1987–1989); feminist-postmodernist anthologies and monographs are numerous (cf. Grosz 1989; Hutcheon 1988; Lather 1991; Riley 1988; Weedon 1987); and experimental and reflexive writing abounds. Extensive bibliographies are easily available to the interested reader (see Meaghan Morris's seven-pager [1988]).

Manning is not alone in his omission of feminism. Rather, his paper is an exemplar of a contemporary "trend." With some notable exceptions (e.g., Cheal 1989; Denzin 1986), "what's happening now" is the erasure of feminist agendas from the "standardized" academic blackboard. For example, Charles Lemert's "Selected Bibliography of Postmodernist Social Theory," distributed at a 1988 American Sociological Association Didactic Seminar, lists forty references. Although seven are women (a "hefty" 17.5 percent, which by "standard" standards might seem a goodly proportion), only two of those references are "about" social theory; only one is written by a (philosopher) social scientist. At best, two items usable, citable, includable in the developing canon. Similarly, Dena Targ (1989), after reviewing recent mainstream family sociology chapters and prominent summaries of the field, found that although some feminist substantive issues, such as family violence and housework, have been added to the canon, the feminist critique of theory, method, and praxis is missing. Georgia NeSmith (1989) reviews modern histories, history texts, and historiography and finds that the male or masculine-identified is (still) the subject of history; if women are included, they are "added on" to the "master narrative of male agency" (3). Both Gil Musolf's (1989) ambitious review and reconstruction of symbolic interactionism and Jeffrey Alexander and Paul Colomy's (1989) similarly ambitious project on "neofunctionalism" omit feminist contributions and forgo dialogue with feminist critiques. This paragraph could get very long and tiresome.

To speak of this and like this, I know, risks identifying my remarks as exemplars of that "awesome genre," *nagging* (Morris 1988). Nagging does not work in sitcoms, cartoons, or everyday life; it is a "powerless text." The nagger's speech, becoming "insufferable," gives way to "frenzy or silence" (Morris 1988, 15). Women, unable to find voice in which to publicly complain, take refuge in madness or depression (Heilbrun 1988, 15). One way out, which women have taken, is to speak to each other. Another way is to defer to the male discourse, to be interruptible in scholarship, too.

There is another choice, though; one I now take: to reframe the sociological discourse as a feminist-postmodernist practice. This frame, I am convinced, gets us out of Baudrillard's desert, swinging a lariat, singing. Let me begin with a mininarrative about feminism and postmodernism.

Feminist theory has been and is driven by political practice, the dismantling of the subordination of women. Feminist political practice, moreover, is ideologically inseparable from personal practices, as coded in "the personal is the political." Theory is thus built from "lived experience," and the dualities between "theory" and "praxis," researcher and researched, subject and object, and so on, are routinely challenged by the feminist methods of "knowing." Like the postmodernists who came after them, feminists have critiqued as partial, interested, and situated the presumed universal, disinterested, and ahistorical truth claims of androcentrism. But unlike the postmodernists, feminists refused to let go of the "quasi-metanarratives" embedded in theories of ideology, macrostructures, interaction, hermeneutics, and so on, because these were the theories necessary for social critique and political change. Indeed, feminism even created some "quasi-metanarratives" of its own (e.g., those found in the work of Nancy Chodorow and Carol Gilligan). Ingrained systems of thought kept intruding, and feminist theory found itself, on occasion, essentializing gender and universalizing "woman." But now again political practice is redirecting theory.

The contemporary women's movement is built upon the idea of "alliances," rather than the universalized and essentialized identity, "woman." The underlying premise of the contemporary movement is that "whereas some women have some common interests and face some common enemies, such commonalities are by no means universal; rather they are interlaced with differences, even with conflicts" (Fraser and Nicholson 1988, 102). Political action is based on this patchwork quilt of overlapping interests, rather than on a single unifying thread. As such, "it is already implicitly postmodern," a multiple site of "feminisms." The plurality of practices pushes us to rethink our critical inquiry, to guard against ossification—to create a theoretical counterpart to the praxis, a postmodernist feminism that is complex, multilayered, multisited, and which speaks of solidarity as it speaks of complexity and diversity, the kind of speaking necessary for overcoming the oppression of women in its "endless variety and monotonous similarity" (Rubin 1976, 160).

Throughout academe, locally and internationally, feminists gather in interdisciplinary feminist-postmodernist study groups, much as we gathered in the 1970s in "consciousness-raising" groups. The union between feminism and postmodernism in academia is thus being (at least partially) situated within frankly feminist sites, and feminist sites are always potentially sites of political action. Intrepid feminists are being drawn to postmodernism like bees to honey, taking that which is nourishing, leaving behind the toxic and nontransformable. The intellectual excitement amongst the doers rivals that of their earlier "discovery/creation" of feminism.

In their dialogue with postmodernism, feminists have been unwilling to let go of ethical and political issues; rather, they are the "themes" to be "written into" our writing, to be accountable for, to be called upon. Although these themes are absent from Manning's summary, they are at the core of feminist postmodernism. For feminist postmodernists the struggle is to unite the strengths of the postmodernist critique with the strengths of the feminist critique. The struggle is a political, moral, and intellectual one. Is there something for sociologists to learn from their analyses? Can a feminist postmodernism help frame a progressive future for sociology?

A first move, I think, is to reconsider "the distrust of metanarratives." Who says the postmodernist critique requires us to forswear "large historical narratives" and "analyses of societal macrostructures" (Fraser and Nicholson 1988, 101)? No philosophical basis within postmodernism requires sociology to abandon the theoretical tools it needs to address the historically situated and culturally embedded ideologies, structures, and processes that have reproduced, and continue to reproduce, power imbalances. Indeed, despite its caterwauling, postmodernism itself has not forsworn metatheory or analysis. Rather, it inscribes its own metanarrative based on the loss of a privileged position for Andro-Eurocentric truth. Like nasty boys on a playing field who are losing the game, some are not content to simply take their bats and balls and go home; they want to tear up the field so no one else can play. We need to be skeptical about the "human condition," currently universalized as the "postmodern condition," by those who are, because of their academic sinecures, by and large, free from the oppressions of the situated conditions of class, race, ethnicity, and gender.

The postmodernist insistence, though, that theorizing must be grounded in explicitly historical and cultural ways, even if not fully practiced by the high priests, matches contemporary feminist political practices and, consequently, has a privileged place in feminist postmodernism. Generic, ahistorical categories like "reproduction," "mothering," and (yes, even) "sexism" are displaced by specific culturally and historically situated social practices. Cross-cultural and transhistorical research does not look for "laws" but for differences. Gender itself is inflected by class, ethnicity, race, age, and sexual preference; gender is viewed as but one "strand" in complexly constructed identities. Feminist work is pragmatic, variegated, using different methods and categories depending upon the problem. Rather than the colorless rope in Manning's metaphor, feminist postmodernism images a "tapestry composed of threads of many different hues" (Fraser and Nicholson 1988, 102).

This brings us to issues of representation—how do we speak "the tapestry?" Representational issues are of feminist concern, even when the representation is not seemingly about women or women's issues, because wherever text is being produced, there is the question of what social, power, and sexual relationships of production are being *reproduced*. How does our writing, including this writing, reproduce a system of domination and how does it challenge that system? For whom do we speak and to whom do we speak, with what voice, to what end, using what criteria? The issues are entirely too complex to do justice to them in this brief space, so let me just offer a way of thinking about them.

The feminist impulse has been to "give voice" to those who have been silenced, to speak for others—even for constituencies to which one may not belong. This impulse, of course, raises postmodernist questions about authority, subjectivity, and ownership, issues that are of concern to feminist theory and practice. On the other hand, the postmodernist impulse has been to delete the author (who only now is reemerging as a "name function"), to dismantle distinctions between fact and fiction, and to deconstruct the difference between sign and signified. As the speechless are given voice and the power to name and be named through feminist practice, the postmodernist theorist would disempower them by erasing their names, deconstructing their stories, and undermining their grounds for authority. Forging a writing union between feminism and postmodernism is, thus, a seriously difficult task.

All writing creates a particular view of reality; all writing uses grammatical, narrative, and rhetorical structures that create value, inscribe meaning, and constitute the subjects and objects of inquiry. How we choose to write, then, involves many major and minor ethical and rhetorical decisions (Brown 1977; Richardson 1990b). No textual staging is innocent (Foucault 1978). Writing is an intentional activity and, as such, a site of moral responsibility. Whoever writes for/about/of whatever is using authority and privilege. But because there is no such thing as "a thing" speaking of "itself," because "things" are always constructed and interpreted, there is no Archimedean resolution to the problem of speaking for others. There is no getting it right about who or what another is; there is no essence defining what "right" is (Roth 1989). Knowledge is always situated, embodied, and partial (Haraway 1988). We are always viewing something from somewhere, from some embodied position. Consequently, the problem becomes a practical-ethical one: How can we use our skills and privileges to advance the case of the nonprivileged?

One answer is to reinscribe the earlier feminist insistence that we "listen to the voices" of the silenced; that we tell the stories of those who have been textually disenfranchised; that we "hear" the "personal as political." But that we write these stories in such a way that the writing "resists its own subordination to a putatively more significant practice of production," to rules of writing that reproduce sociology's "thoughtless" adherence to an ontology of eternal subordination, a "generically unalterable" enveloping society (Agger n.d., 3, 7). One way of doing this rewriting — of interrupting the reproduction of sociological knowledge as the "cartographer of domination" (Agger n.d., 4)—would be for sociology to embrace the narrative both as a means of "knowing" and as a method of "telling" the sociological. Telling stories would not be marginalized or masked but acknowledged and celebrated.

People live by stories (Heilbrun 1988). They attempt to shape their lives by the available narratives. If the available narrative is limiting, people's lives are limited, textually disfranchised. Collective stories that are based in the lived experiences of people, and deviate from the cultural story, provide new narratives; hearing them helps individuals to replot their lives because they provide an alternative plot to absent or powerless texts. At the group level, collective stories help overcome the isolation and alienation of contemporary life and link disparate persons into a collective consciousness. Rather than culture as "collocation shards," we can write here a postmodern culture that is a product of situated persons, creating transformative and liberatory narratives.

Now we are constructing the history of postmodernism within sociology. We are naming its progenitors, framing its issues, and claiming its projects. My effort has been to construct a "feminist speaking position," to move to the center that which has been excluded and marginalized. Such a move, I believe, not only brings the work of actual women into the discourse but also provides an exemplar of how sociology can be a political-moral actor in a postmodernist discourse and a postmodernist world. I propose we write narratives, including the one about postmodernism, in which the previously subordinated are actors in the discourse, are speakers whose voices matter.

PART 2 CROSSING BOUNDARIES

THE SEA MONSTER

AN ETHNOGRAPHIC DRAMA
BY LAUREL RICHARDSON
AND ERNEST LOCKRIDGE

[The characters are Laurel, a sociologist, and Ernest, a novelist. They live together, and they have been writing and talking about writing for years. There is also the "Discussant" who lives in Laurel's study.

The drama begins in a colonial revival home in the heartland of America, where Laurel—who has been invited to be a "Discussant" of "Ethnographic Novels" at the Society for the Study of Symbolic Interaction – Stone Symposium at St. Petersburg Beach—is waking up.]

ACT ONE

Scene One: A white and blue bedroom.

Laurel (interior monologue): I woke up feeling just a Little bit Postmodern. My vital signs aren't good, my mirror's smudged, and my underpinnings aren't back yet from the French Laundry. By high noon, my prose gets the grippe, my poetry transforms into cross-stitchery, and the Clay Figure I am sculpting turns itself inside out, walks off on bronze-plated soles, and declares in the Key of B-Sharp (also known as "C") that It is the Word. By dusk, I swing from the horns of the baby bull moon, trilling, "jumbled genres . . . jumbled genres . . . gembreld jumbles — jumjen — genjum."

Why do I write as I do? Why do I write at all?

> jumbled genres
> jumbled genres — come out to play

                    —come out to say
                              —jumbled genres
                              —jumbled genres
                                        —can they make you free
                                        —OH! Dear,
                                                  eth-no-gra-phy?

Free at last? Free to break every convention? Free not to write? Not to speak? Free to dance, hum, fingerpaint the sociological?

I yearn for my student days, when writing consisted of letters home, doggerel, term papers. There was more time then.

Scene Two: Laurel's study.

Laurel (muttering to herself): Forget the idea of "universals." The same words and techniques mean different things in different contexts. When we talk of "ethnographic novels," are we saying horses are cats because they both have tails and aren't dogs?

Scene Three: The Kitchen Table. It is large, old oak, and round. Ernest and Laurel are deep in talk.

Ernest: In its beginnings, the novel was a commentary on or embodiment of the society within which and about which it was being written. So, Samuel Richardson, Henry Fielding, and Laurence Sterne—in his more quirky way— wrote novels about society. Certainly, the same is true of Austen, Dickens, Thackeray, Balzac, Zola, Tolstoi, etc., etc., and up to the present, Barbara Pym, Beryl Bainbridge, Fay Weldon, Richard Wright, John Updike. So, you can say that the phrase "ethnographic novel" is a redundancy.

Laurel (to herself): Postmodernism says show your process; interrupt your textual staging. If I interrupt myself enough again and often enough again and yes she said and yes again, I'll not have to "really" begin, will I? What is Really? What is Begin? Is this "displaying" my process or a quintessential postmodernist fritter? Enough, already. REALLY BEGIN!

Scene Four: Laurel's study.

Laurel: I am NOT going to comfort myself with modernity and write a taxonomy of writing issues and strategies. I am NOT going to do that.

Scene Five: The Worthington Bike Path. The Lone Scholar Laurel, with stun gun, is walking and muttering sotto voce. The scene takes two hours and thirteen minutes. She exits at the Park of Roses, smiling, saying, "Lived Experience."

ACT TWO

Scene One: Laurel's Study. The Computer Monitor.

THE DISCUSSANT'S ESSAY

The issue is not "really" ethnographic novels, but the writing of lived experience.

Some of us have been drawn to postmodernism like tourists to Paris in April (the cruelest month), and like tourists, upon returning StateSide we proudly show our snapshots, talking about how we don't have any authoritative grounds to stand upon, and "we" aren't, anyway. We're just moving subjectivities — recombinant vapors.

But how we theorize about *lived experience* and how we experience *lived experience* are at odds. Feelings and emotions occupy a primary discursive space in our daily individual and collective lives. We *experience* our lives as personal, emotionally meaningful, narratively knowable, and tellable. We care about things — including, for some of us, the postmodernist debates. We like having "identities" and sharing those with others with whom we identify. In unprecedented numbers, people, including those who have been to Paris, join social movements, go to recovery, co-dependency, and Twelve-Step Programs — where they tell the stories of their lives and feel the "magic" of shared feelings in a like-feeling community.

And, so our own *lived experience* as ethnographic writers is antipodal: As the postmodernist stance humbles us and stills our claims as authoritative speakers "about" or "over" a subject, this emotionally open moment privileges us as speaking subjects, whose stories must be heard, whose power comes from within.

INTERRUPTION OF ESSAY: INTERIOR MONOLOGUE

Laurel: I am finding this piece very hard to write. I am writing about my life. I always do. We always do. Now, my life is set in the interstices of contradictory discourses. The more I write, the more intensely I feel the epistemological stance of postmodernism. The less certain I am about the value of writing. That is the experience I am living right now.

INTERRUPTION OF INTERIOR MONOLOGUE: LIVE INTERACTION

[Laurel is stressing out at the computer. Ernest enters, looking concerned.]

Laurel (choking): I'm writing about writing about writing "lived experience."

Ernest: Lived experience is that which is known through the five senses, and the good fiction writer creates a world through the five senses. If you want to render lived experience, you have to learn fictional techniques. Take a fiction-writing course. Read great fiction writers.

INTERRUPTION OF ALL INTERRUPTIONS

The chilly room, the smell of brewing mocha java coffee, the hum of the electric clock, and Blue Cat lounging on top of the computer monitor distract her from her writing task, but not from her feelings. She is feeling . . . she is feeling . . . very uncomfortable "playing" at writing fiction. She gratefully stops the experiment.

RETURN TO DISCUSSANT'S ESSAY

Do we really want to write novels? Do we really want our readers to believe that the "worlds" we talk about are imaginary? If so, then, our products will be judged as fiction, an intensely competitive domain, and we will lose the political and moral force that we have as ethnographers, persons with skill, talent, and a point of view toward "real" worlds. Do we want to trade off what we have for—what—the freedom? prestige? game?—of "doing" novels?

As qualitative researchers, we use literary devices in writing biographies, collective stories, case histories, and ethnographies. We need not give these up. We cannot, however, write from inside the heads of anyone but ourselves, without losing credibility as ethnographers. We can only write "accounts." And, maybe that's why we're experimenting so much with our writing: We know from our own lived experience that life as subjectively experienced is the key to understanding the cultural and the sociological. And we want to write that.

We have a few options, though. First, we can write about ourselves — our own subjectivity. Then, we are not writing "novels" though, we are writing autobiography. Second, we can continue to write ethnography, but ethnography that is more reflexive. Third, we can write what I think of as "combination genres." In combination genres, fictional stories, field notes, analysis, reflexivity all can coexist as separate (and equal?) components. Each part takes meaning and depth in the context of the whole text. Writers of combination genres clearly demarcate what is intended to be read as "fiction" and what is intended as "ethnography."

We can write "our" material in many different ways, for many different audiences. That is why we call it "material." We can take pleasures in the crafting and recrafting. For those who are talented enough, both ethnography and fiction are possibilities. For others of us, an ethnography, which is consciously infused with literary devices, and which rejoices in, rather than recoils from, the partial vision and situated knowledge of our own "lived experience" is a worthy contender.

ACT THREE

Scene One: SSSI-Stone Symposium, St. Petersburg Beach. Laurel and Ernest walking hand in hand on the beach. Laurel picks up the most beautiful shell she has ever seen and slips it into her side pocket.

Scene Two: Ernest and Laurel are in their hotel room. Ernest holds the shell under warm water to wash off the sand. Out of its pink slit thrusts a long, muscular brown tongue with knobs and spikes, licking ferociously around the porcelain basin.

Ernest: Hey, Laurel. Come and look at this.

Laurel: (*screams*) OH! It's Alive!

Ernest: Yeah, and you had it in your pocket all that time.

Laurel: OOH—I can't stand it. Do something!

Ernest: Well, I've got my Swiss army knife.

Scene Three: Ernest returns the conch to the Gulf of Mexico. Laurel returns to her writing pad.

Curtain

AFTERWORDS: COAUTHORING
"THE SEA MONSTER"

I KNOW the exact moment when I decided to make Ernest Lockridge a coauthor of the "The Sea Monster: An Ethnographic Drama." In that moment my internal conflicts regarding authorship, ownership, ethics, and power in and over the text were resolved. In that moment, I knew with certainty that Ernest had to receive credit for his contributions to "my" text. I did not know what the consequences of that decision would be.

Because of my interests in narrative sociology and alternative representations, I had been invited to discuss the "Ethnographic Fiction" papers at the 1990 Society for the Study of Symbolic Interaction (SSSI)–Stone Conference at St. Petersburg Beach. But how would I "discuss" "ethnographic fiction"? What criteria would I use? Literary? Scientific? What were the issues? What were my thoughts?

After reading the "ethnographic fiction" papers, I decided not to critique them individually. How rude it would be to praise someone's work, perhaps, and not another's. How painful are invidious comparisons, much less outright criticism. I had once experienced a nasty public critique of a poem made all the worse because I thought I was going to be praised, as surely these writers thought now. The occasion was a women's writing conference, and Margaret Atwood had chosen one of my poems to xerox for discussion. Her assault on the poem felt more humiliating than any public criticism I've had of my sociological work. I imputed to the "ethnographic fiction" writers deeper personal vulnerability for their creative offerings than for "scientific" offerings. If I couldn't say something equally "nice" about all of them, I'd rather say nothing at all about any of them—a complex respeaking of a maxim of my mother's, I realized. Better, much better, to use my time to discuss general issues. But which ones? And how? Irritability marked my days.

The preparation of my remarks was taking an inordinate amount of time and thought, particularly for somebody else's project; I had no intention of ever writing something I would call "fiction," whether tagged as "ethnographic" or not, although I did want to respond to the "fiction" with my own genre-bending piece. I like transgressing boundaries, seeing what is on the other (forbidden) side.

Wrestling with the issues—fact/fiction, truth/fiction, science writing/fiction writing—was like battling a many-headed monster, a postmodern "Hydra." Every time I cut off a head, two grew in its place. Hercules' solution—to cauterize the wounds—did not work, for try I was would, my pen would not a cautery be.

At this time, my postmodernist studies group was reading Luce Irigaray. Issues about embodiment surfaced: an "I" (whatever it might refer to) who was an "author" (whether only of my own text or more democratically of all the texts I read) sitting (oh, body!) at a computer (with eyes and hands, mine) engaged in constructing text. Scholarly work was locally situated, in bodies on bums. Perhaps my "body" could lead me somewhere new, if I would only follow it.

I began to write about my body and how it felt while I was trying to think/write about "ethnographic fiction." I also began to vary where I put my body while doing scholarly activity—upstairs, the bike path, the kitchen table. I liked the kitchen table, half sitting, a leg under me, a narrow-ruled pad and a razor-point pen in hand.

The kitchen table is the place where Ernest, my husband, and I have shared three meals a day for seventeen years. He is a professor of English, teacher of creative writing, and a novelist. Sitting around the oak kitchen table at meals and off times, we spent hours, it seems, but maybe only a few, talking about "ethnographic fiction." We had similar ideas but different feelings. He felt, I think, impatient with the whole topic, while I felt impatient with *myself* in relationship to the topic. I was exploring new terrain in fits and starts, while Ernest was hiking over familiar land. What he had to say was fascinating, and, equipped with pen and pad, I began to take "field notes" on two topics, the history of the novel and fiction-writing techniques.

Soon, my discussant's paper began to take intellectual shape under nine unspecified headings. I called it "Writing the Hydra: Nine Heads in One Body." Before long, I had "real" "characters"—Ernest, myself, and a Discussant—scenes, locations, motivations, and conflicts, the makings of a play. Through a play, I realized, I could talk about the embodiedness of my writing/thinking process, legitimately quote Ernest, avoid citing "the literature," and simultaneously do both seriousness and playfulness, a nice postmodernist thing.

But time was running out. I liked the first two acts, but the third one was a cop-out. Act II consisted of arguments for a variety of different writing strategies; Act III, entitled "Moral," consisted of one line said by an unspecified Chorus: "Let us not beheads the Hydra." Cute, maybe, but not much payoff for the listener; not much to say for my genre-bending efforts.

With less than two hours left before the session, Ernest and I went walking along St. Pete Beach. I obsessed about the play but also found the most beautiful seashell I had ever seen, which I put in my pocket. When we returned to our hotel room, Ernest washed the sand out of the shell. "Out of its pink slit thrusts a long, muscular brown tongue with knobs and spikes, licking ferociously around the porcelain basin." Very squeamish, my face puckered and I screamed, "Oh, it's alive!" "Yeah," said Ernest, and "you had it in your pocket all that time." I did a little involuntary oh-yuck dance and screamed again, "Do something! I can't stand it." Ironically, Ernest said, "Well, I've got my Swiss army knife." But, rather than slicing it up, Ernest returned the conch to the beach, and I returned to "Writing the Hydra."

When Ernest came back, he found me scowling, writing, scratching out my writing, writing, scratching, scowling. Ten minutes to show time, and I was trying to rewrite Act III; I wanted it to be about the living conch as a metaphor for what sociological writing could be, and how much it terrified me. "Help," I said.

An exasperated and caring Ernest picked up a pen and wrote a new Act III, the dialogue and description I have quoted above. At that moment—the moment he took pen to paper, the moment he physically authored "my" text and wrote as he did, I knew he had to be a coauthor. I knew this, not simply because he wrote upon my text—editors do that all the time—but because *what* he wrote was not me, not in my voice, not in my style, and not exactly what had happened, which would have been my concern as an ethnographer. *What* he wrote, moreover, was "right" for the text: It *showed* differences between fiction writing and ethnographic writing. Rather than talking as an informant about "fiction writing," he was doing it, here and now, in "my" text. The text performed what it preached. By his action, he had transformed the text into a site where two separate approaches—styles, voices, personae—were coexisting. The easy agreement of "point of view" between the discussants "Laurel" and "Ernest" was contravened by the striking stylistic differences in their writing.

I felt relief that the writing crisis was over, but also the pang of loss: I had voluntarily given away my "ownership of the means of enunciation." The loss felt even greater when Ernest suggested a new title for the piece, "The Sea Monster: An 'Ethnographic Drama,'" a concrete, metaphoric, and playful title, with an appropriately ironic subtitle. He had slain the "Hydra."

There are different potential readings of our writing. Ernest and I have discussed these. Some might say, and it is my preferred reading, that the text represents the nexus between postmodernist disruption and modernist narrative. The "play" itself is a disruption of normative discussant writing; and within the play, the tonal rupture between the first two acts and the third is a disruption of notions of the unified self, author. But the play also fits modernist criteria for a play; there are scenes, characters, locations, narrative drive, crisis, and resolution.

Other readers of my account of our writing, however, might say that Ernest had appropriated my text, sexualized, masculinized it, penetrated it, even "raped" it with his pen, and that I had either "asked for it" ("Help") or been unable to defend myself against his male force. Most curious, this reading reverses the usual concern of the ethnographer — that the ethnographer is appropriating somebody else's text. If I had not given Ernest coauthorship, or if I had not told the story of the construction of the text — if he had just continued to appear in the text as a character, like other ethnographic "characters" — would readers think he had appropriated the text? Raped it?

There is no doubt that his voice brings a masculine sexual energy to the text. His words (slit, tongue, thrust, lick) are not ones I would write about a conch, living or dead. But the "rape reading" misses the crux of the issue in rape or in textual construction: Who has the power to have his or her will prevail? The power over the text remained mine. What would constitute the "text" was under my control, just as it is when I quote from interviews with men/women/children — others whom I "allow" into my text. This is the same power men have traditionally held in the domestic sphere, bosses over employees, parents over children, priests over supplicants, and judges over the accused — the power to decide when and how to flex their power. I had given Ernest "coauthorship" but not "coauthority."

When we returned home from the Stone conference, I sent "The Sea

Monster: An 'Ethnographic Drama'" to *Symbolic Interaction* (SI). My interests, not Ernest's, were in publishing in a sociology journal. In the cover letter, I described the piece as a well-received "oddity," which I hoped would find "a home in SI." Placatingly, I offered to add a prologue, epilogue, and bibliography. But the editor, David Maines, accepted "The Sea Monster" as submitted. It was published with but one editorial change, intentional or not I do not know: the ironic quotes around "ethnographic drama" were deleted. For a long while, I was mortified by their absence, and I penned them in on the reprints lest people think I thought there was such a thing as an ethnographic drama, much less that I had written one—well, co-written one.

Perhaps the lack of ironic quotes finally inspired me, perhaps I would have been inspired anyway, but before long I was writing what I proudly called ethnographic dramas. In dramas, I found a way to "give voice" to multiple positions, reflect upon or spoof my own, and thereby write pieces that *show* how openness and reflexivity *look* and *feel*, rather than simply talking about it.

I also learned why despite my wrangling, Ernest and I never wrote that mystery novel I wanted us to. Sharing a point of view is not the same as sharing the same voice, the same style, the same way of showing, knowing. We could write a "play" with characters with different viewpoints, a postmodern dialogue, but we could not write a piece of fiction or sociology with a unified voice and perspective.

What we say depends on how and *with whom* we say it. Some of the things we want to say—such as about difference and sameness, whether it be about fiction and ethnography or about race, gender, and ethnicity categories—might be better communicated through "showing." Showing, I submit, can happen when different voices deeply penetrate our texts. Voices do not deeply penetrate when they are interview snippets or homogenized story (re)telling. They do penetrate more when the voices become "characters" in dramas, but most deeply when the voices become embodied, take form, as legitimated coauthors, writing different meanings in differing styles, rupturing "our" texts.

This writing-story about "The Sea Monster" is clearly a partial story, not the only one I could have written, but the one I wanted to write, needed to write. I needed to set the record straight, give Ernest his due credit, which extended beyond coauthorship in a sociology journal, and I needed to release the emotional hold the "The Sea Monster" has had on me.

But something unexpected happened on my way through this material: It was here that I discovered, for myself, the methodological and theoretical relevance of an unheralded genre—of what I came to call the "writing-story"—stories of how texts are constructed, the genre that I have now deployed in the construction of this book. Ironically, I found the power of the genre by writing my story about coauthorship as *my* story, not a shared one; I found it by not allowing another voice to penetrate the text.

RESISTING RESISTANCE

NARRATIVES

A REPRESENTATION FOR COMMUNICATION

Models of communication are, then, not merely representations of communication but representations for communication: templates that guide.
    JAMES W. CAREY, *COMMUNICATION AS CULTURE*

LIKE a much desired child, this piece was named before it was birthed, seen, held. I named it "Contemporary Resistance Narratives," wanting it Oh-So-Badly to be one. But like many a desired child, it has been neither wholly controllable nor wholly capricious. It has cockily renamed itself "Resisting Resistance Narratives: A Representation for Communication." Please bear with her, for she is still young, a bit brash, self-centered, and demanding. But she has written in a part for you, too. Please everyone join the Symbolic Interactionist Chorus.

Symbolic Interactionist (SI) Chorus:
There is a dazzle in worldly greatness which no young mind or heart can resist. (Edgerton Brydges, *Autobiography*)

The stories of our lives.

SI Chorus:
How can we write the stories of our lives to minimize the reproduction of the bad and the ugly?

How can we re-present lives?

SI Chorus:
How do we write those stories / lives so that they are symbolically, materially, and aesthetically appealing?

I submit we cannot do so by representing our lives as *resistance* narratives.

SI Chorus:
Resistance. n. Any force that tends to oppose or retard action.

Resist. v. To strive or work against whether by inertness or active force, physically or mentally.

I have thus far resisted seduction by and addiction to the dominant resistance /
metanarratives of Marxism and Freudianism. My intent here is not to dwell
upon them.

SI Chorus:
Resist v. To keep from giving in or enjoying, abstain from.

Like mixing vodka with Lowenbrau, a combined dose of Marxism and Freudianism can produce a false consciousness and a blustery ego. Both narratives
situate contemporary travails in generic historical forces (Marxism in preexisting structures, Freudianism in preexisting child-rearing practices) beyond the
control (but not the knowledge) of the intellectual, but both, nevertheless,
posit a future that will be "theirs." Neither privileges human agency. Contemporary Marxism obliterates the lived experiences of individuals, while contemporary Freudianism blithely metaphors out human agency, speaking of a
mother's love for her child as "object relations."

SI Chorus:
Resist. v. To keep from giving in or enjoying, abstain from.

In resistance narratives, whether meta or mini, however, narrative is not the problem, and narrativity neither can nor should be resisted. At issue is not whether we should write narratives—we always do—but how the stories we tell do and do not reinscribe tyrannies, large and small—do and do not improve the material, symbolic, and aesthetic conditions of our lives. Whenever we write, we are telling some kind of a story, or some part of a larger narrative. Narratives provide meaningful explanation of how events are causally linked. In a story "something" happens because of something else; the connections between the events is the meaning.

Some of our stories are more complex, more densely described, and offer greater opportunities for transcendence; others are more abstract, distanced from lived experience, and embedded in dominant hegemonies.

SI Chorus:
Today, when I got I up . . . (chorus members simultaneously speak aloud of their day) . . . *And now I am reading this passage aloud with other "S-I'ers."*

Even when we think we are not telling a story, we are, at the very least, embedding our research in a metanarrative about, for example, how science progresses or art is accomplished (Lyotard 1979). Quite wondrously, the convention paper's format reveals its own narratively driven subtext. Just listen to us: theory (literature review) is the past or the (researcher's) cause for the present study (hypothesis being tested), which will lead to the future—findings and implications (for the researcher, researched, and science.)

In a compelling narrative, we believe, not necessarily in the facticity of the story, but in its credibility. Things hold together; they make sense. Credibility is accomplished, in part, through the artistry of the teller—the selection of details, the tone, the images, metaphors—and, in part, through locating the story within a larger context of genre. Readers bring to the story preexisting expectations regarding that genre's structure; writers reinscribe those structures by writing through them, glossing, using words from a particular domain to construct believability.

There is nothing inherently wrong with using familiar representational structures; change for change's sake seems somewhat adolescent.

SI Chorus:
RESISTANCE
(*A Found Poem, Adapted from Funk and Wagnalls*)
. . . passive . . .

apparent
true
frame
frictional
aero
lateral
magnetic
ohmic

. . . least . . .

What if the elements of the representational structure are themselves problematical? What if the genre undermines its own agenda?

If we think of the narratives we construct as "resistance" narratives, we have dialogically tied ourselves to that which we oppose. Just as the atheist is forever tied to theism, the antiabortionist to abortion, the anticommunist to communism, and the postmodernist to a variety of "posts," resistance narratives are tied to that which already has legitimacy, to that which they are resisting.

Stories written as resistance narratives, thus, are weak representations: reactive stories that keep alive the dominant culture in the psyches of the nondominant, and stories that continue to materially profit the dominant, because the dominant is the text and/or subtext of the work. Women's Studies has been acutely aware of this as a practical/political dilemma but has displaced the core narrative issue into a debate about where/how Women's Studies should be housed/taught. Mainstreamed or separated? Similarly, contemporary Marxist and Freudian theorists speak within discourses that limit what can be said, and to whom. The overwhelming majority of supposedly liberating narratives are weakly presented, called resistance narratives or counternarratives, subaltern speakers, or marginal voices. Conceived and written as responses to dominant discourses, they reinscribe rather than circumvent. Positioning one's story as reactive makes it reactive.

SI Chorus:
The dam resists the river.

Do we have alternatives? James Carey's thoughtful essays can move us along, I think. Carey argues that our models of communication "create a particular corner of culture that determines, in part, the kind of communicative world we inhabit" (1989, 32). Carey discusses two of these models: the informational and the ritual.

The informational model tends to be privileged in academia. Transmission of knowledge assumes some previously held knowledge base that the "new" knowledge adds to or attacks. Knowledge, like capital, can accumulate. Or knowledge, like missiles, can be fired at hostile or captive enemies. Knowledge is metaphored as possessions or battlefields. Greed and conflict. Have / have-not; win / lose. Position / resistance / counterresistance.

Carey suggests, however, that we might foreground a different and older meaning for communication, namely, communication viewed as *ritual*, a "representation of shared beliefs" (18). Under this formulation, communication, including the stories we tell about the stories we tell, is tied to ceremonies that draw "persons together in fellowship and common faith" (18). Communication is reunited with its etymological siblings: "community," "communion," and "commonality." Communication as "community" invites participation, association, locale, temporality, entrustment, and, most important, empathy. It privileges human agency.

Problems of communication . . .

SI Chorus:
Ah, bring forth will you "problems of communication"—that "semantic crucifix to ward off modern vampires" (Carey 1989, 33).

Problems of communication, then, or the kinds of stories that we can write, the kinds of lives we can thereby live, are thus most strongly linked to the kinds of communion we can create, not to the hegemonies we can resist. It is through association, community building, sharing, and empathy that we have some hope of repairing and transforming culture.

How then can we re-present lives? How can we write lives so that our writing has mattered? Following Carey, I think, that one way to begin the re-presenting of lives, including our own sociological ones, is to create new forms of telling, new rituals for sharing.

> SI Chorus:
> *So that's why you've written me into your text . . .*

Yes, I invite you to experiment with form — to write lives differently in shape and style and format in order to build a new communal understanding of what constitutes sociological "knowledge," an understanding that embraces ritual and that moves beyond the battlefields of attack and counterattack. Such understanding shows. It does not "resist."

Social science, dance, sculpture, painting, literature. An exemplary text comes to life and creates life.

> SI Chorus:
> *It is. It is itself*

Let's do it!

> SI Chorus:
> *Let's do it!*

AFTERWORDS: TRYING COMMUNITY

TWICE yearly—for the annual and midwestern Society for the Study of Symbolic Interaction (SSSI) meetings—Norman Denzin or-ganizes cultural studies–postmodernism sessions. Some of us (David Altheide, Patricia Clough, Carolyn Ellis, Andrea Fontana, Andrew Herman, John Johnson, Michael McCall, and Alan Shelton) have now become "regulars," although there always seems to be room at the table for newcomers. The way it works is that I contact Norman and tell him I would like to be on the panel, and Norman says, "Fine. What's the title of your paper?" I make up a "working title" based on what I'm thinking about right then, knowing full well that a paper, with some title about something, will be written. I like having a deadline, the routine, and the trust.

On my way to becoming a "regular regular," Norman asked me to take part in the 1990 midwestern SSSI symposium inspired by James Carey's book *Communication as Culture* (1989). My feminist-postmodernist studies group had gone off on a Marxist toot, a theoretical position to which I had never cottoned. I had trouble understanding how avowed feminists — poststructuralists ones, especially — could link arms with and stroll alongside a dead man who ignored live women. Marxism, staging itself as "science" and peddling a metanarrative of a class-bifurcated society, had not and could not deconstruct itself; it was, I felt, grossly androcentric in tone, content, and goal. One could not use Marxists' tools to dismantle the Marxists' house — to riff on Audre Lorde. Would I end up at serious odds with my postmodernist community? These were trying times.

I also loathed the argumentive style — nasty, loud, perseverant, and rude — that I associated with the Marxists I had known in graduate school; I feared my PMS group would proselytize among the campus Marxists. Having academic discussions with Marxists was like having meals at my Uncle Frank and Aunt Marie's when I was a child. Everyone spoke at once; no one seemed to listen to anyone else; the volume steadily rose. Uncle Frank was an alcoholic. He repeated himself, louder each time and more demanding until he overcame all resistance to his voice or he passed out. Father believed a soft voice was becoming in a woman. I sat, struck mute, at Frank and Marie's table.

But, in actuality the PMS women didn't act like Frank and Marie's family or like the graduate students I had known. Amongst my fellow PMSers, a Marxist-feminist speaker, Patti Lather, was already becoming my on-campus theoretical, pedagogical, and emotional comrade. Thinking I might learn something by intellectually joining the "feminist materialist girls," I entitled my 1990 paper "Contemporary Resistance Narratives." But I couldn't write that paper; my resistance to resistance narratives was too robust.

Hale and hardy, too, was my desire to build community within the Society for the Study of Symbolic Interaction, where we could try out different forms of representing the sociological and different ways of communicating with each other. I don't know how it happened, but I conceptualized the paper, now called "Resisting Resistance Narratives," as a responsive reading. I wrote parts for myself and parts for the "Symbolic Interactionist Chorus," conceived of as a Greek chorus, warning, chanting, commenting. I handed out the Chorus parts to the audience, who readily partook. It was my first audience participation "performance" piece. I was showing what I was telling, trying to create a nonhegemonic communication that could produce a culture of association and empathy. Someone handwrote me a note: "Are you always this outrageous?"

Until recently, I had judged "Resisting Resistance Narratives" as (but another) playful moment in my academic career, but as I read it now, I see it as a pivotal piece in my life. I refer to "her" as a "desired child," willful; be patient with her, I ask the listener. The Chorus then asks the questions I asked in my earlier work, how should we write, thereby "universalizing" my personal quest. The "chorus" is both the voices in my head and the audience; I conflate them, making me feel the historical and the personal as the contemporaneous and the social. The Chorus helps me spoof traditional scholarship by speaking dictionary definitions of *resist* and *resistance*, even turning Funk and Wagnalls's words into a found poem. At one point, I have each member of the Chorus simultaneously speak aloud the separate stories of their day: Nonconsciously, I had re-created the din, the babble, of Uncle Frank and Aunt Marie's table. But here and now I was not mute. I was the convener, the speaker, the voice that could arise from Bedlam and make sense.

The sense I wanted to bring home—and that is the right metaphor—was simple: How we communicated affected the kind of community we could be. I wanted a community that valued empathy, entrustment, good spirits, participation, human agency, and ceremony. To get there we needed to try new forms of communication, new rituals for representing shared beliefs. We needed forms that privileged communication's etymological family: community, communion, communal, and commonality. We needed to celebrate the kinds of communion we could have, not the hegemonies we could resist.

Now, when I read "Resisting Resistance Narratives," I see beneath its surface my then unnamed desire to create within sociology a community of like-minded people sharing rituals and beliefs around the sacred—a "church." I wanted a safe place, spiritually renewing, not destructive, competitive, or hostile. At the conclusion of the piece, the Chorus (which I now image as a temple or church chorus) twice professed my hidden zeal, an activist's "Amen," not simply for alternative forms of representation, but for alternative forms of community. I rejoin the Choir: "Let's do it!"

FOREWORDS: BELONGING

TALK about resistance! When Norman Denzin asked me to contribute a review chapter on "representation" for the *Handbook of Qualitative Research* he was coediting, I said, "No. I couldn't possibly do so such a chapter." I was no longer able—psychologically or emotionally—to write a "review" chapter of anything, even of something I liked and knew something about. The idea of writing a "review" intensified my issues with sociological writing. Would I be writing new rules for representation in qualitative research? Inscribing a new canon? Providing summaries and categories of knowledge that I devised—as if I could—and then presenting them as—what? truth? fiction? Or, more boringly, would I just be going over materials I had already written about in *Writing Strategies*? Most selfishly, I was not willing to divert my attention from my "own" projects.

Even now as I write to complete this manuscript by its deadline, my peripheral vision catches piles of manuscripts on the left side of my desk. Many of them have deadlines, too. Journal reviews, proofs, copy-edited articles, American Sociological Association session papers, graduate students' papers, general exams, symposia. My irascibility grows looking at the piles, thinking about them, writing about them. They feel like intrusions into the emotional center of my life, now, the completion of this manuscript. Playing with a manila envelope string is Maxwell, a young, gray tiger "humane society" cat that we've adopted.

The piles of manuscripts are, of course, the material representations of involvement in a "community," a community I have claimed to want to belong to. Academic community entails commitment to others, involvement with others' projects and products, a willingness to suspend one's individual needs, for a while, for the betterment of the whole. To tithe time, as it were. Without each of us giving, gracefully, to each other, how could either the community or our individual contributions be sustained? How awful I would feel if I were totally disconnected from this community: if no one asked me to do anything anymore.

(These thoughts sound like I'm in "church.")

I decide to spend the weekend "clearing my desk" of all those professional "intrusions." I grow less irritable and impatient as the piles shrink. There is actually a kind of pleasure to be had here. By the time I am writing these forewords, I am thinking of the piles as links to colleagues, reciprocities, and reminders that I am writing this book for someone besides myself. The desk is lighter; and so am I.

But, when Norman asked me to write the "Representations" chapter, I could not reframe it as anything I wanted to or could do. He extended another invitation, however, saying I could write about anything I wanted to, because he wanted my contribution in the book. I am the third born and last child in my extended family; "being included" is still an emotional live wire for me. Being presented as "my self" is, too, and not the little girl dressed in cousins' "still good" hand-me-downs. I wanted to be included amongst the other qualitative researchers — one of my churchlike communities — but on my own terms. Norman's invitation made that possible. I wrote about what I wanted to read about — "Writing: A Method of Inquiry" (1994). I also provided lots of references and writing exercises.

When I reread my *Handbook* chapter, I'm surprised by its chummy tone — lots of "our's" and "we's." I was writing to a community of qualitative researchers. My desire to belong, and to create community, was on the surface, and embedded, in every sentence of that text. I think the

Handbook chapter has been my most influential qualitative writing. I had thought it was because of its content. Now, I wonder if my tone spoke the longing of others, experienced and novitiate, to feel invited into a community?

For this volume, I have highly abridged that article, deleted the exercise section, altered the tone, and updated the references. I want this new chapter to invite others into a writing community, not just qualitative researchers. To reflect both the spirit and substance of the changes, then, I give this anthology chapter the title I had chosen for my book about writing but which the editor had rejected because it was ambiguous: "Writing Matters." (Is "matters" a verb or a noun? Both.)

In these forewords, then I have modeled the method of writing as discovery. Before I wrote the forewords, I didn't realize how much I would change the proposed chapter, how much anger I have about losing control of a book title, how complex and deep my feelings were about professional networks, or how good I would feel after I wrote these words.

WRITING MATTERS

Writing, the creative effort, should come first—at least for some part of every day of your life. It is a wonderful blessing if you will use it. You will become happier, more enlightened, alive, impassioned, light hearted and generous to everybody else. Even your health will improve. Colds will disappear and all the other ailments of discouragement and boredom.

BRENDA UELAND, *IF YOU WANT TO WRITE*

I HAVE a confession to make. For thirty years, I have yawned my way through numerous supposedly exemplary qualitative studies. Countless numbers of texts have I abandoned half-read, half-scanned. I'll order a new book with great anticipation — the topic is one I'm interested in, the author is someone I want to read — only to find the text boring. Recently, I've been "coming out" to colleagues and students about my secret displeasure with much of qualitative writing only to find a community of like-minded discontents. Undergraduates are disappointed that sociology is not more interesting; graduate students confess that they do not finish reading what has been assigned because it's boring; and colleagues express relief to be at long last discussing qualitative's own dirty little secret: our empire is (partially) unclothed.

Although qualitative research topics often are riveting and the research painstakingly executed, the monographs are underread. Unlike quantitative work, which can carry its meaning in its tables and summaries, qualitative work depends upon people's reading it. Just as a piece of literature is not equivalent to its "plot summary," qualitative research is not contained in its abstract. Qualitative research has to be read, not scanned; its meaning is in the reading.

Qualitative work could be reaching wide and diverse audiences, not just devotees of the topic or the author. It seems foolish, at best, narcissistic and wholly self-absorbed, at worst, to spend months or years doing research that ends up not being read and not making a difference to anything but the author's career. Can something be done? One way to create vital texts is to attend to writing as a method of inquiry.

I write because I want to find something out. I write in order to learn something that I didn't know before I wrote it. I was taught, though, as perhaps you were, too, not to write until I knew what I wanted to say, until my points were organized and outlined. No surprise, this static writing model coheres with mechanistic scientism and quantitative research. But, that model of writing is itself a sociohistorical invention that reifies the static social world imagined by our nineteenth-century foreparents. The model has serious problems: It ignores the role of writing as a dynamic, creative process; it undermines the confidence of beginning qualitative researchers because their experience of research is inconsistent with the writing model; and it contributes to the flotilla of qualitative writing that is simply not interesting to read because adherence to the model requires writers to silence their own voices and to view themselves as contaminants.

Qualitative researchers commonly speak of the importance of the individual researcher's skills and aptitudes. The researcher—rather than the survey, the questionnaire, or the census tape—is the "instrument." The more honed the researcher, the better the possibility of "good" research. Students are trained to observe, listen, question, and participate. Yet they are trained to conceptualize writing as "writing up" the research, rather than as a method of discovery. Almost unthinkingly, qualitative research training validates the mechanistic model of writing, even though that model shuts down the creativity and sensibilities of the individual researcher.

One reason, then, that qualitative texts might be boring is that a sense of self is diminished as we get homogenized through professional socialization, rewards, and punishments. Homogenization suppresses individual voices. We are encouraged to take on the omniscient voice of science, the view from everywhere. How do we put ourselves in our own texts, and with what consequences? How do we nurture our own individuality and at the same time lay claim to "knowing" something? These are both philosophically and practically difficult problems.

In some ways, "knowing" is easier, though, with a postmodernist consciousness because it recognizes the situational limitations of the knower. Qualitative writers are, thankfully, off the "science hook," so to speak. They don't have to try to play deity, writing as disembodied omniscient narrators claiming universal, atemporal general knowledge; they can eschew the questionable metanarrative of scientific objectivity and still have plenty to say as situated speakers, subjectivities engaged in knowing/telling about the world as they perceive it.

A particular kind of postmodernist thinking—*poststructuralism*—links language, subjectivity, social organization, and power (cf. Weedon 1987). The centerpiece is language (see "Value-Constituting Practices"). Different languages and different discourses within a given language divide up the world and give it meaning in ways that are not reducible to one another. Language is how social organization and power are defined and contested and the place where our sense of selves, our *subjectivity* is constructed. Understanding language as competing discourses, competing ways of giving meaning and of organizing the world, makes language a site of exploration, struggle.

Language is not the result of one's individuality, but rather language constructs the individual's subjectivity in ways that are historically and locally specific. What something means to individuals is dependent on the discourses available to them. For example, being hit by one's spouse is differently experienced if it is thought of within the discourse of "normal marriage," "husband's rights," or "wife battering." If a woman sees male violence as "normal" or a "husband's right," then she is unlikely to see it as "wife battering," an illegitimate use of power that should not be tolerated. Experience is thus open to contradictory interpretations governed by social interests rather than objective truth. The individual is both site and subject of discursive struggles for identity. Because the individual is subject to multiple and competing discourses in many realms, one's subjectivity is shifting and contradictory, not stable, fixed, rigid.

Poststructuralism thus points to the *continual co-creation of self and social science*: They are known through each other. Knowing the self and knowing "about" the subject are intertwined, partial, historical, local knowledges. Poststructuralism, then, permits — nay, invites — no, incites us to reflect upon our method and explore new ways of knowing.

Specifically, poststructuralism suggests two important things to qualitative writers: First, it directs us to understand ourselves reflexively as persons writing from particular positions at specific times; and second, it frees us from trying to write a single text in which everything is said to everyone. Nurturing our own voices releases the censorious hold of "science writing" on our consciousness, as well as the arrogance it fosters in our psyche: Writing is validated as a method of knowing.

Having some sense of the history of our writing practices helps to demystify standard practices and loosen their hold on our psyches: Social scientific writing, like all other forms of writing, is a sociohistorical construction and, therefore, mutable (see "Narrative Knowing and Sociological Telling"). Since the seventeenth century, the world of writing has been divided into two separate kinds: literary and scientific (for a discussion of "science writing," see "The

Collective Story"). Because literary writing, by the eighteenth century, was taking a second seat in importance, status, impact, and truth value to science, some literary writers attempted to make literature a part of science.

By the late nineteenth century "realism" dominated both science and fiction writing (Clough 1992). Honoré de Balzac spearheaded the realism movement in literature. He viewed society as a "historical organism" with "social species" akin to "zoological species." Writers deserving of praise, he contended, must investigate "the reasons or causes" of "social effects"—the "first principles" upon which society is based ([1842] 1965, 247–249). For Balzac, the novel was an "instrument of scientific inquiry" (Crawford 1951, 7). Following Balzac's lead, Emile Zola argued for "naturalism" in literature. In his famous essay "The Novel as Social Science," he argued that the "return to nature, the naturalistic evolution which marks the century, drives little by little all the manifestation of human intelligence into the same scientific path." Literature is to be "governed by science" ([1880] 1965, 271).

Throughout the twentieth century, crossovers—uneasy and easy, denied and acknowledged—have characterized the relationship between science and literary writing. Today, scholars in a host of disciplines are involved in tracing these relationships and in deconstructing scientific and literary writing (cf. Agger 1989a, 1989b, 1989c; Brodkey 1987; Clough 1992; Nelson, Megill, and McCloskey 1987; Simons 1990). Their deconstructive analyses concretely show how all disciplines have their own set of literary devices and rhetorical appeals such as probability tables, archival records, and first-person accounts.

Particular social science writing conventions have shaped ethnographies. Needful of distinguishing their work from travelers' and missionaries' reports as well as from imaginative writing, ethnographers adopted an impersonal, third-person voice to explain an "observed phenomenon" and trumpet the authenticity of their representations. John Van Maanen identifies four conventions used in traditional ethnographies or what he calls *realist tales* (1988). First, there is *experiential author(ity)*. The author as an "I" is mostly absent from the text, which talks about the people studied; the author exists only in the preface establishing "I was there" and "I'm a researcher" credentials. Second, there is *documentary style*, with a plethora of concrete, particular details that presume to represent the typical activity, pattern, culture member. Third, *the culture member's point of view* is claimed to be presented through their accounts, quotations, explanations, language, cultural cliches, and so on. And fourth, the author claims *interpretive omnipotence*. The ethnographer's "no-nonsense" interpretations of the culture are claimed as valid. Many of the classic books in the social sciences are realist tales. These include Kai Erikson's *Everything in Its Path* (1976), William Foote Whyte's *Street Corner Society* (1943), Elliot Liebow's *Tally's Corner* (1967), and Carol Stack's *All Our Kin* (1974).

Other genres of qualitative writing—such as texts based on life histories or in-depth interviews—have their own sets of traditional conventions (cf. Mischler 1986). In these traditional texts, the researcher proves his or her credentials in the introductory or methods section and writes the body of the text as though the quotations and document snippets are naturally there, genuine evidence for the case being made, rather than selected, pruned, and spruced up for their textual appearance. Like ethnography, the assumption of *scientific authority* is rhetorically displayed in these qualitative texts. Examples of traditional "life-story" texts include Lillian Rubin's *Worlds of Pain* (1976), Sharon Kaufman's *The Ageless Self* (1986), and my *New Other Woman* (1985).

EXPERIMENTAL WRITING

In the wake of feminist and postmodernist critiques of traditional qualitative writing practices, qualitative work has been appearing in new forms; genres are blurred, jumbled. I think of them as *experimental representations*. They transgress the boundaries of social science writing genres. Working within the "ideology of doubt," experimental writers raise and display postmodernist issues. Chief among these are how does the author position the self as a knower and teller? Who is the writer? Who is the reader? For the experimental writer, these lead to the intertwined problems of subjectivity/authority/authorship/reflexivity, on the one hand, and representational form, on the other.

Postmodernism claims that representation is always partial, local, and situational and that our self is always present, no matter how much we try to suppress it—but only partially present, for in our writing we repress parts of ourselves, too. Working from that premise, we are freed to write material in a variety of ways: to tell and retell. There is no such thing as "getting it right"; only "getting it" differently contoured and nuanced. When experimenting with form, ethnographers learn about the topic and about themselves that which was unknowable, unimaginable, using prescribed writing formats. So, even if one chooses to write a final paper in a conventional form, experimenting with format is a practical and powerful way to expand interpretive skills.

Social scientists are now writing *narratives of the self* (Denzin 1987; Ellis 1995a, 1995b, 1995c; Geertz 1988; Kondo 1990; Krieger 1991; Lawrence-Lightfoot 1995; Quinney 1991; Ronai 1992; St. Pierre 1995; Steedman 1986), *fiction* (cf. Shelten 1995; Stewart 1989; Visweswaran 1994; Wolf 1992), *poetry* (Brady 1991; Diamond 1982; Prattis 1985; Richardson 1992c), *drama* (Ellis and Bochner 1991; Paget 1990; Richardson and Lockridge 1991), *performance science* (McCall and Becker 1990), *polyvocal texts* (cf. Butler and Rosenblum 1991; Schneider 1991); *aphorisms* (Rose 1992), *visual presentations* (Gammell, McCall, and Taylor 1995; Harper 1987), *mixed genres* (Dorst 1989; Ellis and Bochner, 1996b; Fine 1992; Glassner 1991; Hooks 1990; Lather and Smithies 1996; Linden 1992; Pfohl 1992; Slobin 1995; St. Pierre 1995; Trinh 1989; Ulmer 1989; Walkerdine 1990; Williams 1991), and *cybertexts* (Epstein 1996; Herman 1995).

In traditionally staged research we valorize "triangulation" (Statham, Richardson, and Cook 1991). In that process, a researcher deploys "different methods"—such as interviews, census data, and documents—to "validate" findings. These methods, however, carry the *same domain* assumptions, including the assumption that there is a "fixed point" or "object" that can be triangulated. But in postmodernist mixed-genre texts, the writers do not triangulate; they *crystallize*. There are far more than "three sides" by which to approach the world.

I propose that the central imaginary for "validity" for postmodernist texts is not the triangle—a rigid, fixed, two-dimensional object. Rather, the central imaginary is the crystal, which combines symmetry and substance with an infinite variety of shapes, substances, transmutations, multidimensionalities, and angles of approach. Crystals grow, change, alter but are not amorphous.

Crystals are prisms that reflect externalities *and* refract within themselves, creating different colors, patterns, arrays, casting off in different directions. What we see depends upon our angle of repose. Not triangulation, crystallization. In postmodernist mixed-genre texts, we have moved from plane geometry to light theory, where light can be *both* waves *and* particles.

Crystallization, without losing structure, deconstructs the traditional idea of "validity" (we feel how there is no single truth, we see how texts validate themselves); and crystallization provides us with a deepened, complex, thoroughly partial understanding of the topic. Paradoxically, we know more and doubt what we know.

WHITHER AND WHENCE?

Although a postmodernist consciousness gives greater freedom to present texts in a variety of forms to diverse audiences, other constraints arise from self-consciousness about claims to authorship, authority, truth, validity, reliability. Self-reflexivity unmasks complex, political/ideological agendas hidden in our writing. Truth claims are less easily validated now; desires to speak "for" others are suspect. The greater freedom to experiment with textual form, moreover, does not guarantee a better product. The opportunities for writing worthy texts—books and articles that are "good reads"—are multiple, exciting, and demanding. But the work is harder. The guarantees are fewer. There's a lot more to think about.

One thing to think about is whether writing experimentally for publication is a luxury only open to those who have academic sinecure. Should only the already tenured write in experimental modes? Are the tenured doing a disservice to students by introducing them to alternative forms of writing? Will teaching them hereticisms "deskill" them? alienate them from their discipline? These are heady ethical, pedagogical, and practical questions. I struggle with them in my teaching, writing, and collegial discussions. I have no definitive answers, but I do have some thoughts on the issues.

First, there are many different avenues open for the sociological writer. There is no single way—much less "right" way—of staging a text. The same material can be written for different audiences—positivists, interactionists, postmodernists, feminists, cultural studies researchers, policy makers, and so on. That's why it is called material. Like wet clay, it can be shaped and reshaped. Writing in standard ways does not prevent writing in other ways. Most important, understanding how to *rhetorically* stage a dissertation or journal article increases the likelihood of its acceptance. Even radical messages can be published in conservative journals, if the writer follows the rules (Agger 1989c). Consequently, deconstructing traditional writing practices is a way of making writers more conscious of writing conventions and, therefore, more competently able to meet them and to get their messages into mainstream social science.

Second, writing is a process of discovery. My purpose is not to turn us into poets, novelists, or dramatists—few of us will write well enough to succeed in those competitive fields. Rather, my intention is to encourage individuals to accept and nurture their own voices. The researcher's self-knowledge and knowledge of the topic develops through experimentation with point of view, tone, texture, sequencing, metaphor, and so on. The whole enterprise is demystified. Even the analysis-paralysis that afflicts some readers of postmodernism is attenuated, when writers view their work as process—not as a definitive representation.

Third, writing practices can improve traditional texts because writers relate more deeply and complexly to their materials. The writer understands the material in different ways. The deepened understanding of a self deepens the text. The texts will be less boring because the writer will be more consciously engaged in its production, more present to self and others.

Finally, contemporary experimental writing is a harbinger: Qualitative research has been and will continue to be changed by and through it. Respected journals—such as the *Sociological Quarterly*, *Symbolic Interaction*, *Journal of Contemporary Ethnography*, *Qualitative Inquiry*, and *Qualitative Sociology*—already publish experimental pieces. The annual *Studies in Symbolic Interaction* (edited by Norman Denzin) showcases evocative writing. Presses such as Rutgers University, University of Chicago, University of Michigan, Indiana University, University of Pennsylvania, Routledge, and Sage regularly publish experimental work by both well-known and lesser-known authors. A new press, AltaMira, has a series dedicated to alternative ethnographic representations (edited by Carolyn Ellis and Arthur Bochner). Traditional ethnographers write more reflexively and self-consciously. Even those opposed to postmodernism legitimize it through dialogue (Whyte 1992). Throughout the social sciences, convention papers include transgressive presentations. Entire conferences are devoted to experimentation. At least three well-respected interpretive programs—at the University of Illinois (under Norman Denzin), University of South Florida (under Arthur Bochner and Carolyn Ellis), and University of Nevada–Las Vegas (led by Andrea Fontana)—teach about alternative representations. All of these changes in academic practices are signs of *paradigm changes*.

In the 1950s, the sociology of science was a new, reflexively critical area. Today, the sociology of science undergirds theory, methods, and interdisciplinary "science studies." In the 1960s, "gender" emerged as a theoretical perspective. Today, gender studies is one of the largest (if not the largest) subfield in the social sciences. In part, science studies and gender studies thrived because they identified normative assumptions of social science that falsely limited knowledge. They spoke "truly" to the everyday experiences of social scientists. The new areas hit us where we lived—in our work and in our bodies. They offered alternative perspectives for understanding the experienced world.

Today, the postmodernist critique is having the same impact on social sciences that science studies and gender have had, and for similar reasons. Postmodernism identifies unspecified assumptions that hinder us in our search for understanding "truly," and it offers alternative practices that work. We feel its "truth"—its moral, intellectual, aesthetic, emotional, intuitive, embodied, playtime pull. Each researcher is likely to respond to that pull differently, which should lead to writing that is more diverse, more author centered, less boring, and humbler. This is a time of transition, a propitious moment. Where this experimentation will eventually take us, I do not know. But I do know that we cannot go back to where we were.

> Willing is doing something you know already—there is no new imaginative understanding in it. And presently your soul gets frightfully sterile and dry because you are so quick, snappy, and efficient about doing one thing after another that you have no time for your own ideas to come in and develop and gently shine. (Ueland [1938] 1987, 29)

PART 3 FIELDING ETHICS

FOREWORDS: GOOD CATCH

Benign neglect by the "relationships in vector space" chair, yet another new chair appointed by the dean, after the last unseated himself, gave me two years of exquisite pedagogical excess. Faculty were asked to submit our teaching preferences to his secretary. Thinking like my cat, Blue, on this matter, I went on the cat's principle, noted by Joseph Wood Krutch, "that it never does any harm to ask for what you want." I wanted graduate teaching and I asked for it: qualitative methods, feminist theory, gender, and advanced seminars in writing ethnography. I don't know if the chair studied my request—his prime concerns, besides reading "proofs," were hiring, salaries, and promotions—but the secretary approved my two-year plan. For the first time in my academic career I felt a seamlessness among theory, research, and teaching.

Other sociology faculty acted on the cat principle, too, and the department ended up offering one seminar for every 2.2 sociology graduate students. Some seminars had no enrollees and were canceled, giving those faculty even less teaching than usual. Because of my feminist-poststructuralist network (PMS), though, my graduate offerings were oversubscribed with students enrolling from diverse disciplines. These students experienced the same exhilaration that we PMS faculty had experienced in having "found" each other a few years earlier. The seminars provided a "safe space" and time for them to try their voices, reframe their academic experiences, and develop alliances.

I experimented pedagogically. I developed "Writing Communities," in which students shared writing drafts and worked collaboratively.

Several of those communities persisted for years, supporting students through their dissertations. I taught feminist-poststructuralist theory by grounding the theory in the lives of the students; they wrote about their own writing, their discipline's writing, their own "feminist story of their lives." They wrote individually and collectively.

Feminist poststructuralism began to feel "natural" to the students. They learned to think in and through a new language. Their final papers, "normal" graduate term papers and genre-breaking experiments, were excellent—many accepted for presentation or publication. Not since the early 1970s when I taught the "gender seminar" that never stopped meeting, and which created community among many—Judith Cook, Judi DiIorio, Tim Diamond, Mary Margaret Fonow, Harriet Ganson, Betty Kirschner, Diane Vaughn, and others—had I felt such sharing of power, such passionate scholarship.

I brag on, I know. I do feel proud. Not like a mother; that is not the relationship; the students were not my children; they were not in a playpen; this was not academic day care. Rather, I felt we were in this together, stretching the boundaries of feminist pedagogy, testing what its possibilities might be. Today, three of those students—Amber Ault, Carla Corroto, Elizabeth St. Pierre—join members of the 1970s "gender seminar" as colleague-friends.

I know I romanticize a bit here about the feminist seminars. There was the session seven weeks into the quarter in one seminar where the students applied the "doubt authority" message of poststructuralism to me, the readings, the course, everything. One "Writing Community" sandbagged the writing assignment; another glossed over it. I was furious but hid it. I was experiencing close up and in my face, in my "safe space," what more traditional social scientists feared could happen to their academic routine. Dismissal. One student thought I would be proud of them for resisting my authority. Another woman wrote me a year later apologizing for using the "safe space" of our class for venting her rage toward the rest of her graduate education.

During these two years of graduate teaching, I was happily prolific. Stimulated by graduate students' questions and projects and relieved of "small" (n = 70) upper-division classes and "medium" (n = 400) introductory courses, I wrote papers about poststructuralist theory, feminism, pedagogy, and ethnographic research, revised an anthology, and completed two books. I record these publications here not so much to brag as to acknowledge the impact graduate teaching had on my writing life.

Ethical issues kept resurfacing in the seminars and in my writing. I wrote an impassioned convention paper entitled "Who Excludes Whom? Whom Excludes Who!" (not anthologized here) where I asked: Who owns the discourse? Who can take part in the debates? When and how do we inscribe privilege? erase it? In a feminist-poststructuralist world, the answers are not glib. More, the answers are not necessarily abstract. Indeed, I found myself embroiled in symposia where the lived experience of the "politics of writing" would test my "theory" and me.

One bizarrely occasioned symposium centered on William Foote Whyte's 1943 classic ethnography *Street Corner Society* (*SCS*). W. A. Marianne Boelen comes forward fifty years after the publication of *SCS* to challenge its "truth." She claims that Whyte made things up (meetings, conversations) and that she knows the "true" and "real" story about the Cornerville boys because "she was there"—thirty-five to forty years *after* Whyte's study. Although Boelen is not an ethnographer, on the one hand, and provides little to document her assertions, on the other, the editors of the *Journal of Contemporary Ethnography* decided to make her essay the centerpiece of a special journal issue. Catapulted from the sidelines, or less generously, plucked from the bleachers, Boelen plays "quarterback" in the *Street Corner Society* debates. Three social scientists join "her" team, although we don't follow her lead. I am one, and I write "Trash on the Corner: Ethics and Ethnography" (included here). All of us play anew in the old (ethnographic) field. In "true" postmodern fashion, the classic, kitschy, and avant-garde are hitched. Everything old can be made new, can be reread through troubling lenses. But with what human consequences?

TRASH ON THE CORNER

ETHICS AND ETHNOGRAPHY

H ow is knowl-
edge created? By and for whom? And with what consequences for individuals,
groups, and society? This symposium is an opportunity to reflect upon the
production of texts, including the text(s) we are creating by holding this symposium. Why "trash" *Street Corner Society*? Why now? And why am I here?

I'm standing on my corner—the sociology of sociology—and I'm watch-
ing all the folks go buy *Street Corner Society*. It may well be the best-selling sociology book ever. In its three different editions (1943, 1955, 1981), *Street Corner
Society* has sold more than 200,000 copies. That's a lot of people on a lot of different corners.

William Foote Whyte's ethnography *Street Corner Society (SCS)* legitimated
participant observation as a method, stimulated research on small groups,
linked social psychology and sociology, dislodged the popular notion of the
socially disorganized "gang," and provided a ready counterexample to the twin
accusations that "sociology is only common sense" and "sociologists can't
write." Which ethnographer has not profited from William Foote Whyte's
work, directly or indirectly? Based on *SCS*'s longevity, huge sales, wide classroom use, and contributions to sociology, it is a classic, as canonical as ethnographic texts get. William Foote Whyte is a revered elder.

A near half-century has passed since the publication of Whyte's doctoral dissertation, *SCS*, in 1943. We write about it now in a radically different context
from that in which it was produced. Some refer to the present intellectual context as "postfoundational." The core of this postfoundational climate is *doubt*
that any discourse has a privileged place, any text an authoritative "corner" on

the Truth. Characteristic of this worldview is the challenge of all authority: the "death" of the "author"; the "deconstruction" of canonical texts; and the erasure of normative ways of "knowing" and "telling." Margaret Mead and Sigmund Freud have been accused of being frauds, and Paul de Mann, one of the founders of the antifoundational movement, has been unmasked as one (Lehman 1991). So, who's next? Are we looking for a scandal right here in Soc-City?

The postfoundational sensibility locates the construction of knowledge in humanly situated social practices. One's practices reflect biographical, historical, and particularized social locations. Accordingly, each of us sees from "somewhere." No one can be "nowhere" or "everywhere." We are always on some corner somewhere. And, because we are standing somewhere, each of us harbors some ideological preference and political program; our writing is how we act out our (often hidden) desires to affect the course of history.

In what follows, I will look at different "texts." My intent is to illustrate the problems of both foundational and postfoundational "text making." My desire is to "enact" a text that ties together and transcends the other texts by situating all of them in the human practice of "storytelling" that produced them.

THROWING STUFF OUT

The "mirror room" in Aladdin's castle fascinated me as a child. Positioning myself between two mirrors and looking just the right way over my shoulder, I could see myself see myself see myself see myself ad infinitum. The notion of infinite regress has shaped my career in the sociology of knowledge. I am enamored with the idea of reflexivity and the human and temporal processes through which my and others' texts are created, staged, and disseminated. I am adamantly interested in how knowledge is "made." This interest brings me to this symposium, although my comments are different from those I originally imagined.

As an associate editor of the *Journal of Contemporary Ethnography* (*JCE*), I reviewed in 1989 an earlier version of W. A. Marianne Boelen's article. Although I did not recommend the article for publication, I was excited about the possibilities for a revision, and I was intrigued by the emotional energy behind the text. Some of my reviewer's comments on that version were as follows:

I think the paper should be framed in terms of General Ethical Issues and Social Science as Fiction or Fact. . . . Here we have a case where the actors are looked at, and they in turn "reconstruct" what they did *then*—and how Whyte did them "wrong"—even though they had not read the book! I love the possibilities here of construction and reconstruction, and the emergence of new shared stories by the actors—and their stake in a particular version of truth, Whyte's stake, and the author of this paper's stake!

Issues around the social construction of writing research are the subtext of this paper, and they should be brought forward. How is Whyte's (or anyone's work) affected by the academic setting? How have our ethical responsibilities (so defined) changed toward actors in settings? Why don't we "replicate" field work? Whose story construction, at what time, is credible?

And/or the author might want to write a book—a book about "her" Street Corner Society. Presumably, more was collected than just how the actors in Whyte's book differ from how Whyte described them. I think a woman's view of this ethnic culture would be most interesting, particularly if framed within the poststructuralist context of shifting positions, partial truths, and the breakdown in ethnography of the "hoax" that science and literature are discrete genres.

Boelen's text had definitely struck my "postmodernist/writing" chord. I had been writing about "writing strategies" and was beginning to analyze the rhetorical devices deployed in classic ethnographic texts. Thus, when Patti and Peter Adler, editors of *JCE*, announced to the board in 1990 that a special issue would be devoted to the "Whyte materials"—a revised article by Boelen, a response by Whyte, and discussion by yet-to-be-named ethnographers—I speedily asked to be named "ethnographer." The project felt historically momentous and personally propitious.

For several months, I anticipated receiving the materials. When I read them, though, my heart sank. Gone from Boelen's article was the emotional core, the driving force behind her writing. Struggles with the postmodernist writing issues did not replace the lost energy. Rather, the new paper was sixty typewritten pages of "ho-hum" indictments. The Whyte (1992) and Ralph Orlandello (pseudonymed Sam Franco in *SCS*) (1992) documents (included in the symposium) have rejoined most of those. I decided to reread *SCS* and compare editions 1, 2, and 3. I also scanned some ten other books authored or co-authored by Whyte. The more I read, the less substantial I thought Boelen's critique to be. Worse, her article was virtually oblivious to normative ethnographic and social scientific procedures, as well as feminist and postmodernist critique of those procedures. Why, I kept wondering, are we doing this symposium? Should I withdraw? But I was hooked. My heart went out to the people in this developing drama, and my head was obsessing over the issues.

Substantively, Boelen (1992) is kicking down a door Whyte himself opened in 1955. She points out problems in Whyte's text that he himself had already pointed out in the second edition. For example, she faults him for not studying family structure; Whyte tells us in *SCS* that he recognizes the importance of the family but that his interest lies elsewhere. Why denounce Whyte for studying what he wants to study? That's what makes ethnography humanly connected: the ethnographer cares about the project. She accuses Whyte of constructing the idea that Cornerville was a slum; Whyte has already told us that "Cornerville" looked like "his picture of a slum" and that it met the sociological indicators of a slum (dense housing, dilapidated housing, insufficient facilities); Boelen can disagree with the indicators and the label "slum," but this does not change the material reality of Cornerville, 1936–1940, which is Whyte's focus. She argues that Whyte should have discussed the "old country's" cultural role in the production of street corner culture, although he had already raised the question himself; she does not, however, ask her informants about that role; she assumes a contextual continuity and/or that activities are the "same" regardless of context; she does no empirical work to check out those assumptions, nor does she attend to the postmodernist critique of those assumptions.

I cannot position Boelen in relationship to her own text and the one she critiques. She is riled over Whyte's "trashing" nomenclature — slum, gangs, rackets — but fails to contextualize her own riled-up-ness. Does she really believe that because there were only a small number of racketeers, their influence had to have been negligible? She claims she wants the "voices" of the street corner boys to be heard, but she solo authors her text; the other "voices" are rarely present in her text and are wholly mediated through her own voice. Finally, her subtext is that there is but one "corner on the truth" and that she has it and Whyte did not. The idea of a single "take" on the complexities of human lives is naive and antihuman. Our understanding of our own and others' lives is enhanced by multiple and multifaceted readings.

What makes the Boelen text particularly disheartening, though, is what is not there — its absences. According to her own account, she did field work on twenty-five different occasions over a period of nineteen years in Cornerville. The published outcome is the text in this symposium (1992). I do not understand what hold *SCS* or "street corner society" has had over her; I do not understand why her energy is directed toward "trashing" *SCS* rather than writing her own book on, for example, "family in Cornerville." Boelen is a woman who has knowledge of Italian, understanding of gender dynamics within the Italian community, some training in field methods, and access to the people in *SCS*. Why hasn't she used her gender to get access to the women of Cornerville, the Aphrodite girls, the Allini sisters, Mrs. Mallory, the wives and daughters of the corner and college boys? These are the "voices" that are truly absent in everyone's texts. I feel the loss — what we could have learned had Boelen been willing/able ethnographically to pursue the gender issues she raises in her critique. I feel the failure of feminism in not having reached her. Why does she want to keep standing on the men's corner?

What in her text stimulates intellectual reflection and response? For me, it is the issue of the production of knowledge. Boelen invokes an ethical maxim: let your hosts read/comment upon your work. I find this both a false universal and a shallow resolution, because it elides over the complexities of the human practices that constitute research.

PICKING THROUGH STUFF

A continuing puzzle for me is how to do sociological research and how to write it so that the people who teach me about their lives are honored and empowered, even if they and I see their worlds differently. Among the issues that hound me are whose authority counts when; how can/should authorship be claimed; where do validity/credibility/reliability fit; how does one's writing reflect one's social privileges; what part of my biography, my process, is relevant to the text; how do I write myself into the text without being self-absorbed, unduly narcissistic; how can I write so that others' "voices" are not only heard but listened to; for whom should we write; what consequences does our work have for the people we study; and what are my ethical responsibilities for those consequences? These are not only my personal issues, they are ones that engage (enrage) both feminist and postmodernist researchers. A veritable writing industry has been spawned over these issues, an industry to which I contribute and to which I am dedicated. Reflexivity, I believe, will help us shape "better" ethnographies and better lives for ourselves and those who teach us about their lives.

Although the metatheoretical language desiccating ethnographic practices had not yet developed when William Foote Whyte wrote *SCS*, he nevertheless struggled with many of the language issues. In Appendix A, "On the Evolution of *Street Corner Society*," appearing in the 1955 (and 1981) edition of *SCS*, Whyte tells us a story about himself and his relationship to his work. This was a pathbreaking account of ethnographic methods.

The stuff that William Foote Whyte tells us can be sorted into different heaps. When it is twined with the story within *SCS* and the documents that make up this symposium, we have a veritable "landfill" of ethnographic problems. In what follows, I shall pick briefly through only a few of the heaps. These are biographical positioning; ethnographic fact and/or fiction; relationship to informants; and the odor of ethnographic research.

Biographical Positioning

What to write about yourself in a research text is a puzzling postmodernist problem. The problem as I now see it is to discover and write about yourself without "essentializing" yourself by the very categories you have constructed to talk about yourself and without "valorizing" yourself because you are talking about yourself. In Appendix A, William Foote Whyte chooses to tell us something about his background. In so doing, he "positions" himself in relationship to his research. What characteristics did he inscribe in this marginalized and belated text as presumably relevant to his work?

William Foote Whyte tells us he was a child from a "consistent upper-middle-class" background, a Swarthmore graduate, a Harvard fellow, and a would-be novelist with no adventurous life experiences to recount, just embarrassment from his own youthful "insincere dabbling" in the economic reform of the Philadelphia slums. "Oppressed by the sense of [his own] dulness," he desires to enter and know about a world different from the unremarkable one he has inhabited, much as Lincoln Steffins, a role model, had done before him (1981, 287).

Writing against the stereotypes of the upper-middle social class, Swarthmore, and Harvard, Whyte tells us that he is a liberal who lacks verve. A cynical reader might find this stance a rhetorically excellent move for staving off the hounds of academia, particularly as *SCS* was a popular success. A less cynical reading is simply that Whyte listed what he "really" thought mattered. Unremarked are Whyte's race and gender. Yet being white and male were the necessary tickets for entry into Cornerville, and for having the time and support to do the study, a four-year tenure as a Harvard Society of Fellows recipient.

Whyte does not stand alone among his generation of researchers, though, in eliding over their own (white) race and (male) gender. That was the standard, unacknowledged historical practice, and it has shaped the course of ethnography, the suppression of how the researcher's social characteristics shape "knowledge." Could Whyte today rewrite his biographical positioning? Could he tell us *how* his race, class, gender, age, sexual orientation, ethnicity, and religion — to name a few social characteristics — affected what he knew and how he knew it? And why has he not used the opportunity that this symposium provides to do at least some of that biographical work? Through concrete, self-reflexive analyses of specific projects we might come to recognize our own and others' social positionings as both constructed and constructing of knowledge.

Ethnographic Fact and/or Fiction

The postmodernist understanding is that all writing — scientific and literary — depends upon literary devices not only for adornment but for conveying content. Grammatical tropes (such as the separation of subject and object) and deep-seated metaphors (such as "social *structure*" and "theory *building*") form our fundamental ideas about what constitutes knowledge and how it is to be expressed. They go unnoticed. Writing always involves ideological, aesthetic, and ethical decisions. There is no innocent writing, including this.

Some would argue that all ethnographic writing is "fiction," because no "facts" ever exist in and of themselves, only as interpreted facts. However, if ethnography claims to be *only* "fiction," then it loses any claims it might have for groundedness and policy implications; and the ethnographer is doomed to fail in competition with those who have mastered the art of fiction writing. The direction for ethnography, it seem to me, is not to deny its social scientific grounding but to take this historical opportunity to explore its grounds for authority, partial and limited as they may be. There is a burgeoning literature on these and related writing topics, but it is beyond the scope of this paper to discuss them all (for a review, see Richardson 1990b). Rather, I will focus on some of Whyte's writing choices as illustrations of negotiating the "fact/fiction" dilemma facing ethnographers.

The 1936 North End of Boston, "Cornerville," with its dilapidated housing, children overrunning its narrow and neglected streets, and young men standing on corners, looked to Whyte like the kind of community he wanted to study. It looked like a "slum." He wanted his study to culminate in a book that was the story of "particular people" and the "particular things that they do" (1981, xix). He believed that "the general pattern of life is important, but it can be constructed only through observing the individuals whose actions make up that pattern" (1981, xix).

This seemingly innocuous writing goal, however, challenges how most sociologists "do" sociology. Unlike the numbers, masses, groups, trends, statistics, and categories that clutter the sociological world, Whyte's world is composed of *particular* people doing *particular* things. If *"there are no human beings in it,"* Whyte asserts in his introduction to SCS, *"then the picture of society is wrong"* (1981, iv; italics added). His major writing concern, then, is to write a general sociology based in real human beings' lives. How can this be done?

Whyte's way of writing "the individual . . . in his social setting and observed in his daily activities" (1981, xvi) privileged the narrative way of knowing. Narrative is the primary code through which humans organize their experience into temporally meaningful episodes. Unlike the logico-empirical code, which dominates sociological writing and looks for universal truth conditions, the narrative mode is contextually embedded and looks for particular connections between particular events. But Whyte in SCS does more than privilege narrative; he enters the domain of the novelist.

Novelists write narratives with "plots," "characters," "dialogue," and "settings." Causality governs narrative sequence. A "story" is a narrative event arranged in a time sequence. A "plot" is a narrative time sequence also, but *causality* is emphasized. "If it is a story we say 'and then'? If it is a plot we ask 'why?'" (Forster 1954). Just below the surface of SCS is Whyte the would-be novelist, using fiction-writing (not just literary) techniques to rhetorically accomplish his goal of writing a sociology with humans in it. The sociology he wrote is not the static snapshot of community studies but a story through time, a "plotlike" story of "characters." Stated another way, Whyte's purposes pushed/pulled him into deploying fiction-writing techniques. With them he could write a text about humans and social change that the logico-empirical mode would have prohibited.

Whyte deploys many fiction-writing techniques. He gives his settings fictional names: "Cornerville" and "Eastern City." He gives the people of Cornerville fictional names. They tell us about themselves in extended stories; we go with them to the corner, the bowling alley, the restaurant, the club, and so on. We follow the trajectories of corner boys and college boys through intertwining plots. We know that Whyte is "making up" some of the text—such as the names—but we tend to overlook other things he has obviously "made up." For example, he tells us in his appendix that he did not take notes in the field and tape recordings were not used. Nevertheless, Whyte treats us to pages and pages of text that are presented as if they are verbatim quotations from "characters." He stages monologues in the first person, uses ellipses and dialect, all ways of suggesting verisimilitude. The different "characters" sound different. Chapter 1, which sets the style and tone for the rest of the book, for example, begins with about six pages of "speaking" in small type attributed to Doc. "Doc's story" is clearly Whyte's rendition of Doc's story. Doc speaks the way a fiction writer might have him speak in order to establish his character, his relationship to other characters, and his role in the upcoming narrative. The different characters, moreover, sound different, and we come to think of them as different individuals. "Voice control" is an unheralded trope, then, through which Whyte advances his thesis.

Could he have "invented scenes" such as the bowling alley one, which Boelen's informants say never happened? Perhaps he could; perhaps he did. But does it matter if he did? Is "scene building" much different from naming characters and "quoting" them? Do any of these fictional techniques detract from the *general* sociological points that Whyte wishes to make; or is it, conversely, because of these techniques that he was able to make his points *and* generate an abundance of research projects in his wake?

Yet Whyte's book is *not* fiction: It is decidedly not a novel. He claims to have done an ethnography based upon his participant-observation and alliances with key informants, particularly Doc. Cornerville is a "real" identifiable neighborhood, and the "characters" are "real" identifiable people. This is what we need to think about next.

Relationship to Informants

Are there any generic rules for how ethnographers should "treat" their informants? Or does the nature of the traditional ethnographic project with its visiting scientist and scholarly product ineluctably situate us so that we are, finally, offensive, rude, and the ethnographic project invariably "trashy?" Postmodernist writers decry speaking for others and seek a principled solution by using their skills and privileges in the service of those they have researched. But will this attempt at the recuperation of the ethnographic project work in actual practice? Or are the human relationships and human practices upon which ethnographic research depends unassailably contradictory to the writing of ethnography as traditionally conceived? Is it possible to both serve the host community and serve yourself in a sociology text that bears your name as author? Let us look at Whyte and Doc as they appear in *SCS* and in the texts about *SCS* in order to concretize and explore some of these questions.

Whyte dates the "true" beginning of *SCS* to his first meeting with Doc on the evening of February 4, 1937 (1981, 290), some eighteen months into his fellowship. Whyte did not take notes from this meeting but tells us that Doc offered to help him gain entry and make sense of Cornerville. "Just remember you're my friend," said Doc (1955, 291), and you'll be accepted.

In the beginning, Doc was Whyte's sponsor and key informant, but before long Whyte "ceased to treat him as a passive informant," discussing with him "puzzling problems," ideas, and observations. Doc became, in a very real sense, a collaborator in the research" (1981, 301). Doc once commented to Whyte, "'You've slowed me up plenty since you've been down here. Now when I want to do something, I have to think what Bill Whyte would want to know about it and how I can explain it. Before, I used to do things by instinct.'" (1981, 301). Doc was a sensitive observer and interpreter of his own and others' lives; some of the interpretations in *SCS* are more Doc's than Whyte's. Whyte says that it is "impossible to disentangle" the interpretive contributions of the co-researchers, himself, and Doc (1981, 301). As a final act of collaboration, Whyte showed drafts of his 1940 work to Doc, whose "criticisms were invaluable" for revisions. Did Doc like what he read? According to Whyte, Doc "would smile" and say: "This will embarrass me, but this is the way it was, so go ahead with it" (1981, 341).

Five years after the publication of *SCS* Whyte visited Doc. Doc's reaction to the book, according to Whyte, seemed to be one of "pride and embarrassment" (1981, 346). Doc had discouraged the corner boys from reading it, saying, "'No, you wouldn't be interested, just a lot of big words. That's for professors'" (1981, 347). He also discouraged the editor of the *Italian News* from reviewing it, and anyone else from reading it. For a few years, Doc guest-lectured at Harvard and Wellesley classes, but then there was an estrangement between Whyte and Doc. Letters went unanswered by Doc; letters went unsent by Whyte. Doc gave Whyte "the impression that he had a lot of other things to do and was not eager to see" him (1981, 348). His last letter asked that Whyte "henceforth not tell anyone who 'Doc' was" (1981, 347). Doc died in 1967, still estranged from Whyte.

What *SCS* material might have embarrassed Doc? Why does Boelen claim that Doc's sons say *SCS* ruined their father's life? Doc is positioned in Whyte's research in three ways: corner boy, informant, and co-researcher. As a corner boy he is a "little guy" at "the bottom level" (1981, xvii) of a society in which upward mobility is possible, as witnessed by the rise of the college boys (1981, 105). The college boys rose not only because they had more "intelligence and ability" than Doc and the corner boys (1981, 195), but also because the corner boys did not "cultivate the middle class value of thrift" (1981, 106). Corner boy leaders are expected to help out clique members economically; prestige and influence depended upon one's ability to be a "free-spender." "The corner boy is tied to his group by a network of reciprocal obligations from which he is unwilling or unable to break away" (1981, 107). Even when Doc's political future depends upon his breaking away from his friends, he does not. Whyte tells us, "He continued to act for other people just as he had before. He was powerless to change" (1981, 108). But life changes him. Despite Whyte's "periodic efforts to find him employment" (1981, 325), Doc is plagued with unemployment and lack of funds. As a consequence, he loses his leadership status in his gang. He comes to suffer a "nervous breakdown" (1981, 207) and "psychosomatic dizzy spells" created by his "role loss" (1981, 266). Might not Doc be humiliated by these textual revelations about himself?

But Doc is also a key informant, a genuine "insider" who paves the way for Whyte and legitimates his study. He tells Whyte on their first meeting to "just remember you're my friend" (1981, 290). Doc initiates Whyte into the ways of Cornerville friendship. Doc judged a man's worth by his "loyalty" to his friends and his "behavior in personal relationships" (1981, 107). Corner-boy friendships enacted certain codes of "silence," such as equivocating rather than offending a friend; dissembling rather than embarrassing a friend; not asking certain questions; and face-to-face politeness, concealing one's feelings rather than confronting or hurting a friend.

Did Whyte violate the spirit of these friendship norms? He embarrassed Doc, personally, but even more so he put Doc in an untenable position relative to his friends. Doc was introduced in the first chapter as a key informant. He felt, according to his son's accounts in Boelen's text, that he was thereby "made responsible for the entire contents" of *SCS*. Rhetorically, he was. A goodly portion of *SCS*'s validity rested on how well Whyte could stage Doc as a credible and sensitive insider who told Whyte the "truth." This is standard ethnographic writing convention through which truth claims are justified. But *SCS* is not always flattering to Doc's friends. The most important thing in Doc's life, his relationships to his friends, had thus been sabotaged. Doc's sons claimed that their father carried a "guilt complex" into his grave because he had introduced Whyte to Cornerville as his friend. Boelen says Doc grew paranoid about the book, never returned again to the corner, and ended his life withdrawn from even his closest friends. Whyte, too, has remained troubled over the source of the estrangement between him and Doc.

Third, Whyte saw Doc as a co-researcher, whose interpretations were intermingled with Whyte's. Ultimately, however, Whyte single authors *SCS*; Whyte receives the fame and "fortune" associated with the book. The fortune probably seemed immense to Doc, who was habitually underemployed. He might well have thought Whyte profited from Doc's insights and at his socioemotional expense. Might Doc feel betrayed? " 'Never,' " says Doc in *SCS*, would he " 'turn against a friend' " for economic profit (1981, 107). Is this what Doc sees Whyte as having done? Does Doc think that Whyte has sold out his friend, just as a college boy would?

Odors

Ethnography is a human practice with consequences for all concerned. To do the kind of ethnography that Whyte did almost guarantees that some members of the host culture will hurt and that Whyte himself suffer. Cornerville is a particular place with particular people. They can identify themselves. The actual people are not hidden in numbers, trends, or as a generic "someone." The "characters" in *SCS* are real people with real ongoing lives and relationships. Whyte depended upon his friendship within Cornerville to do his research, but the norms of the subculture required he not offend his friends. If he tells the story as he sees it, which he did, he is bound to offend, to hurt the people who helped him, to violate their sense of trust. Moreover, in a subculture that values "sharing resources," Whyte's apparent failure to share authorship or royalties with Doc shows him to have been an ungrateful friend. Finally, because the task required of Doc—to be self-reflexive about his life and friends—changed him, undermined his previous dependence on his "instincts," he could never go home again, but, unlike Whyte, he had nowhere else to go. In brief (grief), Whyte could not simultaneously meet the ethics of "science" and the ethics of his host culture.

But not everyone in Cornerville was hurt by Whyte's project. Ralph Orlandello (pseudonymed Sam Franco in *SCS*) testifies (1955, Appendix B, and in this symposium) to the contrary. Over the years, Whyte successfully interceded on Orlandello's behalf (1955, 349–354, and this symposium); Whyte is still helping him with his "major book," begun in 1977, on Cornerville. Orlandello has enjoyed employment as a "social researcher/trouble shooter" in the military and industry; he sees himself "protected . . . for the rest of his life" through his "sociological insurance policy" (Whyte 1981, 366). Orlandello credits his success to the "the training and 'feedback'—well fortified with friendship" bestowed upon him for over forty years by Whyte (1981, 375). Ralph Orlandello thus has everything that Doc wanted and did not get: economic success and continuing friendship. Now comes the crucial ethnographic question: How was Orlandello as the character of Sam Franco positioned in Whyte's text? In the 276 pages of text, Franco appears only three times (1981, 248–251, 257–258, 260–261). No chapters bear his name; his words do not begin or end the book; he is quoted only three times and only on two adjacent pages (1981, 260–261). Whyte does not call him a "key informant" or "co-researcher" but later says that Orlandello (Franco) was more of a help than his presence in the text would suggest. Orlandello appears as a speaker validating Whyte in Appendix B of the 1981 edition of *SCS*, and in this symposium in a similar function.

Is there any connection between "Sam Franco's" absence in the text and the real-world advantages Orlandello has accrued through his attachment to *SCS*? I believe there is. I submit he got his rewards because Whyte could "help" "Franco" in ways he was unable to help Doc, and that "Franco" did not have to bear the burden of validating the book—he only had later to enjoy the prestige of validating its author.

LEFTOVERS AND NEW STUFF

Ethnography is a human practice with human problems. What I have had to say about Whyte's work and dilemmas are general ethnographic problems. Boelen's text, I think, can be partly redeemed as a plea to look at these problems. We, as ethnographers, have to sort through our own "garbage." How is it possible to situate ourselves as participant-observers in the lives of others and not affect them? The social skills we use to do ethnographies attach us to real human beings. They connect us to people in deeply human ways. And then, we become (solo) authors of "true" texts that have unintended, often hurtful, consequences for those who have trusted us. Ironically, the more successful the ethnographic project, the greater its appeal, the wider its audiences, and the more research and attention it spawns, the greater the ethical problems for its writer, and the greater the chances for human pain and alienation.

I have been drawn to the story of the estrangement between Whyte and Doc; it is the emotional crux of this paper, and I have constructed a "plot" to explain it. I have found myself impelled to make "sense" of the materials, both as a "foundationalist" and as a "postfoundationalist." I do not know if the story of "Doc and Whyte" is "true," but it feels humanly plausible; and I want it to be true. I want it to be a metaphoric story for the plights of ethnography—plights situated in human lives. When we bring real humans into our stories, our ethnographic writings might be "right," but what we do to our hosts might be very "wrong."

Do we have to "give up" ethnography? I do not think so, but we will have to seriously and self-reflexively "deconstruct" our practices, so that we can "reconstruct" them with fewer negative consequences. I am convinced this will require different methods (e.g., participatory research, autobiography, and critical methods), "breaking genre" (e.g., the poetic representation of the social, performance science, and community authorship), and a deep rethinking of who/what constitutes the author/subject of research. I hope this paper itself stands as a miniexample of genre breaking and the reconstitution of what "constitutes" a "subject."

Afterwords: Replay

I N "Trash on the Corner," my contribution to the *Journal of Contemporary Ethnography*'s symposium on *Street Corner Society*, I write about ethics, fact/fiction, and Boelen's missed opportunity to write about the women of Cornerville. I speak of my human concerns for the players — Whyte, Boelen, the informant, "Doc," and other members of the "Norton Gang." To both W. A. Marianne Boelen and me, Whyte responds as a modernist ethnographer. He deploys an informant (Ralph Orlandello) to back him and discredit Boelen's claims; and he reads my article as a critique of his "science," not as an opportunity to explore literary intrusions into "science writing" and the ethical and human consequences of doing research.

This week — four years after the symposium — I received an article of Whyte's to review; it's about the symposium, Boelen, me (Whyte 1996). I had read another version of the article two years earlier. Whyte is still trying to prove that he is a "scientist" who "told the truth." I regret that contemporary ethnography does not catch his imagination, that he views poststructuralism as an attack upon himself and his life. But mostly I feel weary replaying the symposium.

My critique of Whyte, I now realize, has probably hit him at two levels. Rather than acknowledging the research-principled, kind, and moral Whyte, who has tried to protect identities, I ask him, for example, how he could quote "Doc" verbatim when he didn't tape-record him. Rather than accepting his research dedication, I obliquely challenge the "science-truth" of his work. By pointing out the literary licenses he must have taken to construct a narrative, I have joined forces in his mind, I think, with Boelen.

But, in addition to the "science problem" in *Street Corner Society*, I confront Whyte with an irreconcilable human problem: Whyte's text has diminished the informant Doc's life. And now my writing, like Boelen's, is causing Whyte continuing grief. Whyte's life, like Doc's and Boelen's — and mine, too, if I would let it — is tied to *Street Corner Society*: to the fact that Whyte did research in a real community and published that work in such a way that the participants knew who they were as "characters" in the book.

We can never fully know what consequences our work will have on others. We cannot control context and readings. But we can have some control over what we choose to write and how we write it. At this point in my life, for example, I could not do a community study like *Street Corner Society*. I wouldn't want to take responsibility for how I brought the "community" into my text (theory, debates, and so on); I wouldn't want to "give voice" to real, live people who know each other and could identify each other in my text. For me, it might be "text"; for them, it is life.

Reviewing Whyte's article, thus, presents me with yet another ethical problem: How can I simultaneously honor Whyte and protect myself from spending (yet more) time backtracking onto old terrain? I temporarily resolve the problem through thinking pedagogically: What does Whyte have to teach me and (my) students about writerly questions? So, I ask him writing-technique questions like how he decided what "scenes" to write up. I don't know if his revision will answer them, but I'm afraid that he'll read those questions as yet more challenges to his authority, as more pesky — or painful, or improper — repetitious reminders, and not as the intended tribute to his ethnographic influence.

You see, an ethnographic project beckons me. There is this Park of Roses about a mile south of my house where my father walked my son,

Josh, as I now walk Josh's son, Akiva. Weddings—my older son Ben's, too—bar mitzvahs, graduation parties, memorial services. Ashes spread. Women alone; older couples, gay couples, friends, families, Japanese visitors. I love this "safe space."

Some of the rose bushes date from the seventeenth century.

FOREWORDS: BACKHAND

Alan Sica, editor of *Sociological Theory*, got my name from Steven Seidman, who got it from Ben Agger or maybe Jeffrey Alexander. (None of these men have I ever met.) Sica was putting together a symposium on postmodernist theory for the journal, and he needed a feminist-postmodernist. He had asked the well-known philosopher Linda Nicholson, but she had declined. Would I do it?

What could I say? I mean, just think of what I *could* say. The article I wrote, "Postmodern Social Theory: Representational Practices" (greatly abbreviated here), spun off on Sica's invitation and addresses issues of access to writing "theory." Who can do it? Who can take part in the debates?

I grounded my paper in my feminist-theory teaching experiences, proposing that sociologists *teach* people how to sociologically "interview" themselves, tying personal experiences to historically situated circumstances. I proposed that the resultant "self-writing" be recognized as sociological theory. The article offered a radical departure from the standard practices of theorists, which I considered both fictive and elitist. I was pretty proud of myself for breaking down old dualities (theory/research, sociologist/sociologized) and democratizing sociological knowledge making.

Seized by the applied possibilities, I took the State of Ohio Social Work licensure exam, the last opportunity for Ph.D. sociologists to "grandfather" into social work. I might want to facilitate "life-writing" groups some day, I thought; teach older people, especially, how to interview themselves; write sociobiographies. Social work might even be an alternative or supplementary career: "sociotherapy." Ethical considerations and pedagogy extended into potential future roles. I passed the test. There was life after academia.

POSTMODERN

SOCIAL THEORY .

REPRESENTATIONAL PRACTICES

STEPHEN Seidman suggests that the quest for foundational and general theories be abandoned (1991). In its place, he proposes sociologists write social theories as social narratives that "clarify an event or social configuration" and "shape its outcome." He calls upon sociologists to construct broad social narratives that serve as social critiques. In these narratives, sociologists would detail the social changes desired and the consequences of those changes for the individual and society. Justificatory appeals for change should be made to local "traditions, practices and values." The community's values become the ultimate realm of moral appeal. In Seidman's story of sociological theory making, sociologists are pragmatic actors in a political arena, advocates of morally situated public discourse.

As a postmodern sociologist, I welcome the advocacy and pragmatism Seidman proposes. I have three issues, however, with his general position, and three issues with his particular version of a postmodern narrative.

First and generally, as a marginalized speaker, I am suspicious of the "appeal to local standards" as the final moral arbiter. Whose locality? How can one's individual situatedness be separated from the grounds of different access to power, and therefore to determining what constitutes "local standards"? This sounds suspiciously like the U.S. Supreme Court's 1970s ruling on pornography. I cannot find the grounds for justifying the changes I desire in the "traditions, practices, and values" of the sociological theory community. Contemporary sociological theory, as Seidman himself has so well argued, has insulated itself from a larger political and moral world. How can we make moral appeals to a practice that claims amorality? My appeals must of necessity be based on metacommunity or fictive community or alternative community or cross-cutting identities — or — or —

Second, the elevation of sociologists to the role of moral arbiters, elaborators of moral discourse, seems to me at best ironic. I have trouble imagining the same human beings who are nit-picking at each other's putative conceptual cooties as capable/willing of accepting the relevance of the postmodern moral domain, much less elaborating upon it. But, even more problematic to me is the undisclosed lust after power embedded in the proposal. From Comte to Seidman a discipline-serving twist on Plato's maxim has seduced us: If only sociologists were kings! But what specific sociologists does Seidman have in mind? If "generic" sociologists were kings, would anything be different? The marginalized would remain marginalized. Sociologists have no special moral/leadership gifts.

Third, although I strongly share Seidman's desire that sociology enter and affect the public domain, his proposal, I believe, remains overly tied to unexamined assumptions about the nature and "level" of sociological theory. There are many different kinds of "sociological stories" to tell, many different forms in which to tell them, and many different audiences to tell them to (cf. Richardson 1990a).

Seidman suggests writing social narratives that link "event-nation based" theory to public life. But this version of a postmodernist story, although valuable and worth doing, should not be the only version. It has three serious limitations. First, it privileges "macro" accounts, marginalizing or "utilitizing" individual and group narrations, self-reflections, and sense-making. This parallels the hegemonic degradation of the "micro" within sociology. As Seidman himself so convincingly argues, though, individuals have multiple identities, diverse experiences, and are locally situated. Any categorical designation is suspect. The "stuff" of "events" is not situated in the events but in microlevel experiences and meaning making. The personal is the basis of the political. This is the "level" at which social theory must be constructed. Second,

Seidman's position strips people of their agency *as* social theorists; sociologist continue to own the means of sociological enunciation. Their lust for power goes unchecked. Third, it privileges the sociological prose-text. If sociological theory is to be a viable human resource in the postmodern world, then individual and group stories need to be sociologically told, although not necessarily told by sociologists and not necessarily told in sociological prose.

The recent feminist movement gives witness to the empowerment of individuals through the telling of their own lives. The major metaphor of the contemporary American women's movement is "voice"—speaking, naming, breaking silence. Telling their own stories. Journals, diaries, personal letters, autobiographies, poems, and biographies of ancestral women are forms in which women have been giving voice and creating collective identities. Sharing their stories has led to a renaming of what constitutes "social theory," how it is constructed, and who can do the theorizing. Feminist theory is locally situated, grounded in a woman's experiences. It is constructed through "checking out" its assertions through diversity and multiplicity. Accordingly, a woman can theorize about her own life, thank you, and write bona fide theory. What feminist theorists are doing now is deconstructing their own stories, including the "gender story," and writing diversity, multiple identity, shifting subjectivity, and so on.

We as sociological theorists can take a lesson from feminist theory and practice. People make sense of their lives for the most part in terms of specific events, such as getting a job, and sequences of events, such as an occupational career. Few people articulate how the sociological categories of race, gender, class, and ethnicity have shaped their lives or how the larger historical processes such as the demographic transition, service economies, and the ecology movement have affected them. Yet, as C. Wright Mills cogently argued (1959, 5), knowledge of the social context leads people to understand their own experiences and to gauge their "own fates." This is the promise of the "sociological imagination."

Postmodern sociologists have unique opportunities to fulfill the promise of the sociological imagination. They can write the lives of individuals, groups, and collectives, grounding social theory in people's experiences and celebrating diversity and multiplicity. By so doing we move closer to social history, giving voice to silenced, marginalized, or inarticulate people. It is a way of using sociological skills and privileges in less self-referential and self-serving manners.

But there is another more participatory way to use our skills and privileges. We can *teach* people how to sociologically "interview" themselves; how to tie personal experiences to historically situated circumstances; how to construct social/personal theory. We can name the writing of one's own life *as* social theory. What I propose here is thus a radical departure from current sociological practice. It breaks down the dualities of "research/theory," "theory/practice," "researcher/researched," and "sociological theory/self-theory." It helps move us out of the moral quagmire raised by postmodernism regarding authorship, authority, and appropriation of people's lives. We lose our privileged place; we do not become philosopher-kings, merely teacher-facilitators. The sociological perspective is still present and we can still write sociology, but we do not command special moral/political/intellectual privileges.

The versions of postmodernist sociology I propose here do not require the death of sociological theory or specialized sociological audiences. Rather, a postmodern sensibility celebrates multiplicity of method and multiple sites of contestation. Postmodernism can expand our understanding of what constitutes social theory, who can do it, and how it might be represented. Such is my hope.

Afterwords: Left Field

Afterwords: Left Field

AFTER the *Sociological Theory* symposium was published, William Bogard (1992) and Mary Rogers (1992) sent in critiques. The editor decided to publish them with symposiasts' responses as "Debate." Calling my response "Hide-and-Seek," I deployed the language of that game as topic headings—"Into the Woods," "Behind Closed Doors," "Beneath the Covers," "All-ee, All-ee, All-ee—All-in-Free" (1992e). The playfulness, though, did not hide my anger; my pen sought defense.

Bogard's contribution to the debate was familiar. "His desire to play theory with the guys on their turf," I wrote, "blinds him to the theory possibilities within my feminist article that is before his very eyes" (Richardson 1992e, 253). I write on—getting still meaner: "Disdaining closed texts as he writes one of his own and believing in the futility of the sociological enterprise as he writes for a sociology audience, Bogard writes a feckless text. He plays the game described by literary theorist Terry Eagleton, in which 'victory is achieved by kenosis or self-emptying: the winner is the one who has managed to get rid of all his cards and sit with empty hands' (Eagleton 1983, 147). Bye-bye, social theory. Bye-bye, sociology" (Richardson 1992e, 253).

Much more problematic for me, though, was the persona of Mary Rogers. She described herself as a teacher in the "backwaters of higher education" and described my narrative stance as "inclined toward hegemonic androcentric notions of power," "disparaging" of some discourses and noncognizant of my privileges. These were serious charges, I felt, and a peculiarly perverse reading of my symposium article, my life.

At the time, Rogers was an associate editor of *Sociological Theory* and a frequent reviewer of submissions. Why hadn't she been invited to be the token woman contributor to the symposium? No doubt my academic credentials (professor at a Big Ten university) and "sponsorship" by men in the poststructuralist community helped put me on the playing field. But my theoretical position helped, too. It was not just a "woman" that the editor sought for the symposium, it was a feminist-poststructuralist woman. That's I. Ironically, Rogers's lack of identification with feminist writing disqualified her from the original tourney.

Competing with other women has never been easy for me. I don't like to pit myself against them academically or fight with them over men's attentions. I don't even like to play tennis against them. I like to work cooperatively with them. My resistance, I know, to "taking on women" can be seen as a doubled-up, pleated sexism: not wanting to fight a woman also means not wanting to lose to one, implying that none is a worthy contender; wanting to work cooperatively with all women means essentializing and romanticizing them.

What I chose to do about Rogers's critique was difficult for me: I took her on. I treated her as I had treated men I had judged as at least my equals. I challenged her assumptions; I asked what she was hiding, seeking. I didn't feel good about it, and I still don't. I don't like writing "shootouts at the OK Corral," and I'm not proud of having roped myself into it.

For several years, I felt uneasy when Mary Rogers's name came up. Then, I went to a session at the American Sociological Association conference where she was a discussant. We smiled handily at each other; we chatted; we were on the "same side." And I still feel grateful to Rogers for bringing me back to the game of Hide-and-Seek.

When I was a child, I liked to play Hide-and-Seek. Two or twenty could play. Boys and girls of all ages played together. Each age had its own advantages. Hide-and-Seek knew no season. Inside and outside we played. Houses, alleys, backyards, and the woods were all game sites. The boundaries were drawn and redrawn, never quite fixed. Hiders became seekers; seekers, hiders. Roles were interchangeable. For me, winning or losing was not what the game was about; it was about being together with others, but on my own, alone, deeply experiencing both existential estrangement and social dependence. Once when I was very young, I hid so well that I was not found. During those long minutes feeling like hours, days, I invented what I later learned was "sociology"—the necessity of social exchange for individual existence.

Like everyone else, I am privileged in some ways, marginalized in others. I am invited into some debates, excluded from others. I am welcomed into some communities, shunned in others. The part of me that is marginalized is attracted to poststructuralism, as I imagine is also the case with others seduced by postmodern theory.

The postmodern game has a flexible, dynamic character. Marginalized speakers can move to the center—witness the publications of both W. A. Marianne Boelen's and Mary Rogers's long critiques in prestigious journals. Witness my inclusion in symposia. There is open-endedness, experimentation, discovery; intellectual life. Everyone can play Hide-and-Seek. Others see what I do not see, not just about themselves but about me; and I can see what I saw differently, later. Nobody has to be a stick-in-the-mud. Poststructuralism makes "old" texts potentially "current," through its rereadings, while some "new" texts are a century old, intellectually.

After my two "good years" of graduate teaching and inclusion in a flurry of symposia, I took a sabbatical. When I returned to my department, yet another new chair was seated—the third one in five years. She was a putative feminist who allegedly sought the position so she could have some control over her own life. She assigned me four undergraduate courses and only one graduate course. Sociology graduate students were advised to avoid qualitative and "foundation questioning" seminars like feminist-poststructuralist theory. The more I was invited to partake in the discipline's debates, the less I would be invited to teach "our" graduate students. The "culture wars" had hit sociology. As I write this, I think of my academic colleagues who have never had the good fortune to teach graduate students. One of my colleagues at a regional campus sued the university for depriving her of the right to graduate students. At the time, I had thought the suit somewhat frivolous. Now, I don't.

Although privileged as a speaker in the postmodern debates, I was sidelined on departmental home turf. The positivist game, rule-bound and moribund, had shut off the debates, closed the stadium, canceled the World Series. The only game in my sports-mad town was "fixed." Limited. Limiting. Poststructuralism was defined as "antirational," and its adherents needed to be "drummed out." "Academic freedom"—a juncture of ethics and pedagogy—succumbed to seventeenth-century notions of science.

In the summer of 1995, the College of Education hosted a symposium series on qualitative methods and postmodern theory. I talked to it about *Fields of Play.* Korean, Chinese, and East Indian graduate students challenged my work. They challenged my right to put the words of others into genres—to call them dramas or poetry, for example—when speakers might not so characterize their own words. They said I had chosen "elitist" forms of representation. They said my work might be "representations" to me, but to others it was "life." In this symposium, I was like William Foote Whyte, challenged about my writing not from science preservationists but from doubly marginalized speakers troubling postmodernism, pushing it in ways of value to them. I left the seminar troubled, tired, and exhilarated.

PART 4

WRITING
LEGITIMACY

LOUISA MAY'S STORY
OF HER LIFE .

.
.
.
.
.
.

i

The most important thing
to say   is that
I grew up in the South.
Being southern shapes
aspirations   shapes
what you think you are
and what you think you're going to be.

   (When I hear myself, my Ladybird
   kind of accent on tape. I think, O Lord,
   You're from Tennessee.)

No one ever suggested to me
that anything
might happen *with* my life.

I grew up poor in a rented house
in a very normal sort of way
on a very normal sort of street
with some very nice middle class friends

   (Some still 'til this day)

and so I thought I'd have a lot of children.

I lived outside.

Unhappy home. Stable family, till it fell apart.
The first divorce in Milfrount County.

So, that's how that was worked out.

ii

Well, one thing that happens
growing up in the South
        is that you leave. I
always knew I would
    I would leave.

    (*I don't know what to say . . .*
    I don't know what's germane.)

My high school sweetheart, Tom, and I married,
and went north to college.
                    I got pregnant and miscarried,
and I lost the child.

    (*As I see it now it was a marriage*
    situation which got increasingly horrendous
    where I was under the most stress
    and strain without any sense
    of how to extricate myself.)

It was purely chance
that I got a job here,
and Tom didn't.
I was mildly happy.

After 14 years of marriage,
That was the break.

We divorced.

A normal sort of life.

iii

So, the Doctor said, "You're pregnant."
I was 41. John and I
had had a happy kind of relationship,
not a serious one.
But beside himself with fear and anger,
awful, rageful, vengeful, horrid,
Jody May's father said,
"Get an Abortion."

I told him,
"I would never marry you.
I would never marry you.
I would never.

"I am going to have this child.
I am going to.
I am. I am.

"Just Go Away!"

But he wouldn't. He painted the nursery.
He slept on the floor. He went to therapy.
We went to Lamaze.

> (*We ceased having a sexual relationship directly*
> *after I had gotten pregnant and that has never again*
> *entered the situation.*)

He lives 100 miles away now.
He visits every weekend.
He sleeps on the floor.

We all vacation together.
We go camping.

I am not interested in a split-family,
her father taking her on Sundays.
I'm not interested in doing so.

So, little Jody May always has had a situation which is normal.

Mother—bless her—the word "married" never crossed her lips.

(I do resent mother's stroke.
Other mothers have their mothers.)

So, it never occurs to me really that we are unusual in any way.

No, our life really is very normal. I own my house.
I live on a perfectly ordinary middle-class street.

So, that's the way that was worked out.

iv

She has his name. If she wasn't going to have a father,
I thought she should have a father, so to speak.

We both adore her.
John says Jody May saved his life.

O, I do fear that something will change—

v

(Is this helpful?)

This is the happiest time in my life.

I am an entirely different person.

With no husband in the home there is less tension.
And I'm not talking about abnormal families here.
Just normal circumstances. Everyone comes home tired.

I left the South a long time ago.
I had no idea how I would do it.

So, that's the way that worked out.

(*I've talked so much my throat hurts.*)

Afterwords: "Louisa May" and Me

"Louisa May's Story of Her Life" is a narrative poem I created
from an in-depth interview with "Louisa May," an unwed mother. I
used only Louisa May's words, syntax, and grammar. My desire was to
integrate the poet and the scientist within me and to explore the epistemological bases of sociological knowledge. But transforming a transcript into a poem has transformed my life. "Louisa May" entered my
worldview, turning me into "Woman who Accepts She cannot Control
all She Sees," a woman who is learning to accept outcomes, whatever
they might be. The earlier, feistier sociologist is replaced somewhat by
a gentler, more consciously revealing, more accepting poet-sociologist.
She is not less analytical, though, nor without humor.

I have read the poem "Louisa May's Story of Her Life" in her voice
and accent in many different settings — conventions, poetry venues,
public lectures, and sociology, women's studies, social work, and history classrooms. Responses have been strong, and the consequences to
my self have been many. "Louisa May," thus, has been a crystallizing

experience, for me, and a crystallizing representation for others. Crystals reflect, refract, change, and grow.

Like a crystal, "Louisa May" has multiple facets; I keep discovering more. What we see, I keep learning anew, depends upon the angle of repose. Even as I write this, I have made a sad discovery: All my good jewelry is missing, lost, presumed stolen. The platinum and diamond wristwatch my father gave my mother, engraved on the back "Rose from Tyrrell—12.25.45," the antique garnet earrings my husband gave me, the sapphire ring I gave myself to mark the end of a book tour, and other pieces. Thirteen in all. Even as the story unfolds, Louisa May's words are in my mind—"that's the way that turns out."

"Louisa May" is emblematic of a poststructuralist methodology—crystallization—a methodology that generates alternate theories and perspectives for writing and for living, deconstructing traditional notions of validity, glancingly touching some projects, lighting others. None of this had I foreseen. She has indeed transformed my relationship to my work and revealed to me a story of my life.

Because "Louisa May" has been prismatic, deciding which Louisa May project (facet, theory, rhizome) to tell about here has been difficult, like choosing one angle for peering into a crystal. Turning the question in my mind over to the Louisa May in my mind, though, the answer comes more easily. "Go with the original story line. Show the intellectual and emotional journey."

Appearing in chronological order, then, the three articles in this part, "Writing Legitimacy," tell two interwoven stories of illegitimacy: Louisa May's story and the research story—its production, dissemination, reception, and consequences for me. There are multiple illegitimacies in the stories: a child out of wedlock; poetic representation of research findings; a feminine voice in social sciences; ethnographic research on ethnographers and dramatic representation of that research; emotional presence of the writer; and work *jouissance*.

I had thought the research story I told in the three articles was complete, not necessarily the only story that could be told, but one that reflected fairly, honestly, and sincerely what my research experiences have been. I still believe that. But missing from the research story, I realized, were the personal, biographical experiences that led me to author such a story.

The idea of "illegitimacy," I have come to acknowledge, has had a compelling hold on me. The working title of this book had been "Texts of Illegitimacy." In my research journal I wrote:

> My career in the social sciences might be viewed as one long adventure into illegitimacies. To wit: my dissertation on "Pure Mathematics," in which I sully the field by showing it was not so pure, but materially based; an unfinished 1965 ethnography on Le Leche League, an organization dedicated "to better mothering through breastfeeding," a thoroughly illegitimate discourse, then; "The Door Ceremony," a critique of pure etiquette, whose publicity in a 1973 Op-Ed section of the *New York Times* was read by a university trustee while in Hong Kong, who then alerted the Provost, who intervened, without the entire sociology department's blessing, on behalf of my tenure and promotion; my text, *Dynamics of Sex and Gender*, co-edited anthology, *Feminist Frontiers*, and other feminist writings for three decades; *The New Other Woman*, a study of single women in long-term relations with married men, a trade book which brought me fifteen minutes of fame, television spots, book tour, and froze my salary; an aborted unwed mother project; and an unceasing attraction to poststructuralist critiques of authority, science, and science-writing fueled by my exploration of and desires for writing deeply theoretical sociology in alternative forms—poetry, drama, responsive reading, personal essays.

Why am I drawn to constructing "texts of illegitimacy," including the text of my academic life? What is this struggle I have with the academy—being in it and against it at the same time? How is my story like and unlike the stories of other academic women, struggling to make sense of themselves, to retrieve suppressed selves, to act in their own deepest self interest?

I have come to some understanding, now, of how "Louisa May" is grounded in my own childhood experiences. Surely as we write "social worlds" into being, we write ourselves into being.

Forewords: Synchronicity

THE "schoolgirl" within responds to "assignments," the "feminist" to "collective projects," and the "pioneer woman" to the unmapped. When Norman Denzin asked me to take part in a 1992 Society for the Study of Symbolic Interaction postmodernist-cultural studies session whose goal was to build bridges between cultural analysis and lived experiences, the "schoolgirl," "feminist," and "pioneer woman" joined hands, jubilantly.

Much of my work has been stimulated by invitations to join an ongoing conversation or help set future agendas. Much in my texts are responses to others' texts, others' questions; my engagement with poststructuralism is an engagement with a collective project. I am dependent upon others' work, and I give in to a kind of synchronicity, that the questions asked by others are the ones I need to ask myself.

In "The Poetic Representation of Lives: Writing a Postmodernist Sociology," I applied poststructuralist theory to matters close to home: ethnography, symbolic interactionism, qualitative methods, representational practices. In addition to the theory talk, I read the poem "Louisa May's Story of Her Life" at the conference. I was exuberant.

I note now how quickly I identified myself as a "symbolic interactionist," how easily I slipped myself into that category of knowers, how I felt I would belong here, that the center of symbolic interaction was a poststructural and feminist one. Perhaps like an academic Ruth, I felt that their questions were my questions; or, maybe I felt like an academic Naomi—my questions would be their questions. Probably, in true postmodernist fashion, I constructed myself as *both* Ruth *and* Naomi, following "us" wherever "we" go.

THE POETIC REPRESENTATION
OF LIVES.
.
.
.
.
.
.

NORMAN Denzin presents an enticing challenge for symbolic interactionism at this postmodernist juncture: to build an interpretive framework that takes as its subject matter the production, distribution, and consumption of cultural meanings, the analysis of texts that contain these meanings, and the connection of these meanings to the worlds of lived, interactional experience. To do this requires a shift in how we articulate our work into and out of larger bodies of theorizing (cf. Carey 1989, 94). One way to shift that articulation is to alter our cultural alliances, to speak more of poetry and politics and less of metaphysics, science, and disembodied methods (cf. Agger 1989a; Brown 1977; DeVault 1990).

"Louisa May's Story of Her Life" is both a poem masquerading as a transcript and a transcript masquerading as a poem. The subtext is political. My intent is to display through Louisa May's story an interpretive framework that demands analysis of its own production, distribution, and consumption as a cultural object and of itself *as a method* for linking lived, interactional experience to the research and writing enterprises of sociologists. I do not claim that the framework and method are the only ones worthy of producing sociological texts, but I offer them at this historical moment as ways for seeing through and beyond sociological naturalisms.

[Here I read the poem that opens this section, "Louisa May's Story of Her Life," in Louisa May's hill southern accent.]

THE PRODUCTION OF THE TEXT

One evening Louisa May told me, a sociological interviewer, the story of her life. I transcribed the interview into thirty-six pages of prose text and shaped it into a poem/transcript. What possessed me to do so?

What possessed me to do so was head-wrestling with postmodern issues regarding the nature of "data," the interview as a interactional event, the representation of lives, and the distribution of sociological knowledge: The core problems raised by postmodernism concerning these research problematics seemed to me resolvable — or at least rethinkable and reframable — by shaping sociological interviews into poems, rather than into prose representations. This conviction arose from my experiences as a poet and as a sociologist and deepened the longer I worked with Louisa May's story. Once spoken, once experienced, the integration of the sociological and the poetic seemed simultaneously bounded and unbounded, closed and open. Not the only way, I hasten to add, but a pleasing and credible way to write the postmodern.

In the routine work of the sociological interviewer, the interview is tape-recorded, transcribed as prose, and then cut, pasted, edited, trimmed, smoothed, and snipped, just as if it were a literary text, which it is, albeit usually without explicit acknowledgment or recognition of such by its sociological constructor. Normatively, underlying this process is the belief that the purpose of the text is to convey information, as though information consists of facts or themes or notions that exist independently of the context in which they were told, as if the story we have recorded, transcribed, edited, and rewritten as snippets is the true one: a "science" story. Using the standard conventions and procedures of qualitative sociological writing (not to mention the conventions of positivist writing), we conceal the lived, interactional context in which a text was co-produced, as well as the handprint of the sociologist who produced the final written text. We also mire ourselves in "Derrida's Dilemma" (Denzin 1990), or the problem that transcribed materials do not recover the reflexive basis of accounting/storytelling.

In shaping Louisa May's story, I have tried to reframe these problems through poetic representation as a method of revelation of context and labor, and as a method for undoing Derrida's Dilemma.

Let me begin the argument for poetic representation of lives, then, with the nature of the sociological interview. Such interviews are essentially interactional speech events created in particular contexts; interviews are themselves examples of lived experience. The interactional nature of the interview engages the interest of a postmodernist sociology, which reflects upon how its own texts are produced (see especially Mischler 1986). An interview, for example, is now theorized as a jointly constructed "text" arising from the intersection of two subjectivities, the interviewee and the interviewer, but with the two participants not having equal billing: The interviewee is the creative voice; the interviewer, the facilitator (cf. Patai 1988). The privileged status of the interview as "science" or "fact" is thus challenged, as it takes its place alongside other human ventures.

Louisa May's story arises in the context of an interview; the context is written into the poem. From start (*"The most important thing"*) to finish (*"I've talked so much my throat hurts"*), Louisa May reminds us that her story was constructed in a live interaction of a particular kind, the sociological interview. She frames her life for us. She speaks a story, comments on her life, *"a normal sort of life,"* and talks in asides, written in italics, to the interviewer, about the interview, the tape recorder, *"what's germane,"* *"what's helpful."* She speaks emotionally about her mother, friends, sex life, voice, not as story line but as private asides to a listener. Yet and still, Louisa May is the center of the story, not the interviewer, the context, or their relationship.

The poem may seem to omit "data" that sociologists' want to know. But this is Louisa May's narrative, not the sociologist's. She does not choose, for example, to talk about her educational level or her employment. The questions the poem raises for readers about Louisa May, thus, reflect their own particular subtexts, not universal texts. If they wonder, for example, how Louisa May supports herself, are they tapping into stereotypes about "unwed mothers"? If they feel they cannot understand her unless they know about her schooling, are they telling us something about their own relationship to education, its meaning in their own lives? More generally, have the concepts of sociology been so reified that even interpretivists cannot believe they "know" about a person's life without refracting it through a sociologically prescribed lens?

In writing Louisa May's story I drew upon both scientific and literary criteria. This was a greater literary challenge than a sociological one because Louisa May used no images or sensory words and very few idioms. The poem, therefore, had to build upon other poetic devices such as repetition, pauses, meter, rhymes, and off-rhymes. Without putting words in her mouth, which would violate my sociological sensibilities, I used her voice, diction, and tone. I wrote her life—as she told it to me—as a historically situated exemplar of sense-making. Her life, as she speaks it, is a "*normal one.*" The political subtext, as I wrote it, is "Mother Courage in America."

According to the oral historian Dennis Tedlock (1983), when people talk, whether as conversants, storytellers, informants, or interviewees, their speech is closer to poetry than it is to sociological prose. He claims:

> conversational narratives THEMSELVES
> traditionally classified as PROSE
> turn out, when listened to CLOSELY
> to have poetical qualities all their OWN (109)

Everybody—literate and nonliterate, adult and child, male and female— speaks using a poetical device, the pause. Indeed, in American speech, estimates are that about half of the time we are speaking, we are not; we are pausing (Tedlock 1983, 198). And some 25 percent of pauses cannot be explained by physiological needs for breath or grammatical demands for closure, such as at the ends of sentences or clauses (Tedlock 1983, 198).

In poetically representing lives, the sociologist/poet writes in the pauses, signals them by conventions such as line breaks, spaces within lines and between stanzas and sections. The sociologist/poet chooses how and where and why and for how long quiet will counterpoint the sound, thus creating a text that mimics more closely the actual conversation and that builds upon both sounds and silences.

When we listen to or read the text, "Louisa May's Story of Her Life," rather than being swayed into thinking we have the one and only true story here, the facticity of its constructedness is ever present. By violating the conventions of how sociological interviews are written up, those conventions are uncovered as choices authors make, not rules for writing truths. The poetic form, moreover, because it plays with connotative structures and literary devices to convey meaning, commends itself to multiple and open readings in ways that straight sociological prose does not. The poetic form of representation, therefore, has a greater likelihood of engaging readers in reflexive analyses of their own interpretive labors of my interpretive labors of Louisa May's interpretive labors. Knowledge is thus metaphored and experienced as prismatic, partial, and positional, rather than singular, total, and univocal.

The poetic representation of lives, moreover, derides the dazzle of Derrida's Dilemma. Transcripts, Derrida argues, are fairly accurate approximate renditions of literal social reality, but they do not recover the reflexive process through which the knowledge is created. That is, when people speak, they are deferring their thoughts; their thoughts are in the process of creation and transformation (cf. Denzin 1990). But, I would propose, poetic representation reveals the process of self-construction, the reflexive basis of self-knowledge, the inconsistencies and contradictions of a life spoken of as a meaningful whole for two reasons. First, a poem is a whole that makes sense of its parts; and a poem is parts that anticipate, shadow, undergird the whole. That is, poems can themselves be experienced as simultaneously whole and partial, text and subtext; the "tail" can *be* the dog.

Second, an experiencing person is a person in a body. Poetry can re-create embodied speech in a way that standard sociological prose does not because poetry consciously employs such devices as line length, meter, cadence, speed, alliteration, assonance, connotation, rhyme and off-rhyme, variation, and repetition to elicit bodily response in readers/listeners. Universal in social and religious ritual poetry, for example, is a three-second line length (Tedlock 1983). Apparently, we bodily experience the present as a three-second interval. When rhythm is added to a line, we respond physiologically. Meter feels good. Similarly, when the poet adds cadence, rhymes and off-rhymes, repetition, and variation, our neurons are made happy. Thus, poetry, built as it is on speech as an *embodied* activity, touches both the cognitive and the sensory in the speaker and the listener.

Lived experience is lived in a body, and poetic representation can touch us where we live, in our bodies. Thus, poetry gives us a greater chance of vicariously experiencing the self-reflexive and transformational process of self-creation than do standard transcriptions, and a greater chance of relieving us of Derrida's Dilemma.

CONCLUSION

If our task as symbolic interactionists is to build an interpretive framework about the production of cultural meanings and the connection of those meanings to lived experience, then we need to devise strategies that reveal and extend our own processes of sociological production, since "sociology" is and will continue to be the framework in which we as sociologists cast our understandings of other cultural productions. That is, we need to attend to our own factory and salesroom.

Casting sociological interviews into poetry can make visible the underlying labor of sociological production and its sales pitch (conventional rhetoric), as well as its potential as a human endeavor. A "sociopoetics," then, at this postmodernist juncture, is both framework and method for representing the sociological.

FOREWORDS: THE TRUTH
OF CONSEQUENCES

CAROLYN Ellis asked me to contribute to a book she and Michael Flaherty were editing on "investigating subjectivity," and I wrote about the consequences to the self of having transformed an in-depth interview into a narrative poem. Carolyn's feedback was rev-elatory. I found myself engaged in "real"—not imagined—dialogue with a colleague, soon to be friend, with whom I shared multiple over-lapping interests—writing, feminism, qualitative research, sociology, symbolic interaction, the self. Her questions pushed me into greater self-revelation about my attitudes toward sociology, reasons for having written "Louisa May," the seriousness with which I take my work, and how I had been impacted by it, emotionally and—ah, I actually said it in print—spiritually.

On rereading "Consequences to the Self," I see how I define myself and Louisa May through sociological categories, although I cajole other sociologists to stop doing so. A sociological consciousness holds me, deeply.

The Louisa May project resonated with a variety of readers and has generated a veritable "mini-industry" of "poetic representation" in dif-ferent academic projects and disciplines. Prismatic work reflects back upon itself while creating new images. New projects include literacy re-search; writing across the curriculum; English as a second language; the staging of social problems; performance sociology; ethnographic poetry for publication; and the First Annual Louisa May Poetry Reading at the SSSI-Stone Conferences.

But this mini-industry has not been without problems. One is that I have been labeled "antirationalist." Talking with those who so label me reminds me of how energy-draining it was in the 1970s when I tried to explain feminism to people who bashed it, knowing "all" about how awful it was.

More painful—and rage-making—though, are the accusations that by writing poetic representations I have abrogated my ethical responsibilities as a qualitative researcher. I have been accused of not disciplining myself and my "disciples" to "abide by the rules of the [ethnographic] craft" (Swalbe 1995, 397–398). Even worse, I have not enforced "guild rules" that check our "artistic pretensions and excesses" (411). My "irresponsibilities," thus, are many: failure to patrol ethnography's boundaries; refusal as a qualitative researcher to align myself with those who would discipline and punish poststructuralist ideas; and, worst of all, not making nice-nice with those already well-situated and secure within the academy, i.e., the anti-"antirationalists."

Policing is always about bodies, though, isn't it? It's not just about ideas, but about people. What real live people are included or excluded through different visions of ethnographic practices?

Here is something I have learned from teaching qualitative methods and reading letters sent to me about my work: People from marginalized and devalued cultures find the turn to alternative ethnographic representation as beckoning, welcoming. They see it offering them the possibility of both joining the qualitative research community and honoring their responsibilities to their traditions and cultures. They are not undisciplined in their attention to craft or exclusionary in their practices. They envision themselves—as I envision myself—doing both "standard" and "nonstandard" ethnographic work, as full-fledged members of a socially responsible, culturally complex, qualitative community.

Consequences of Poetic

Representation .

Writing the Other, :
Rewriting the Self •
•
•
•
•

This paper is consciously self-revelatory, but my purpose in writing it is sociological, not confessional. Social scientists inherit an academic culture that holds authority over them; that culture suppresses and devalues its members' subjective experiences. For social scientists to make their lived research experience the centerpiece of an article seems Improper, bordering on Gauche and Burdensome. I have not, I hope, ventured beyond Improper.

I have breached sociological writing expectations by writing sociology as poetry. This breach has had unexpected consequences on my sense of self, which may be of sociological and methodological interest to others struggling with alternative forms of representing the sociological. By violating the norms of sociological production and dissemination, I have felt the power of those norms, their role in suppressing lived experience, and the exhilaration of writing nonalienating sociology.

The Lived Experience

Why did I choose to breach the norms governing sociological interview writing? Why did I not simply paraphrase Louisa May's life, write it as case study, or quote her words as evidentiary text? What happened when I read and discussed the poem in different discursive sites? What were the consequences to my Self?

I wrote her life as a poetic representation for several reasons known to me, and surely many that are not. First, for several years, I have been wrestling with the sociological representation of lives (1988a, 1990a), which resulted in a monograph on writing qualitative research (1990b). In that book, I argued that no matter how we stage the text, we — the authors — are doing the staging. As we speak about the people we study, we also speak for them. As we inscribe their lives, we bestow meaning and promulgate values. I concluded that the ethically principled solution to issues of authority/authorship/appropriation required using my skills and resources in the service of others less beneficially situated. My conclusions were satisfying as rhetorical, aesthetic, and philosophical abstractions; but how to write substantive sociology that pleased me was still elusive.

Second, upon reflection, I realized there were few substantive (not theoretical or methodological) sociology texts that I enjoyed reading or could point to as models for my students (cf. Brown 1977 on "style"). Even when the topic was ostensibly riveting, the writing style and reporting conventions were deadening. Nearly every time sociologists broke out into prose, they tried to suppress (their own) life: passive voice; absent narrator; long, inelegant, repetitive authorial statements and quotations; "cleaned up" quotations, each sounding like the author; hoards of references; sonorous prose rhythms; dead or dying metaphors; lack of concreteness or overly detailed accounts; tone deafness; and most disheartening, the suppression of narrativity ("plot," character, event). Unlike literary literature, which I read for the experience of reading and which could touch me emotionally, sociological texts were either skimmable — the cream risen to the top in abstracts or first sentences of paragraphs — or dreary.

Third, I had signed a book contract about voluntarily single adult mothers. Although I had collected the interviews and the manuscript was overdue, I could not get myself to write the book. I found myself clutching at my own throat at the thought of writing "straight" sociological prose.

About this time, a part of me that I had suppressed for over eight years demanded attention: the part that writes poetry. Writing poetry is emotionally preoccupying; it opens up unexpected, shadow places in my self. As a kind of time-saving/snaring-two-birds-with-one-net strategy, I decided to fashion material from an unmarried mother interview into a poem. That, I thought, would get me started on the contracted book, acknowledge my need for poetry/play, and, maybe — just maybe — provide a new strategy for resolving those horrid postmodernist writing dilemmas. Once uttered, however, the idea of the union between the poetic and the sociological was compelling. Like a charismatic idea, it developed a life of its own. It proffered sociological life writing that was endearing, enduring, and endurable—bounded and unbounded, closed and open—sociological writing that I would want to read and write.

During my off-duty quarter, I enrolled in an intensive, advanced poetry workshop at the university. I was fully immersed in poetry for three weeks: every day, three hours in seminar, three hours writing poetry, and another hour or so reading it, and only it. No sociology. I felt adventurous.

Of all the available interviews, I chose to work on Louisa May's, not because she was intrinsically more interesting than other women I interviewed, but because the literary and sociological challenges were great. If I could "do" Louisa May, I felt, I was onto a "do-able" method.

Because I had decided, for sociological veracity, to utilize only the words spoken by the interviewee in the construction of the poem, Louisa May posed a difficult literary problem. For the most part her speech was bland and unconcretized, almost entirely devoid of images, metaphors, and poetic language. She used some literary devices that I felt captured her "poetic essence." For example, she characteristically used large words (e.g., "extricate") and complex sentences, and she had a distinctive "hill southern" rhythm in her speech. In renarrativizing her story, she told it through dialogue and conversations. Like the Ancient Mariner and the Wife of Bath, Louisa May used the literary device of weaving the listener into her story.

Sociologically, the task of empathetic understanding—feeling that I was "getting it right"—was difficult because Louisa May and I differed in many ways: She was an unmarried mother; southern; rural; Christian; from a poor "broken" family. Not only did she belong to different sociological "categories," she positioned herself differently than I did, emotionally and ideologically: Things "turned out" for her, she didn't "make" them happen; her life was "normal"; she liked being "middle-class"; she had succeeded in escaping from her background; she had distance from but not disdain for her child's father; she spoke no guilt. I was born and raised in Chicago, into a cultural/religious/class mixed marriage. My father, an attorney, was from a mainline Episcopalian "Daughters of the American Revolution" family but was reared by Christian Scientists; my mother, a graduate of the eighth grade, was a Russian Jewish immigrant. I have seen myself as having "agency" in the world: Things don't just "turn out"; I make them happen. I experience my life as far from normal; yet I do not choose to escape my background, nor do I think, finally, I could, despite all my claims to agency and independence. I am comfortable on the (intellectual, sociological) margins.

Louisa May was, then, in many ways, my "other." Her language stylistics, her sociological background, and her fix on the world were near opposites to mine. Could/should I write from this "other" subject position? Here I was careening fast again into an emotional and pragmatic struggle with the same postmodernist issues of "authorship"/authority/appropriation that I had sought to escape through the poetic representation of the sociological. Challenged, I chose to write through my perplexities.

The poem went through innumerable computer screen revisions, nine hard copy drafts, two critical readings by the professor, and two critiques by workshop participants before becoming the version published here. Writing the poem took the better part of four weeks. During that time, Louisa May moved into my psychic interior in a way that no interviewee of mine ever had. She moved in the way poetry does. She's not yet moved out.

I have presented "Louisa May" to diverse audiences; sometimes "Louisa May" has stirred up heated controversy. Poets have responded with sociological analyses of how "normalness" is constituted, as well as discussion of genre boundaries and authorship/expropriation. Did I "steal" Louisa May's voice? Poetry audiences, identifying with Louisa May, have tearfully requested I pass on words of encouragement to her. General audiences have discussed implications for family and child policy. Academics have had diverse responses: Oral historians have noted that the poem captures "essence" in the way prose does not, and that there are methodological lessons here for them; women's studies audiences have discussed the poem as a method for revealing conventional forms of reporting "findings" as patriarchal strictures—with poetry "feminizing" the product and its production; and postmodernist theorists have discussed the work as an important turn for both theory and research on social scientific writing. Some interpretivists have welcomed the breach as an opportunity to rethink sociological representation. Other social scientists have challenged the "validity" of the poem, demanding to see the transcript, although not to hear the tape, see a videotape, or talk directly to Louisa May. Some feminist social scientists have assumed that I am Louisa May. I doubt if the very existence of Louisa May would have been challenged had I reported it conventionally.

Thus, I have been variously accused of exploiting Louisa May, of fabricating her, and of being her. But I also have been applauded for writing Louisa May's "core"; for touching an emotional center in the listener; for showing how patriarchal strictures have controlled the writing of social science "findings"; for problematizing interpretive methodological practices; and of providing policy makers with a different slant on "unwed mothers."

Because of the unexpected hold on my psyche stemming from the creation of the poem and because of the unexpected and intense receptions of "Louisa May," Louisa May has changed my life. Through writing "Louisa May," I am rewriting myself.

Consequences to the Self

I have identified five ways the experience of producing and sharing "Louisa May" has changed my life. First, I find myself using Louisa May's words in my daily discourse. I find myself saying—even more so, feeling—"so that's the way that turned out." Louisa May's words enforce an acceptance of that which cannot be changed. When my younger son missed a family holiday, I validated his decision with the mantra "that's the way that turned out." Sometimes, I say her words with a touch of irony, amusement. When my department put forward an unworthy candidate (in my mind) for a prestigious honor, I saw this as an ironic "turn of events" rather than as a "plot."

Second, speaking Louisa May's words has had a transformative effect on deeper, more spiritual parts of my self. I speak her point of view, not as hers, but as mine. A dramatic example of how speaking Louisa May's words has transformed my point of view happened in a favorite place, the Shenandoah National Park, an area close to Louisa May's heart, too. My husband and I planned an easy day hike, the 7.5-mile Hoover-Laurel loop. During the hike out I thought and talked about death, about how quickly and unexpectedly death can happen, just one wrong turn. We don't know how things are going to turn out—only, as Louisa May would say, that they will. Therefore, I reasoned, this is the time in our lives, as is any time in any life, as Joseph Campbell would say, "to follow our bliss."

We reached Laurel Prong, but a new trail had been blazed with the old color, which we guilelessly followed. Trail ran into gravel road, but gravel road dead-ended at groves of trees, half-century high. Nothing made sense. Dark fell. We "slept" that night in the woods, with one windbreaker jacket between us, a full moon, six ounces of water, no guarantee of finding our way back, visions of Laughing Wolf gently pulling the blanket, Night, over us, and, as we discovered the next day, twenty-two miles of wilderness hiking under our boots and twelve more to go before we left the area, called since before the Civil War and to this day "The Wilderness," inhabited, now, by some four hundred bears, each a night roamer with a twenty-square-mile territory.

We survived for me to tell how things turned out, including how my internalized sense of life had altered; how I now find the apparent paradox of simultaneously succumbing to life's turns and taking charge by "following one's own bliss" as compatible, complementary visions.

Third, I feel more integrated. The suppressed "poet" and the overactive "sociologist" have found each other. The two separate writing "voices" were united in Louisa May's poem. This is a union I have desired and avoided for nearly two decades while I wrote sociology as "Laurel Richardson Walum" and poetry as "Laurel Richardson" and "Alexis Tyrrell." About a decade ago, I named myself "Laurel Richardson" in both writing arenas; but only now do I bring the two forms together. One tangible outcome is that I have returned the advance and contract for the book on unmarried mothers, because I cannot write (at least at this time) the kind of conventional sociology that the contract (and my own proposal!) called for. I do not know where the integrated self is heading, but the energy for writing (living) is immense.

Fourth, I am better able to step into the shoes of the other, as well as into the other's body and psyche. I am more attuned to lived experiences as subjectively felt by the other. This has affected my willingness to know myself and others in different ways. For example, in multicultural classrooms, I have been more willing to risk potential conflictual situations by "modeling" listening to and then speaking from nondominant positions, even if those positions undermine the grounds of my authority within the classroom. My positionality is subject to critique. Similarly, I ask my feminist theory students to critique and rewrite their work from an other's position. My research interviewing, on the one hand, requires less effort because it is easier now to "travel" unencumbered by my own baggage to the other's world (cf. Lugones 1987); but, on the other hand, it is more difficult to choose to do interviews, because I am more cautious, more contemplative, about what "doing research" means.

Fifth, Louisa May brings me to different sites and allows me to see familiar sites in new ways. Disillusionment is one of the outcomes. When, for example, a symbolic-interactionist conventioneer asks me to "prove" Louisa May exists by showing him the transcript of my interview (as if transcripts were real), or when my feminist-postmodernist reading group wants to know about the "validity" of the poem, I experience deeply the hold of positivism on even those I consider my allies, my intellectual companions. In the chasm, I experience isolation, alienation, and freedom, exhilaration. I want to record what they are saying; I want to do field work on them. Science them. My romanticized vision of a postmodernist sociology shaken, I seek alternative sites for sharing sociology. Louisa May's life takes me to poetry bars, literature conventions, women's studies classes, social work spaces, and policy-making settings.

I take pleasure in feeling I am a sociological revolutionist in community with others who are questioning how and for whom we write sociology. My feminist mission has intensified. I desire to problematize sociology's concepts and methods by grounding sociology in lived experiences; to write sociology as "windows on lived experience." I struggle now with ways to unite people's subjective experiences with my sociological utterances. I strive for forms in which sociology can be an affective and affecting discourse, a nonalienating practice.

Representing the sociological as poetry is one way of decentering the unreflexive "self" in order to create a position for experiencing the self as a sociological knower/constructor—not just talking about it, but doing it. In writing the other, we can (re)write the self. That is the moral of this story.

> I am indebted to Louisa May.
> And that's the way
> this has turned
> Out.

Poetics, Dramatics, and
Transgressive Validity.
"The Case of the Skipped Line"

The Presentation

At the 1990 meetings of the Society for the Study of Symbolic Interaction (SSSI) I presented a paper, "The Poetic Representation of Lives: Writing
a Postmodernist Sociology." The paper asked: Why prose? How does the
prose trope conceal the position of the author (the sociologist) and prefigure
judgments about the validity of a social science text? For that 1990 program I
transformed an open-ended life history of an unwed mother, Louisa May, into
a five-page poem. Poetic representation could make visible, I argued, both *context* and *labor*.

Louisa May is the speaker in the poem, but I crafted it, using both scientific
and poetic criteria. Reminding the reader, there are two intertwined texts in the
poem. In one text, Louisa May tells us that her story was constructed during
an interview. In the other, she tells us she grew up hill southern poor, married,
went north to college, miscarried, moved to another city, and got divorced.
She's forty-one and single when she becomes pregnant by John, a man whom
she does not intend to marry. She gives her daughter, Jody May, John's last
name, and he visits on weekends; sleeps on the floor. Louisa May is not interested in having a "split family," John taking Jody May away on Sundays. No,
her daughter has a normal life on a "perfectly ordinary middle-class street."
Louisa May has never in her life been happier.

Writing "data" as a poem did two things: First, it changed me, personally, unexpectedly; and second, it exposed the truth-constituting, legitimating, and deeply hidden validifying function of the genre prose. Here are some comments from my process journal:

Whose poem should I write? I think Louisa May's because it's going to be difficult. She uses almost no poetic devices in her normal speech; her background, goals, and perspective are different from mine.

If I can construct a poem which creates a vivid, immediate, emotional experience for the reader/listener using Louisa May's words, then I'm on to something.

I could write my own poem alongside hers, a poem about what it is I don't say during the interview. Me, the deceiver, the deluder — of self and others. My thoughts would be the buried text that needed to be excavated. But then the focus would be on me in a way that it should not be.

I resist beginning the poem because I don't want to be in anyone's head for as long and as deeply as I'll have to be in order to write poetry.

Fourth Draft! I like it. I love this work. I feel I am integrating the sociological and the poetic at the professional, political, and personal levels. I love what I am doing. I love the process.

I am showing a different way of displaying a life. I am deconstructing the formats sociologists have chosen. I'm not just talking strategies: I'm showing them.

Bliss.

In writing sociological findings as poetry, I felt I had discovered a method that displayed the deep, unchallenged constructedness of sociological truth claims and a method for opening the discipline to other speakers and ways of speaking. I could foresee the possibility of building cultural alliances with poetry and politics (cf. Brown 1977; Carey 1989), of taking seriously William Wordsworth's vision of a poetics applied to science:

> The remotest discoveries of the Chemist, the Botanist, the Mineralogist, will be as proper objects of the Poet's art as any upon which it can be employed, if the time should ever come when these things shall be familiar to us, and the relations under which they are contemplated by the followers of these respective sciences shall be manifestly and palpably material to us as enjoying and suffering beings (Wordsworth, quoted in Noyes 1956, 363).

I had in mind writing sociologies that displayed how meaning was constructed and that were helpful to people, and not boring.

In August 1990, I sat at a long table at the front of a conference room, a happy actor in the ritual drama that Norman Denzin organizes each year on postmodernism for the SSSI convention. I was grateful for a respite from my department's obsession with logico-empiricism. In the standing-room-only room, I felt there was space. I could breathe. I could speak and be heard.

Two panelists read their papers. My turn. I handed out copies of the poem, read my paper in my normal voice, while reading Louisa May's poem and words in her hill southern accent. Two more papers were read. Nobody hogged the podium. There was time for discussion. I loved how it all was.

THE DISCUSSION

The ensuing forty-minute discussion period focused entirely on "Louisa May." I became a participant-observer and took extensive field notes, which I later constructed into an ethnographic drama. In the drama, the comments appear in the same order in which they were spoken during the discussion. Following ethnographic conventions, I abbreviated comments but strove for accurate renditions of tone and content. Three of the characters are 1990 panel members—Norman Denzin, Patricia Ticento Clough, and myself. The other characters, members of the audience, are without names or identities, other than gender—ten men and five women. They are treated here as anonymous speakers—speaking positions, not personages.

I had not intended to create an ethnographic drama when I took my field notes. I had planned to write them up as part of a larger paper on the reception of "Louisa May" by different audiences. But I was unable to shape the experience in prose without losing the experience; the material was intractable, unruly, transgressive. But a drama, I thought, could capture and communicate the event.

I beseeched myself with ethical questions. Did I have a right to write this play? Who has ownership of words spoken in a public meeting? Was I plagiarizing? (I decided I was not.) Was I violating some human subjects code? (According to my university's rules, no.) Was I violating some unwritten courtesy code by doing "covert" ethnographic research on ethnographers—and thereby committing academic suicide? Would anyone ever "trust" me again? Would I be attacked? sued?

At the previous year's (1991) SSSI meetings, I had presented a paper, "Ethics and Ethnography" (an earlier version of "Trash on the Corner"). That paper argued that ethnographers always run the risk of hurting their hosts, particularly if they used the norms of the community to gain entrée and rapport and if the published material might not reflect the host's visions of self. Now, here I was in the very ethical dilemma I had discussed abstractly. Would my consternation be less, I wondered, if the dramatis personae were not drawn from my academic family? I resent being "sociologized"; will they? I felt great relief when Norman Denzin and Patricia Clough read the script, consented to the use of their names, and assured me that I had "heard" them. If others recognize their speaking positions in this script, I hope they will also feel that they were heard.

Once the drama was written, I cast members of my family into the roles and tape-recorded them. In addition, using the dramatic convention of the "interior monologue" or "talking to oneself," I left blank time on the tape for me to speak live what I had been thinking but did not say in 1990. I did the ethnographic performance at the 1992 SSSI meetings, using the prerecorded tape and speaking out loud in 1992 what was unspoken in 1990.

The process of constructing the drama led me to reconsider the postmodern debates about "oral" and "written" texts. Which comes first? Which one should be (is) privileged and with what consequences? And why the bifurcation between "oral" and "written"? Originating in the lived experience of the 1990 discussion, encoded as field notes, transformed into an ethnographic play, tape-recorded, performed using both the taped and live speech, and now reedited for publication, the script for *The Case of the Skipped Line* might well be fancied the "definitive" or "valid" version, particularly to those who privilege the published over the "original" or over the performance or over the lived experience. *The Case of the Skipped Line* incorporates in its construction multiple sites of invention and potential contestation for validity, the blurring of oral and written texts, rhetorical moves, ethical dilemmas, and authority/authorship. It doesn't just "talk about" these issues, *it is these issues*.

Below is a script, *The Case of the Skipped Line*, a representation of the 1990 SSSI discussion of the session, "Postmodernism and Cultural Studies."

THE CASE OF THE SKIPPED LINE

An Ethnographic Presentation in One Act and Many Scenes

CHARACTERS: *Norman Denzin, moderator*
Patricia Ticento Clough, panelist
Laurel Richardson, panelist — 1990 and 1992
Male Conferees — 10 different Voices
Female Conferees — 5 different Voices

(SETTING: August 1990. A large hotel conference room at the Society for the Study of Symbolic Interaction Meetings, Washington, D.C. The room is overpacked; people are standing at the back, trailing out into the hall, peering in. The panelists are sitting equidistant behind a long skirted table at the front of the room.)

Norman: Questions — comments? Yes . . .

Male-1: My question is for Laurel. Your oral text — poem — was different from the written poem you handed out. Why didn't you read the poem just as it appeared on the handout? I wonder why you changed it?

Laurel: Easy — my bifocals skipped a line.
Laurel (*interior monologue*):
I'm confused by the question. Reading poetry out loud is a performance art; the evocative, smooth performance of the poem is my priority. It would not occur to me to stop the flow of the poem to pick up the lost line.

Mmm . . . Would someone have commented about a "slip" in a prose text? Would anyone at a sociology conference question the difference between an oral and written rendition of an interview snippet? . . . Ah, I get it: The written text is being privileged over the spoken one! If I hadn't distributed the written text, no one would have thought I had made a "slip." Maybe I shouldn't have handed out the poem . . .

Norman: Patricia?

Patricia: He has not asked an interesting question and Laurel has not given an interesting answer. I want to make it more interesting. Laurel, you slipped — you made a slip. There are no slips. I want to know about the accent that you used when you read the poem and its relationship to slips.

Laurel (interior monologue):
Oh, no, Pat, are we going to get into this Freudian stuff again? Maybe I can fend it off with a minimal negative response.

Laurel: Patricia's question is not interesting to me.

Male-2: (speaking with increasing anger and volatility) What about the reliability and credibility of the original experience? You have collapsed three moments of doing research into one? Because of what you have done, we cannot accept your findings as an accurate story. *(Continues chanting in the background beneath the sotto voce exchange that follows)*

> reliability — validity — cannot accept your findings — inaccuracy — reliability-validity — cannot accept your findings — cannot accept your findings —

Norman: (sotto voce, aside to Laurel, supportively nodding his head) Go on. Aren't you going to respond?

Laurel: (aside to Norman) No, I'm too busy taking field notes. I'm doing science.

Laurel (interior monologue):
Over the years, participant-observation has been a convenient shield. Now, too.

Male-3: What is an accurate realization?

Laurel (interior monologue):
Yeah! A smart male ally in the audience to do answering. Great!

Male-2 (huffily, pointedly, and with great authority): I want to see your transcripts and the poem and reconcile the two.

Laurel (interior monologue):
Why doesn't he ask to hear the tape? Or, speak face-to-face with Louisa May? Why is he so tied to the written word?

Male-2: (more and more huffy and angry) Does the original, the written text, relate to anything? Did you actually do an interview? Is there a Louisa May? If you want to display originality, then how can we trust you? What is the truth here? How do we know that you haven't made the whole thing up?

Laurel (interior monologue):
This is outrageous. I am being subject to a vitriolic, out-of-control, libelous attack on my professional ethics. Why? Because my oral reading differed from a written text? If I had written Louisa May's interview in a normative way, would I be accused of fabricating research? Or is there something deeper in this assault that I don't quite get yet?

Male-4: I'm interested in how the previous questioner shifted from "original" to "originality."

Laurel (interior monologue):
Yeah. Like we should only trust the unoriginal.

Male-5: What Laurel Richardson has presented us is the grounds of Laurel Richardson's loyalty. The poem reflects her loyalty to Louisa May's story. Why didn't you tell us John's story?

Laurel: I am telling Louisa May's story. The material was collected in the context of a larger research project on unwed mothers.

Laurel (interior monologue):
You look satisfied with my answer. You nod your head. Is it because I couched my answer

traditionally¿ Because I spoke of a research project, data set, interviews¿ Because I spoke in the passive voice¿ Or, or you nodding because I confirmed your suspicions that I'm always on the woman's side¿ What if I had said, I am not interested in John's story¿ He is irrelevant. . . . Maybe that is what I am saying.

Patricia: I am asking the question about accent because Laurel's reading was different than what/how we were reading the written text. She's pointing to the difference between poetry and narrative. The narrative voice sometimes takes the "I" of the poem, and I thought it could be Laurel—a poem about herself—and I at times I thought it was about me—my divorce. The poem shows how hard the narrator has to work to make those identifications possible and at the same time to make those identifications invisible. The slips make all that visible again.

Laurel (interior monologue):
I'm stunned. Pat thinks what really slipped out in my reading was my concealed identity . . .

And, smart, very smart, very very smart fast-talking psychoanalytic Patricia, identifies with Louisa May. Identifies. Can merge. The poem is working . . .

Mmm . . . Maybe Patricia is right. Maybe, all mothers ARE *deeply quintessentially unwed mothers . . .*

Male-3: The poem evokes bodily and sensory experience. I don't accept the written text as the denotative reading. I reject the idea that she "slipped" in her oral presentation. I will not privilege the written text over speech.

Patricia: Laurel's was a slip. But her slip is prior to the text. . . . Was there a text before the slip¿

Norman: What is this obsession with the REAL—with the REAL—with the idea of an "original" text¿

Male-2: (*furious*) People are losing their f——ing minds!!! We must make a distinction between her life and her speech. These are methodological and technical issues. The interview was obviously flawed. There is no reliability or validity here.

Male-3: Don't you get it? She's problematizing reliability and validity. She asks questions about that which you take for granted. She doesn't have the authoritative spirit.

Laurel (interior monologue):
THANKS. *Keep talking . . . keep talking.*

Female-1: I saw a dramatization of the Ollie North trial, and through it I could see Ollie North differently. That is what this poem is doing. We see unwed mothers differently. We see beyond the veil of data.

Norman:—as though cinematic realism is verification. As if doing something like it is supposed to be done makes its real and true . . .

Male-6: What are the concepts? What do we learn about someone's life?

Laurel: In the poem, Louisa May talks about her own social mobility, her normalness because she lives a middle-class life.

Laurel (interior monologue):
I can't believe I'm doing this, that I am succumbing to the conventions of soc-talk . . . That I am defending myself by talking concepts.

Patricia: The poem is about *my* life.

Male-6: So, it's a T.A.T. test?

Male-1: What is sociology? What about the grand narrative? the sociological deviant man? the mobility man? How do we represent the sociological without the grand narratives?

Male-7: If we lose the grand narratives that we cannot love, we lose . . .

Male-3: It may not be such a loss.

Norman: Many thanks to our panel. If anyone has more comments, perhaps they can talk to the panelists privately.

(*Applause, groans, papers rattling, feet shuffling. Conferees come forward and form a loose queue.*)

Female-2: I didn't know you had that accent in your background, Laurel, that you were from the south. I could see how your identity sometimes blurred with Louisa May's.

Female-3: I know you were talking about yourself, Laurel, and that is good. We should be able to talk about ourselves. But when we disguise and hide our identities, we just feed the woman's problem — the denial of self.

Female-4: You're very talented.

Female-5: The space was suddenly filled with male voices, loud and booming. We women couldn't breathe. We were gasping for breath.

Male-8: You brought life into the room, dispelling weight and negativity. We could breathe. I want to do work where we can breathe.

Male-9: I liked your poem. I, too, tried writing fiction some years ago. I sent a piece to the ASR — of course, it was summarily rejected.

Male 10: All this happened, Laurel, because you were wearing orange.

CURTAIN

THE INTERPRETATION

How to interpret my lived experience? How to explain the discussion? I offer an interpretation that has the virtue of meeting a criterion favored by both poets and scientists: parsimony. The interpretation explains both the masculinist and feminist responses to "Louisa May."

"Louisa May" revealed the phallocentrism of sociological discourse. The revelation of how sociological knowledge is constructed was a revelation of phallocentrism. The heated controversy over the "skipped line" was a fig leaf, a cover, a covering up, a covering over of that which Adam had but "Louisa May" put asunder: the phallus. The case of the skipped line is the case of the missing phallus. "Louisa May" was felt below the belt.

The content, form, method, and presentation of "Louisa May" are not "antimale," a familiar and conservative stance that binds feminist dialogue to phallocentrism, as atheism is tied to theism. No, "Louisa May" is something qualitatively different; the work is outside the phallocentric discourse; the phallus is unremarked, absent, simply irrelevant; and yet, "Louisa May" is at a disciplinary conference, presented and legitimated. This shift to an *unremarked* gynocentric world, I believe, stimulated the energetic responses from both masculinist and feminist speakers.

Louisa May is a voluntary unwed mother who chose to raise her daughter without a husband. She is a marriage resister, celebrating a peaceful, husbandless world. She claims the patriarchal right to language, the power to name. Her daughter's first name, Jody May, echoes Louisa May's and portends the reproduction of a happy, manless future for Jody May and other mothers' daughters. In a self-conscious ironic move, she gives Jody May her father's last name, a tip of the pelvis, so to speak, to the father, so to speak; in Lacanian terms, Louisa May displaces the symbolic and embodied father, the source of law and the self-other separation.

Louisa May is also the speaker in the poem. We hear her voice, words, pauses, emphases; in the oral version, we hear her accent, inflections, intonations. In the interview, she did not construct herself as sociologists might. In narrating her life, she decides what is worthy of naming. Education, occupation, and income are not. Louisa May refuses to give way to abstracted identities with which she does not identify; she resists categorization into and through a sociology that constructs and then reifies patriarchal concepts, as though the way to know or know about someone is through their socioeconomic status.

There are three additional women's presences in the paper. First, there is Louisa May's mother, Jody May's grandmother, foreshadowing the triumph of the future of matrilineage. Second, there is the silent character of the listener to

Louisa May's speech. In the poem, Louisa May talks in asides to this listener ("Is this helpful?" "I've talked so much my throat hurts.") Evoked is a private, two-woman space where woman talk is the only discourse. Third, there is the writer of the paper and the crafter of the poem, myself, a woman. That live woman is given time, space, and attention to speak at a convention, to raise questions about sociological knowing and telling.

Interviewing is a standard sociological technique for acquiring knowledge, for "knowing." Interviews are co-created through the intersection of two subjectivities, the interviewee and the interviewer. In the poem, Louisa May reminds us from the opening line ("The most important thing") to the closing line ("I've talked so much my throat hurts") that she is constructing her life story in an interactional context. What we claim to know as sociologists is displayed as constructed knowledge. What happens, then, to our authority? our definitive readings? Questioning the grounds of authority implicitly challenges phallocentrism.

But "Louisa May" represents phallocentric displacement in more immediate ways. The poem confronts and threatens sociological epistemology and ontology. What we know about Louisa May is not just the plot of her life but her feelings, spoken as intimate asides to another woman during an interview. Knowing about emotions requires "emotional work" on the part of the sociologist, including giving up power and privilege within an interview. As a gender class, women are skilled in, sensitive to, and interested in doing this kind of emotional work, and the sociology of emotions is growing rapidly within sociology (Ellis and Flaherty 1992). Might not the masculinist interviewer feel threatened? Can he foresee a future where he is handicapped, perhaps mortally, from plying his trade? These grown men will still be able to watch boys on playing fields and bluster about rationality, but do they fret because they cannot locate the newly mown sociological field, or, if they should find it, do they fear they'll lack the right balls?

Lest these ruminations seem far afield, let me turn to the issue of "telling." Writing Louisa May's life as a poem displays how sociological authority is constructed and problematizes reliability, validity, and truth. Poetics strips those methodological bogeymen of their power to control and constrain. A poem as "findings" resituates ideas of validity and reliability from "knowing" to "telling." Everybody's writing is suspect—not just those who write poems. In sociological research the *findings* have been safely staged within the language of the fathers, the domain of science writing. "Louisa May" challenges the language, tropes, emotional suppressions, and presumptive validity claims of masculinist social science.

Louisa May's poem models a way of telling that creates a bodily and emotional response. The subtext of Louisa May's poem is loss and displacement, bodily experienced, emotionally powerful themes. The deepest loss the poem inscribes is that of the father, the male authority over the staging of knowledge. We feel this loss because poetry joins emotional and intellectual labors.

By settling words together in new configurations, the relations created through echo, repetition, rhythm, rhyme let us hear and see the world in a new dimension. Poetry thus suggests a way out of the numbing, disaffective, disembodied, schizoid sensibilities characteristic of phallocentristic social science.

But to conjure a different kind of social science means changing one's relationship to one's work, *how* one knows and tells about the sociological. The distant, separate "I" of normative sociology that objectifies both the product and the process as "other," outside the self, won't do. That kind of constructed self can neither do the work that faces contemporary sociology nor understand why it is important (Krieger 1991). The relationship to one's work modeled by "Louisa May" alters both social science and the self that produces it. This relationship draws upon feminist ethics and gynocentric values.

In feminist writings of poets and social scientists, the position of the author is linked aesthetically, politically, emotionally with those about whom they write. Knowledge is not appropriated and controlled but shared; authors recognize a multiplicity of selves within themselves as well as interdependence with others, shadows and doubles. Alternate selves are interwoven by common threads of lived experiences. It is this feminist process of "knowing/telling" that led women listening to Louisa May's poem to feel that I was talking about my own life — or theirs. It is this potential for relating, merging, being a primary presence to ourselves and each other that makes possible the validation of transgressive writing, not for the sake of sinning or thumbing one's nose at authority, nor for the sake of only and just writing poetry — which may be ill suited for many topics, audiences, and writers — but for the sake of knowing about lived experiences that are unspeakable in the "father's voice," the voice of objectivity; flattened worlds.

Validating Transgression

"Louisa May," the "Case of the Skipped Line," and, now, also, this paper, I submit, are demonstrations of how transgression looks and how it feels. My intent is not to tell sociologists to write poems or drama — like Poe, most of us will at best be only almost poets. My intention is more radical: find and deploy methods that allow us to uncover the hidden assumptions and life-denying repressions of sociology; resee/refeel sociology. Reseeing and retelling are inseparable.

This text steps outside the normative constraints for social science writing: in-depth interview "findings" transformed into a poem; ethnographic field notes turned into a drama; and sociology with a poetry, drama, journal entries, personal experiences, feminist humor, irony, odd section headings, and very few references. (References are authority moves; disruptions; invite the reader to disengage from the text, like answering the doorbell in the middle of a lively conversation.)

Because the text violates conventions, it is vulnerable to dismissal and to trivialization as commonplace. Quoted here in toto is a dismissive reading of this paper, a reviewer's "Comments": "It is difficult for me to see that this article will be of interest to the readership of *The Sociological Quarterly*. It is too sectarian and other than that intensity [*sic*] I think the piece doesn't really work through its points with care." Excerpted here is a reviewer's trivializing-as-commonplace remarks: "In fact, the poetry only shows what we always do, especially us qualitative types. . . . So, there isn't much new there about the poem." Sure.

I try to write sociology that moves people emotionally and intellectually. When successful, the texts violate sociology's unwritten emotional rules. Social science writing is supposedly emotionless, the reader unmoved. But, just as other social science writing conventions (e.g., prose, passive voice, omniscient narrator) conceal how truth value is constituted, the affectless prose style conceals how emotions are harnessed in service of a presumed truth value. Readers of traditional sociology think they are feeling nothing because what they are feeling is the comfort of Similac, a formula, which maintains the illusion that social science is all intellect. Suppressed are complex, differentiated, intense, and more mature feelings. The suppression of these feelings shapes a sociology that is lopsided — lopped off is the body. How valid can the knowledge of a floating head be?

Postmodernist culture permits us—indeed, encourages us—to doubt that any method of knowing or telling can claim authoritative truth. We have a historical opportunity to create a space for different kinds of science practice. As one possible practice, I have modeled here a feminist-postmodernist practice. In that practice, one's relationship to one's work is displayed. There is a sense of immediacy, of an author's presence and pleasure in doing the work. Lived experience is not "talked about," it is demonstrated; science is created as a lived experience. Dualisms—"mind-body," "intellect-emotion," "self-other," "researcher-research," "literary writing – science writing"—are collapsed. The researcher is embodied, reflexive, self-consciously partial. A female imaginary, an unremarked gynocentric world, centers and grounds the practice. Space is left for others to speak, for tension and differences to be acknowledged, celebrated, rather than buried alive.

AFTERWORDS: FAMILIES

THE palimpsest on our Society for the Study of Symbolic Interaction (SSSI) T-shirts, beneath the words "Interaction Happens"—"S-H-I-T"—hit me when I presented "Louisa May" to the 1992 SSSI meetings. I have told that story here, in prose and in the ethnographic drama "The Case of the Skipped Line," which uses the speaking positions and words of my fellow conferees.

Ironically, as I let go of the illusion that SSSI might be "family," I let my "real" family—brother, sister, brother-in-law, sons, daughters-in-law—into the process and pain involved in my work. Never before had I made my work and my relationship to it vulnerable to them. I had liked keeping the worlds separate, insulated from each other. But now I cast my family into an ethnographic drama and tape-recorded them one summer day when everyone had come from everywhere to celebrate the wedding of my older son, Ben. I liked how my relatives sound reading my colleagues' words—some favorable, most not. I am surprised at how emotionally supportive my family has been, how a decade ago I would have kept the convention experience a secret, a nasty little failure, something to hide from my family. Now, the experience felt less shameful. The discursive site had changed. It was now around my kitchen table. No longer only "close to home," but *at home*.

Sharing responses to my research with my family, I think, opened me to sharing with them the material conditions of my departmental life—for example, a salary twenty thousand dollars less than other full professors. Even as I write this, I can feel my self reading it as though it were someone else's life, someone I don't know very well, if at all, and I am poised, ready to justify the salary differential, ready to take the side of the unknown institution and its players. I know a lot about the power of hegemonic discourse.

A woman who had won the National Book Award for biography came to lecture at my campus. At dinner, the talk turned to salaries and her tale of discrimination. Even though I was also embroiled in an ugly salary dispute, I was unwilling to wholly believe her account. Only much later, writing to the university president in a last gasp effort for intervention in my behalf, did I realize how her story was my story, how difficult it is to write a convincing "plot." So, I shall not dwell upon salary here.

The ethnographic drama had some other consequences, too. My colleague-friend relationships with Patricia Clough and Norman Denzin, named characters in the play, were extended and solidified. I saw for the first time the power of feminist-psychoanalytical thought, espoused by Patricia, as a constructive force in the resettling of sociology into a more interesting and humane posture. I saw how Norman's own biography figured into his postmodernism. That is, I respect the differences between "us" poststructuralists and see how variously marginalized speakers could be attracted to poststructuralism.

But perhaps most significant, intellectually and spiritually (that word, gain), was my conscious desire to create a "performance piece," a ritual reenactment of a murderous drama. I wanted to "play" and to write a play. I wanted "everyone" to understand what had happened; talking about it wouldn't do it; but dramatizing it would. My deep grief surrounding the loss of the spoken word, the oral tradition, surfaced.

My husband and I both have ancestral roots in the Shenandoah. We often hike there. "Can you feel it?" I ask him. "Yes," he says. We veer off the trail into an overgrown clearing. Fallen, scattered, are gravestones, plain, uncarved. No need to carve the names of the dead on stones, for family knew who was buried where. Oral tradition passed on the history. I, who have spent a lifetime writing, mourn for the passing of oral tradition. No one knows the names of the dead, the stories of their lives. I am crying. We set the stones upright and return to our hike.

PART 5

REMAPPING
FIELDS

FOREWORDS: ". . . AND FEEL MOST BRACED . . ."

VIRGINIA Woolf doesn't look at me. She's staring, unblinking, at her own words in calligraphy on a 1981 calendar that I have framed in burnished wood, like an icon, and hung on my wall, eye level, to the left of my computer:

> I do my best work and feel most braced with my back to the wall. It's an odd feeling though, writing against the current: difficult entirely to disregard the current.

I omitted four of those words—"and feel most braced"—from the epigraph to a 1990 essay of mine on values, metaphor, and rhetoric (anthologized here, "Value-Constituting Practices"). Why?

Did I think I could improve on Virginia Woolf?

Did I think sociologists wouldn't get the complex metaphor? that university life didn't "brace" me? that my "heroic" narrative required me to stand up by (for) myself?

Was I questioning the concept of "wall"—boundary, barrier, enclosure?

Was I troubled by the image the words evoked? A frightening memory, me, nine years old, drowning in a quarry, underwater, my back forced against a wall by a current, rescued by a man.

Probably, all of the above reasons and others, too, that I can't yet articulate. Even my choice of quotations, like all my writing, I have come to think of as overdetermined.

Like a mantra, everyday, many times a day, I read Virginia Woolf's words until they became a forgotten presence in my mind; and I saw her looking dark-eyed, unflinching, yet sad, at her words, and beyond. Virginia Woolf drowned herself, choosing a wall-less river, a current against which she would no longer fight, but I never connected the quotation with her death. As I do so now, I shudder.

One afternoon in 1993, I read the quotation aloud. How negative, how constraining, how limiting, I thought—not how depressing or prophetic, as I read it now. Writing "against" the current tied me to the "mainstream" always aware of its speed, eddies, whirlpools, displacing the power and centricity of my own "current." I no longer desired to position my work as "counter" or "anti" or "against," as I had been doing for years. I did not want to write about issues that were uninteresting; and I wanted to write through the "personal" binaries (me/them, good/bad, for/against) that were my walls, invisible to me then, bracing and constraining.

I took down the 1981 calendar that afternoon in 1993 and put it somewhere, "temporarily." I find it now, behind the guest room door, propped on the floor, braced by the wall: Virginia's facing the wall.

Marriage and the Family

Legacy

To comfort the mother
of the third born daughter
her father names her
after his own mother.

The third born becomes a mother.

She learns her namesake died
of pleurisy or suicide.
Her father doesn't remember.
Says it doesn't matter.

Marriage

I used
to think it was
cute to have a lit-
tle shadow go in and out
with me.

The Good Doctor Said

Your son has inoperable
brain tumors. At puberty
he'll get progressively
weaker on his left side
until he takes to bed
catches cold and dies.

Treat him as normal

Lullaby

Time   When he was a baby,
goes   I wondered if he
slowly   would die in his sleep,
thinking   in my sleep.
about
dying
giving
me
more
time
to
think   Joe said it didn't matter
about   Death, he said, is best
dying   after a good night's sleep.

Taking Him to the Vet

He's shameless, Doctor.
Walks around with no clothes.
Growls at pussies,
sniffs.
Pees in public with others
of his sex and species,
impervious to breed.

I do believe he would bite
the hand that feeds him.

At night
He pants and moans and salivates.
He's shameless.

Will his Blue Cross cover?
How soon can you fix him, Doctor?

Custody

See how the orange is segmented:
naturally. How apples resist
paring. How ocean water fills
a glass. My glass. Full tide
hovering at the rim. My hand
holding the ocean still,
still the undertow. See my hand
through the glass.

Being Single Is

drying a wishbone
by the kitchen window
till the bone is chipped

to bits by trinkets
placed beside it,
or it rots, because

there is no one
to take one end
you the other

pulling, wishing
each against each
until the bone

breaks.

Surrounded by Men

Short ones, lover and friend,
beer drinking on the back porch,
comparing the lengths of their
manuscripts, their tenures.
Wisps of Tennyson and Chaucer.

Tall ones, sons, territorizing
the front yard. Shooting rockets,
burning fingers, spilling rock salt.

Commanding the living room, Father,
dead already eight years, today,
swollen with waiting—

If I were a fork, I would know my place,
to the left of the plate, tines beckoning
a hand to cradle me,
me holding meat for the knife.
The blade slips between my tines
scraping edges.
There is no pain, and after
I am bathed in water
and returned to the space
I share with others of my kind.
We nestle together, edges cradling edges.
I am safe in the drawer.
Even the knives sleep.

COMMENTARY

At the "Redesigning Ethnography" conference in Boulder, Colorado, April 1992, I presented ethnographic "findings" as a long narrative poem and as a drama. Some conferees feared for ethnography's future. At the conclusion of the conference, Patti Adler, a conference organizer and coeditor of the *Journal of Contemporary Ethnography* (*JCE*), stood up in the front row of the newly renovated auditorium, full to capacity—no, overfull, with people sitting in aisles and standing along the back window wall. She said with cheeky good humor: We are the ethnographers. We decide what constitutes ethnography.

As I was packing up my briefbag, Patti Adler, turning theory into practice, invited me to send poems, with or without an introduction, to *JCE*. I sent her and Peter Adler (coeditor) "Nine Poems," unadorned, unjustified. Some reviewers wanted to know: How are these poems ethnography? Although I was initially resistant to writing about the poems, I now thank the reviewers because thinking about them affords the opportunity to push contemporary ethnography's envelope—and mine—a little further. I intend these comments, primarily focused on narrative and validity, as suggestive, not definitive, closed, or authoritative.

Poststructuralism proposes that systems of knowledge are narratively constructed. Traditionally, ethnographies, oral histories, social histories, biographies, and other qualitatively based research are constructed with fairly straightforward, obvious, and visible plot lines. The author intends that the reader "gets *the* story." "The story" is understood as taking place within or reflecting a particular social order or culture. Writing ethnography as a long narrative poem or as a drama, then, although transgressing ethnographic representational practices, coheres with the narrative traditions of ethnography. These transgressive writings reinscribe the possibility of "the plot line," the story, even as they challenge the *format* through which the story is told.

In "Nine Poems," however, the narrative is only *implied*. The nine poems are short, *lyric poems*, each a "mininarrative," an episode, representing an emotionally and morally charged experience. The order of the poems implies a plot, but the "spaces" between the poems invite greater readerly responses and interpretive work than would a long narrative poem. The nine poems could, also, be reordered, implying yet different plots. Subsuming "Nine Poems" under the rubric "Marriage and the Family," moreover, implies a *metanarrative*, the sociocultural construction of those two concepts "marriage" and "family" and a seeming "relationship," "marriage *and* the family." The implied narrative would change if "Nine Poems" were subtitled "Marriage or the Family" or "Gender" or "Maturing," or "Socialization" or "Treason" or "Paper Airplanes."

If a goal of ethnography is to retell "lived experience," to make another world accessible to the reader, then, I submit that the lyric poem, and particularly a sequence of lyric poems with an implied narrative, comes closer to achieving that goal than other forms of ethnographic writing.

Lyric poetry comes closer to presenting "lived experience" for literary, sociological, and cultural reasons. "Poems exist in the realm of making (*mimesis*) rather than of knowing or doing; they are representations of human experience . . . not speech uttered by or speech acts performed by individuals who happen to be poets" (Borroff 1993, 1032). That is, lyric poems are consciously constructed through literary devices such as sound patterns, rhythms, imagery, and page layout to evoke emotion. Like the lived experiences they represent, poems are emotionally and morally charged. Lyric poems concretize emotions, feelings, and moods — the most private kind of feelings — in order to re-create experience itself to another person. A lyric poem "shows" another person how it is to feel something. Even if the mind resists, the body responds to poetry. It is *felt*.

Sociologically, each lyric poem represents a "candid photo" or an "episode" or an epiphany. People organize their sense of self around and through such epiphanous moments (Denzin 1989a). Everyday life experiences are not organized around the long biographical account, the epic poem, the life history. Rather, people tell stories about events in their lives; the meaning of the event changes through the invocation of different implied narratives. Not all events, further, are stuffed into the same narrative. A life may have a "plot line," but not everything lived—nor everything of import to the person—fits neatly into "a" plot. We are not characters. Our lives are not morals. They are not even ethnographic narratives.

Cultures provide prefabricated narratives for hooking up the events of our lives. As cultural studies and discourse analysis demonstrate, those narratives are multiple, contradictory, changing, and differentially available. As agents in our own construction, we choose among available cultural stories, apply them to our experiences, sometimes get stuck in a particularly strong metanarrative, often operate within contradictory implied narratives, and sometimes seek stories that transgress the culturally condoned ones. Any or all of these processes through which the self is constructed and reconstructed may be going on simultaneously. Lyric representation mimics the complexity and openness of this human process—shifting subjectivities—by which we come to know, and not know, ourselves, and know ourselves, again, differently.

"Nine Poems" raises a second question about ethnographic practice: validity. In "Louisa May," a long narrative poem I crafted, the reader is told that all the words, rhythms, and sound patterns come from an in-depth interview with Louisa May. In "The Case of the Skipped Line," a drama I crafted from field notes, the reader is told that I followed standard ethnographic procedures—the dramatis personae were "real actors," the event did happen, and the words, intonations, and sequencing of speakers are "truthful." Although I crafted these works, my voice is distinguished from the voices of the ethnographees. In the case of "The Case of the Skipped Line" I did a "member check." Several of the "characters" in the drama verified the accuracy of the drama. I even "performed" the drama in a different but similar setting, and the responses "replicated" the original "findings." That is, although the formats were transgressive, in the production and sharing of these ethnographic works I adhered to a scientific protocol.

In "Nine Poems," however, the reader is not told the source of the poems. No "subversive repetition" of science practices is proffered. The poet and the poems are conflated. Are the poems from the life of a particular person, and if so, is that person one and the same as the poet? Or did the poet compile the poems from interviews with different people or from a variety of texts?

But does it matter—ethnographically—whose life is represented, or whether the poems represent a particular life? These questions are not asked in standard ethnographic codifications, where an "ideal-typic" portrait may be presented or a series of quotes from different interviews are collated under a theme, sometimes (I am told) quotes from the researcher herself secreted in amongst the others. If you care about whether the "I" of the poems is the "I" writing this essay, I ask you to ask yourself, "Why?" Do you have "validity" questions? "Reliability" questions? Truth questions? Emotional identification/disidentification concerns? "Nine Poems" brings these ethnographic issues—always present, usually suppressed—into critical awareness.

If we suppose that "Nine Poems" are a representation of a particular life, they simply fit within the tradition of making an individual (e.g., the "jack-roller," the children of Sanchez, Don Juan) the center of ethnographic writing. But if the poems are thought of as a representation of my own life, then the writing belongs to the newly developing sociology of subjectivity (Ellis and Flaherty 1992). In literary writing and ethnographies of the self, the boundary line is personal; the boundary is between the foreign territory of one person's psyche and that of another. The other that is the foreign territory, the "terra exotic," is the *inner experience*, the inner life of the writer. Writing about the self as both subject and object distances the self from the usual codifications of ethnography, even while the writing points out how the self depends upon social and cultural discourses to "know" itself, to position itself. Lyric poems have the capability of reducing the "distance" between the "I" and the "other" and between the "writing-I" and "experiencing-I" of the writer, and thus move us to rethink the boundaries between ourselves and our "work," help us to feel how ethnography might be situated within the "self" (also see Krieger 1991; Ellis 1991a).

I would submit that the "good" ethnography like "good" literary works invites the reader to *experience* a culture or an event. If one wants to *feel* what the plague was like, one can read Daniel Defoe's *Journal of the Plague Year*, which purports to be factual but is in fact a work of imagination. If one wants to *feel* what it was like to survive the Buffalo Creek disaster, one can read Kai Erikson's *Everything in Its Path*, which is categorized as ethnography and reads like good fiction. If one wants to *feel* what it is like to experience emotional depression, one can read William Styron's *Darkness Visible*, which is a personal account by a novelist that exposes institutionalized medical ignorance, as might a good ethnography. In all of these instances, and many others, the reader *feels* the experience. In this deepest sense, ethnographic writing, then, is allied to the rhetorical and emotional center of literary writing.

How does the lyric poem fit in, then? The lyric poem's task is to represent actual experiences — episodes, epiphanies, misfortunes, pleasures — capturing those experiences in such a way that others can experience and *feel* them. Lyric poems, therefore, have the possibility of doing for ethnographic understanding what normative ethnographic writing cannot.

The question that began this commentary — "How is lyric poetry ethnography?" — must be, I submit, inverted. The question should rather be, "When is lyric poetry *not* ethnographic?" As an opening move to answer that question, I would suggest that had Keats's "Ode to a Nightingale" first appeared in a journal of ornithology, this fact would have forever influenced how the ode was read and understood by the literary critic. Knowledge, as sociologists propose, is always contextual, legitimated by gatekeepers, and always exists inside a metanarrative. For now, "Nine Poems" appearing in the *Journal of Contemporary Ethnography* "is" ethnographic writing.

AFTERWORDS: SACRED SPACES

W HEN I was in graduate school at Boulder, I owned twenty or so books. A shelf of books. I liked touching them, hefting them, piling them up, classifying them — alphabetically, chronologically, topically, by color, size, favorites, ideologically — Parsons to the right, Marx to the left. I liked reorganizing the books but looked forward to the time when

I could afford a "decent library" of my own, where books would have a prescribed place—even a pecking order.

I was the first woman in the sociology Ph.D. program at Boulder. The chair told me then that "I wasn't really accepted—I'd have to prove myself," because there had never been a woman in the program. This was 1958. In January 1963, the program's first woman received her Ph.D.

Hundreds and hundreds of books and thirty years later, I was invited to give a keynote address at Boulder's Centennial Celebration, "Redesigning Ethnography." I was as excited as a hummingbird, but anxious too, the way adults sometimes feel when they return to their parents' home.

Preparing for that conference, I realized that the production, dissemination, and responses to my transgressive writings were leading me to a radical rethinking of ethnography and sociology. I wanted to move ethnography in particular, and sociology in general, out from under "the crisis of representation" and into the "calm of sacred spaces."

I had thought the Society for the Study of Symbolic Interaction meetings would always be a safe space for me, but my heresy—turning an in-depth interview with Louisa May into a narrative poem—destabilized the illusion, self-delusion, that "constructionists" shared the same sanctuary, stood before the same altar. The ethnographic drama *The Case of the Skipped Line* (see "Poetics, Dramatics, and Transgressive Validity"), which I wrote about the reception of "Louisa May," portrays the violation of safe space—mine and "theirs."

Those experiences altered my sense of self and my desired relationship to my work. Reading about and discussing these issues with my feminist-postmodernist studies group, I discovered I was not alone: I was part of a feminist-postmodernist longing, a desire to speak outside the discourse, to transgress, to exceed to excess—to take what I think of as a "spiritual turn," although many of my group members would not use that term.

Thinking about "spiritual turns" is scary for me. Where will it lead? What might I mean by "sacred space?" I know it is not "innocent space" but a space where, minimally, four things happen: (1) people feel "safe" within it, safe to be and experiment with who they are and who they are becoming; (2) people feel "connected"—perhaps to each other, or a community, or nature, or the world they are constructing on their word processors; (3) people feel passionate about what they are doing, believing that their activity "makes a difference"; and (4) people recognize, honor, and are grateful for the safe communion.

Discourses about the ineffable occur in sacred spaces; but so can collegiality, teaching, researching, and writing. Now, I find myself wanting to turn ordinary sites into sacred sites. I'm wanting to create alternative metaphors for ethnographic practices. We become the metaphors we use. We construct worlds in our metaphoric image.

How do we metaphor ethnographic practices? "The Field" metaphors a place — out there — where we go, as temporary, itinerant crop pickers. By "going into the field," we linguistically reify the duality, "me — fieldworker" and "them — crops." The metaphor also separates "writing/analytical mind work" from "data gathering/bodywork." By naming our work "participant-observation"—a term my husband, a novelist, has found particularly amusing because it sanitizes and licenses nearly anything in the name of "science"—by naming ourselves "participant-observers," we alienate ourselves, hide, obfuscate, and scientize. "Exiting" and "entering" the "field" conjure a bad Pinter play, not an engaged life. The distant "participant-observer" or "interviewer" of normative ethnography objectifies both the product and the process as "other," outside the self. Such a researcher can neither do the work of postmodernist ethnography nor understand why it is important.

Can we re-sign ethnography into life-affirming, sanctifying practices? We can, for example, re-sign the in-depth "interview," as an opportunity for "witnessing" another's life, hearing testimony, feeling the multiplicity of selves that is ourself and all selves, shadows and doubles of each other. Instead of "going into" the field, we might embark on a "pilgrimage" or imagine ourselves "walking with" people. In "walking with" we are embodied, self-consciously reflexive, partial knowers, conveners, ministers,—not "insiders" or "outsiders."

Feminist poets and social scientists link themselves aesthetically, politically, emotionally with those about whom they write. Alternate selves are interwoven by common threads of lived experiences. Dislocation, disidentification, displacement, ironically, are experiences of disconnection that make it possible for us to experience "connection." It is this potential for relating, connecting, recognizing the sameness in our differences, of being a primary presence to ourselves and each other, that makes possible the signing of ethnographic research as sacred space.

We can carry on these newly signed ethnographic practices in our classrooms and seminars, too. These can also be "sacred spaces," where teachers model passionate scholarship and where students feel "safe" to err, transgress, because there is space for tensions and differences to be acknowledged, celebrated, rather than buried or eaten alive.

We can continue these practices in the kinds of collegial communities we build. The feminist-postmodernist studies group on my campus has met nearly weekly for about seven years. We are women from many different disciplines — education, art, architecture, mathematics, classics, social work, anthropology, sociology, folklore, political science, music, English. We have bridged the disciplinary differences and created for ourselves a "sacred space," a sanctuary in the midst of the profanity of the university.

And, we can celebrate the sacred in our own writing spaces.

Last summer, while I was in the Shenandoah, my son, Benjamin — who was born to me during my third year of graduate school at Boulder and is now a man — stripped the fifteen-year-old "little house-on-the-prairie" wallpaper from my study walls and painted the space a pristine white. All of my books — hundreds and hundreds, now — he left, tarped over, in the middle of the room. Sociology texts, gender, theory, methods, ethnographies, poetry, writing guides, travel books, art, dream manuals, meditations, women-centered religions, archaeology.

Staring at my books — my life?—piled up and concealed, protected—

from what?—was an epiphany. I didn't know what categories to use to reshelve the books. I didn't know. The old categories no longer made sense, had nothing to do with my work/life. Many once valued books were repugnant now. Other books reflected new but somewhat embarrassing interests, "sacred sites" and bird-goddesses.

I sent boxes of books to Friends of Libraries. The few hundred books left I have organized by topics, not genres. There is lots of open space on the shelves, and nothing on the white walls, save three pictures of family past, family present.

Dualities between "inside/outside," "nature/culture," "science/literature," and "here/there" no longer work for me. Received wisdom regarding boundaries, borders, and limits feels arbitrary and constricting.

This spring, carpenters installed a nine-foot-wide window in the south wall of my study, behind my computer, facing the garden and the bird feeders.

Forewords: Speech Lessons

"Perform for the visitors, Laurel." "A child should be seen and not heard." These contradictory messages from my father found resolution through me taking on a theatrical "role," speaking through a "character," being quietly whoever it was I thought I was when I was only "seen." Once I slyly retorted, "Children should be obscene and not hurt," but I said it softly, nonsatirically, and I don't think Father heard me for he would not have let my impudence pass unpunished.

When I was barely seven and thought I might be Miss America when I grew up, I chose acting as my talent. I borrowed a large brown book from the Uptown library, titled something like "Fifty Monologues Guaranteed to Win Contests." I don't remember a one of them now, but back then I'd curl up in my bed with my dog, Happy, and memorize them. Following the "helpful" directions for emoting, staging, and costuming, I'd practice in front of Happy and my full-length mirror. Each Friday at school we had "show and tell" our classmates and I'd "tell" a monologue; some weeks, my teacher sent me to perform in other classrooms, even my older brother's classroom. Each weekend at home we had "show and tell" the visitors—mostly relatives, sometimes Father's law or political associates—and I'd "tell" a monologue. It was an easy kind of symbiosis, I realize now. The adults (teacher, parents) could take credit for my performance, while I raked in applause and, as a by-product, diminished my brother's value. In good weeks, my performances would diminish him at home and at school.

But then something happened to my unscripted speech. Teachers and relatives complained they couldn't understand me. I talked too fast.

In breakneck speed, I delighted in saying my name—"Laurel Gloria Cookie-Face Talking-Machine Richardson BOING!"—which, except for the "Laurel" and "Richardson," were definitely not my given names. As I write this now, I hear my cousins, aunts, and uncles at Olivet Camp on Lake Geneva, where we vacationed each summer, teasing me, embarrassing me, calling me "talking-machine." Telling me effectively to "shut up." I have just had an "A-ha!": I think my seven-year-old's solution to being told she "talked too much" was to talk faster, to say what she wanted to say in less time, and to evaluate that effort positively—to name herself "Talking-Machine." I marvel at "her" resourcefulness.

But my parents didn't see my fast speech as compensatory. Experts told them the problem was that my brain moved more quickly than my tongue. The solution was to send me to elocution lessons the year I turned seven. I don't know if elocution lessons were supposed to speed up my tongue or slow down my brain, but every Saturday morning for a couple of years, I'd board the Michigan Avenue bus by myself, getting off at the Goodman Theater–Art Institute of Chicago. After my lessons I'd immerse my whole being into the Thorne miniature rooms housed in the Art Institute's basement, free in those days to children. It was a relief to be where I could be quiet, but where I could imagine that if I did talk, my speed would be just right for the tiny rooms; I imagined that small spaces required quick speech, that somehow these were universal laws of time and space.

In the Goodman Theater, "Madame," dressed in burgundy and smelling like lavender, taught "her young ladies" how to warm up and soften their voices, when to "project," when to "demur," and how to sit, stand, and move in ladylike fashions. "A well-mannered woman never shakes a man's hand." "A well-mannered man never offers a woman a handshake, but cradles hers in his. Do not spend time with ill-mannered men." "Hold both your white gloves in your hand, palm up." "Feel the back of the chair with your leg before sitting." "Cross your legs at the ankles." "Walk toe-heel, toe-heel." "Speak when being spoken to." "Smile pretty."

We also practiced increasingly difficult tongue twisters—ironically the faster, the better. We trilled "r's" enunciated "ng's," tongue-tipped "t's," and denasalized "a's," suppressing any hints of "Sheekawge-eze." Before long, Madame advanced me to "acting classes." She cast me in what I considered even then awful, predictably silly children's plays, never as the ingenue, because I was brown-haired, and brown-eyed, as well. But I liked being directed on stage, being told where and how to say my lines. What I liked least was I made no friends there, and no one I knew except my mother ever came to a performance. And I had to share applause with the others, exit, leaving the ingenue stage-center for her ovation.

I'm not sure if the elocution and acting lessons succeeded in slowing down my brain or speeding up my tongue, but they did teach me how to manage my "problem." I learned to treat my thoughts as a script that I was writing and could scan and edit while speaking that which I had already scanned and edited. If anything, my brain was working even faster, writing, editing, scanning, reading, evaluating, taking in how others were responding, giving my tongue less to do. I learned how to cut back what I might say, to limit my speech, to rarely repeat myself, to synthesize, and to take up very little of other people's time with my spoken words. I still have these skills. I can make a point, orally, in a few seconds that might take others several minutes. I can "read" people; students sometimes think I'm "psychic." And I'm easy about relinquishing the floor. These are skills honed since I was seven, I realize as I write this, that are useful to me as an ethnographer, but oh how great the cost—censoring, monitoring, limiting the young self that might have been spoken into being, not because what she might have said was wrong or cruel but because it was "too fast" and "too much."

When I was in my thirties, I participated in a bioenergetics group where we were to go from birth to adolescence in our minds and bodies in about forty minutes. When the leader called time, the other participants were "driving" cars and dancing the twist while I was nine months old, barely walking and talking. There was so much, I felt, to see and assimilate; life was multifaceted, complex, and constantly refracting upon itself. The way to communicate this complexity and therefore to communicate *who I was in this world* would be to do it fast and detailed, telling who I was through my relationship to this "booming, buzzing" reality, before it changed again. Sometimes, nowadays, I meet a child who talks lots and fast. I speak at the child's tempo, support the breath points, and despite our rapid-fire talk—or maybe because of it—I feel a deep sense of connectedness, and peace.

But performing was not the only way to communicate: There was writing. One day in fourth grade, probably after one of my "monologues" or maybe after my excitement with an etymological lesson with which we always started the day, my teacher, Miss West, invited me to sit in the student chair next to her desk, a sacrosanct space that one entered only by invitation. She said that children's plays were "hackneyed"—that was her word—and suggested I write some plays myself. Since I would have done anything to please her, I got my best friend, Gloria Fenner, to turn historical events into dramas with me. Miss West exotically "blue-penciled" the scripts. Bending history somewhat, we wrote in lots of girls' parts. Sometimes I cast myself in the lead. All of this probably sounds like a hackneyed "inspiring teacher story," but my fourth-grade teacher, supporting herself for the while through teaching, "my Miss West," was soon to become a famous novelist. Although I read her novels as an adult, I have only recently realized that the frizzly red-haired, thin author and my frizzly red-haired, Wheat Thin–eating teacher were one and the same: *the Jessamyn West.* I had lucked out.

Writing dramas with friends—never alone—became a major sideline activity for me through high school. In fifth grade, Suzy Verb and I operated a Saturday morning preschool in Suzy's dining room. We charged fifty cents per child, per morning—including snack and supplies. We never lacked for "students." We directed them in plays we wrote for them, and then published the plays in our "Gazette" (sold separately to students' parents); our reviews of our plays were always magnanimous.

My eighth grade girls' club, "Just Us Girls"—innocently acronymed "JUGS" on our pristine white sailor hats—was moved by the plight of a poor sick girl featured one day in the *Chicago Tribune.* We decided to raise money for her through staging a drama — well, melodrama — about her life, sickness, and near death. I think I played the girl, but I am hazy about that. We sold advertising space on the playbill to neighborhood stores and relatives and performed, with lights, costumes, and curtain, to a full house in my basement. We raised forty dollars. A *Tribune* photographer took our pictures, in our "regulation" pyramid pose, wearing our JUGS hats. That picture, our names, and a "human interest" story about us appeared in the Sunday *Tribune*. I got a special mention in "Kup's Column." Probably all of this publicity happened, although I hadn't realized it then, because of my father's downtown connections.

Alpha Girls was the "best" sorority at Senn High School, where I went. Its members were school "leaders" like majorettes, homecoming queens, and cheerleaders. It was also the only sorority that accepted both Jews and Gentiles. At a time when high school social life was totally organized around sororities and fraternities, Alpha was the only sorority I could join. My older brother, a basketball jock and thereby a school "leader," was a member of Alpha Boys. Although it was unprecedented, I was pledged to Alpha my freshman year as a "legacy."

Pledge duties included supplying gum and cigarettes, fetching meal trays, carrying books, washing gym clothes, kissing feet, left one first, and writing a skit about the "actives." Obviously, the skit could not offend any actives and would have to honor the hierarchy established among them. Offensive pledges were called "bad pledge," given demerits, and, if bad enough, dropped from the pledge class. For the first time, I had to think about the consequences to me of writing. As chief script writer, I decided the skit would not razz any of the actives and that the amount of time spent on a particular active would be commensurate with my perception of her ranking in the sorority. Now, I might call my considerations the politics of poetics, or the ethics of writing. The skit was a "success," and for the next two years — until I left Senn, early off to college — I was the chief skit writer for Alpha Girls' parties with Alpha Boys. I wrote a lot of double entendres.

With the exception of adapting, with my college roommate, Thurber's "The Thirteen Clocks" for children's theater, I stopped writing plays after high school. Thinking about it now, I see that playwriting had been for me a vehicle for "becoming a woman," for practicing skills expected of a woman slated to marry a professional man and mother his children. The activity was always on the sidelines, never mainstreamed, always something to do after fulfilling my duties and obligations. I wrote with friends, bonding, practicing the arts of compromise necessary to a future, say, Junior League member. We gently manipulated the guys through double entendres; we could be simultaneously inviting and innocent. We worked with "deserving" children, teaching them, literally and metaphorically, "how to act." We produced plays as charity events, young Lady Bountifuls, transmutating, like alchemists, our base fun into golden nobility. We even got press coverage.

Something more happened to me in high school, though. Madame's and Father's "speech lessons" took on a new dimension. As I was becoming a woman, my voice grew ever softer, "becoming in a woman." I remember speeding up my talk. Did I think that if I spoke softly, fast would be okay? Was I trying to retrieve the sense of self I had previously censored, integrating "her" into the woman I was becoming? By my sophomore year in high school, people routinely asked me to speak louder; they said they couldn't hear me, understand me. "How true," I must have thought, "how painfully true."

The next year, a loud college roommate told me she thought I spoke softly as a control mechanism, making people shut up and strain to hear me. Perhaps she was right; perhaps I had found an "offstage" way both to be "feminine" and to command attention. But mostly I think I had grown shy; I had come to doubt the value of my way of perceiving, organizing, and "wording the world." As an early entrant in the University of Chicago's college, I had plenty of proof of my shortcomings by way of comparison with the truly gifted students around me.

By graduate school, I was speaking quietly—and quickly—in seminars, except when seriously ticked off by the sexism of my peers. ("A female can't understand X [Weber, Marx, social structure, etc.]," a male student would say to me whenever I was besting him in an argument.) My Ph.D. adviser's job placement letter, I learned much later, said I would be a poor teacher because I spoke too softly. He had never seen me teach. He didn't "understand me"; he didn't understand that for me the classroom is a theater, a place to play the role of "professor," to project, to move an audience of students. He didn't know I had theater skills.

But I did have theater skills—reading, performing, and improvising. These I had sharpened at University Theater, a student and community activity at the University of Chicago, when I was an undergraduate in the mid-1950s. I spent much more time with U.T. than I did with my schoolwork. The year my mother had my dog, Happy, put to sleep and I didn't cry about it, I won a "UTEY" for best acting performance by a female. The *Maroon*'s theater critic singled out my performance in "The Member of the Wedding" for two paragraphs of accolades. But I didn't "roll over" for him, and my name never again appeared in his column.

Our director staged "Lord Byron's Love Letter," a one-act in-the-round. Theater-in-the-round was an innovative and risky way to block drama then because it was unfamiliar and brought audiences closer to the action. I played Ariadne, the soft-spoken, unmarried daughter of an aging New Orleans woman, a shopkeeper. From offstage the mother's loud, piercing voice controls Ariadne's actions onstage. The pair's livelihood comes from showing a love letter from Lord Byron to tourists; the pair's emotional life comes from telling about the mother and Lord Byron's romance, from their initial meeting on the steps of the Acropolis to his love letter. Telling the story, the mother's voice fades, gives way to Ariadne's; sometimes, they speak in unison, emotionally as one. As the drama unfolds, the audience believes that Ariadne is Lord Byron's illegitimate child. But the brash couple to whom they are telling the story shatters the myths of Ariadne's life: The letter, they say is a forgery; Ariadne is not Lord Byron's daughter. At the dramatic apex, the couple refuses to pay Ariadne for viewing the "fake" letter. Raising her voice and expressing for the first time in the drama her own emotional life, not her mother's, Ariadne flings her arms, wails, and screams at them, "Canaille! Canaille." (Think "swine," the director said.) A "dramatic" pause—and then the denouement, the mother comes on stage, silent, a broken woman.

Opening night, the audience was quiet at the end of the play and then broke into wild applause and a standing ovation. My parents came to the second night's performance, sitting a few rows back. Before the denouement, immediately following my intense dramatic moment, Mother stood up, opened her purse, and said out loud through her tears, "Here honey, I'll give you the money." She didn't understand why her action mortified me or how it destroyed the drama's resolution. In consolation, I decided I was a really great actress to trick my own mother that way. Later, I thought I wasn't so good, or Mother wouldn't have confused me with the character. Now, I think she was incapable of making a distinction between her daughter and "Ariadne," between reality and theater.

I was a good actress, but not as good as some of the others—especially the community people who brought in Viola Spolin's improvisational techniques. Now, I'm going to name-drop. My "theater troupe" included Mike Nichols, Elaine May, Barbara Harris, Ed Asner, Alex Hassilev, and Sevren Darden. I was part—a minor part, to be sure—of a fledgling "Second City." Called "The Compass Players," we did improvisations on a makeshift stage at the 55th Street tavern "The Compass."

But I didn't have what "they" had. I wasn't determined, driven, the way some of them were. Acting was not going to be my life. A brief fellowship at Actor's Studio in San Francisco after college convinced me I lacked the motivation. I also didn't like how I "became" a character, how the character slipped into my daily life. I didn't like how being tall severely limited my parts. And something else was different: I didn't like the applause. I had grown highly critical of my own performances—they didn't meet my own expectations. So, when audiences generously clapped for me, I felt only contempt for them. But if the applause was merely polite, I was furious. "Pearls before swine—Canaille!" I thought. I was becoming a moody, demanding prima donna, and I didn't like "her" at all.

Like other adults who had talents or hobbies as a child, I put theater behind me. How could I fit hours of rehearsal, method acting, "personality changes" or script writing into an adult life of scholarship and parenting? But how could I completely suppress the "theater" in me? As I write this, I realize that the ease with which I took to sociology and the way I fell in love with it—sociology felt absolutely "natural" and "true" to me—might have had something to do with my theater experiences of playing roles, acting in context, multiple points of view, and knowing that all of the above are constructed, interrelated, and changing. Perhaps sociology for me is one big "displacement," a place where I thought I could undo and redo.

That said, I find myself smiling. How delicious to think of my career in sociology, at least in part, as a restitutive journey, a reclamation of the self, a complex, life-affirming application of "speech lessons."

I use acting skills in teaching, adjusting style to context. Giving conference papers, I mark my text as a script (accents, skip, pause), rehearse it, and check out the "feel" of the room and the "stage" setup. For a fourteen-city national book tour (1985–1986, for *The New Other Woman*), I videotaped improvisational role-plays with "coaches" playing nasty talk show hosts; I practiced "spontaneity"; and I enrolled in "modeling school" to learn good television posture, demeanor, makeup, and clothing. My desires were to spread sociological gospel, sell books, and perform well—flawlessly, seemingly effortlessly. My "professional" acting ego, my "child" ego, and my academic ego were all on tour. I doubt if academics without "speech lessons" would have gone to the same lengths that I had, or have such absurd expectations.

Preparing for the book tour in 1985, I realize now, sent me back into "real" theater, not its surrogate academic "theater of the absurd." After that tour, I experienced a "crisis of representation." Resolution of that "crisis" came through writing, I now realize, *performance texts*—dramas, narrative poems, responsive readings. I found new "best" academic friends and the excitement of "coauthoring" with them new "fields of play." The possibilities for the *fields* of sociology now seem vast, uncharted, unbounded. This summer I have made a tentative first step back into "real" theater.

About this next thing I may be wrong. Sometimes we don't see ourselves as others see us. But this is what I think is true of my life in theater and beyond. The more I "became" a character, the better my performance and the greater my loss of self. Fear and anger about what was happening to me I displaced into contempt for audiences. The danger for me was letting a "role" take me over, letting a "part" in someone else's drama suppress my own self. So, I've not been willing to play the demeaning stock university "parts" for women—"pet," "victim," "good mother," "bad mother," "tagalong," "mistress." Nor have I been willing to play "border guard," "disciplinary police officer," "roll-overer," "science fetishist." These were not the parts I "tried out" for, not the ones I came to academia to play. My contempt for "audiences" has not transferred to students—who I view as co-creators of the "performance" called "education"—but to the "male gaze" of colleagues and administrators, of either sex. I have thus not been completely successful in department politics. But in retrospect, I can't say I'm sorry; I can't say I'd do it any differently—speak more softly or speak more slowly.

EDUCATIONAL BIRDS

ACT ONE

Scene One: It is a chilly September afternoon in a sociology department chair's office. The walls are catacomb drab; there are no mementos, pictures, or plants in the room. Seated at one end of a large conference table are two women: a department chair with her back to the windows, and full professor Z. looking out to the silent gray day.

Chair: I've been reading your work, because of salary reviews—

Professor Z.: —

Chair: —You write very well.

Professor Z.: —

Chair: But is it Sociology?

Professor Z.: —

Scene Two: On leaving the department office, Professor Z. sees Visiting Professor M. at the drinking fountain. The pipes are lead. The university says it's not a problem if you let the water run. Professor M. is letting the water run into his coffee maker. His hair is flat, plastering his head; he's heavy-looking, somber, wearing worn blue pants and a stretched-out dun cardigan, hanging loosely to his mid-thighs. Not the eager Harvard man hired a year ago.

Professor Z.: —Looks like you've acclimated.

Scene Three: It is an overcast November noon at the Faculty Club. Pictures of deceased faculty, men in drab suits, line the room; wrought-iron bars secure the windows. Professor Z. and assistant professor Q., whose five-author paper "Longitudinal Effects of East to Midwest Migration on Employment Outcomes: A Log-Linear Analysis" has made her a member of the salary committee, are having lunch.

Assistant Professor Q.: Everyone says, "You write very well."

Professor Z.: Is that a compliment?

Assistant Professor Q.: "But is it Sociology?"

Scene Four: A cold and dismal January afternoon in the sociology seminar room. During one of the department's "reconstruction" phases, the oak conference table was disassembled and the legs lost. Without a leg to stand on, it lies, in pieces, at the far end of the room next to discarded computer equipment.

The wallpaper is flaking away like mummy wrappings. Assembled are the new graduate students, the graduate chair, and the department chair. The new students are being taught how to teach.

New Graduate Student: (*addressing the department chair*) Can you tell us about the worst undergraduate sociology class you ever took?

Department Chair: Yes. The worst course was one where the professor read *a* poem.

Graduate Students: —

Department Chair: What a waste of time!

ACT TWO

Scene One: A dark day in February. Conferees are assembled in a modern auditorium at State U. for a conference wrap-up. On the stage is an assemblage of well-preened speakers. We tune in near the end.

Feminist-Marxist Discussant: There is great danger here. I like poetry, too, and like to listen to it when it is read well and with emotion, but it is not sociology and not *for* women. Professor Z. is being wrongly paid to write poetry.

Scene Two: A chilly March evening in a conference room in a convention hotel in Metro-City. The room has no windows, one rear door, and an erratic heating system. No one has been outside all day. Professor Z. is at the podium:

Professor Z.: Why Prose? Prose, I submit, is not the only way to represent sociological understanding. Another possible way is through poetic representation. Poetry touches us where we live, in our bodies, and invites us to experience reflexivity and the transformational process of self-creation.

  For this paper, I transform an in-depth interview into a narrative poem. Using only the interviewee's words, diction, rhythms, and other poetic speech components, I try to meet both scientific and poetic criteria. (*Professor Z. reads poem and discusses Derrida, Denzin, and data, poetically represented, which is followed by a discussion period.*)

Conferee 1: Where is the f———king Validity?

Conferee 2: What about reliability?

Conferee 3: Truth? Where's truth?

Conferee 4: And reality?

Conferee 1: You have lost your f———king mind!!!

Professor Z.: (*takes field notes.*)

ACT THREE

Scene One: April, Ballroom A, Convention Center, Mega-City. The sky looks threatening. Chairs—red, yellow, blue—seat an audience of old-guard and new-guard sociologists, anthropologists, communicationists, humanists, scientists, undergraduate and graduate students, policy makers and grant givers, and an untold number of "others." A flock of sociologists in professional drag have assembled on stage. They have grayish skin and prematurely gray hair.

Sociologist 1: My surveys of depression, anxiety, and happiness are definitely sociology.

Sociologist 2: Yes, they are. I do them, too.

Sociologist 3: My statistical research on politics in foreign lands and other times is unquestionably sociology.

Sociologists 4, 5, & 6: Yes, it is. I do that, too.

Sociologist 7: My demographic work is categorically sociology.

Sociologists 8, 9, 10, & 11: Yes, it is. I do that, too.

Sociologist 12: My statistical research on crime and punishment is unequivocally sociology.

Sociologists 13, 14, & 15: Yes, it is. I do that, too.

Sociologist 16: My writing on abstract variables in vector spaces equals sociology.

Sociologists 1 – 15: Yes. Yes. Yes.

Sociologist 17: My Marxist analysis is sociology.

Sociologist 18: My realist tale is sociology.

Sociologist 19: My construction of sociology is sociology.

(*A gust of wind blows up, the sky clears, and a figure larger than life comes out of the woodwork. He walks toward the assemblage on stage.*)

Sociologists 1 – 19: My God, it's Lundberg! Back from the dead. Sociology's father of the operational definition.

(*Sociologist 19 hands him a sheaf of poems, entitled "Higher Education."*)

Lundberg: Hmm. "Higher Education." Why are you giving me these poems?

Sociologist 19: Somebody's trying to pass them off as sociology.

Lundberg: Is it a sociologist?

Professor Z: Yes.

Lundberg: Here we go then . . .

(Chuckling and smiling, he walks off stage and takes a seat in the audience. He puts on his old-fashioned, owlish reading glasses and reads aloud some of the poems.)

CREAMED SHERRY

I do not like creamed sherry,
Nor the parties where it's served.
Nor the hosts who pour it sacredly
As though it had some worth.

I cannot stand the taste of it
Nor the smell or name of it.

Oversimmered hosts
inside shirred shirts
serve the coddled brine
in cutglass incubators
to shells, sitting
side by side in cartons.

Host and parasite sip
the fluid of the chicks.

Brooders, Layers, Peckers.

The weather is poor, the economy's down,
Famine's a bore, the flu's in town.
Randall got married, promotions are rare.
Deans are harried, the movie was fair.

Anne's a good bit, Fanny's too much,
Jill has ice tits, Verna's in a rush,
Bet's a good ass, Judy's too easy,
Eliza has class, Lana's cheesy.

My book will be published by University Press.
My article appears in *Daedalus*.

My son won the MacIver Award.
My conference is held at Harvard.

I cannot stand creamed sherry
Nor the parties were it's served.
It must be made with coddled eggs
To sour semen so.

GEM OF AN ACADEMIC WOMAN

My
facets
polished
reflect
decades of wisdom

Ground
Beveled
Deflawed
Registered
Certified
Purchased
Displayed in Haggerty Hall, Room 114D
Tuesdays and Thursdays, 1 – 3

Only ivy can climb the walls.

WHILE I WAS WRITING A BOOK

my son, the elder, went crazy
my son, the younger, went sad
nixon resigned
the saudis embargoed
rhodesia somethinged
and my dishwasher failed

my sister, the elder, hemorrhaged
my brother didn't speak to me

my ex gurued and overdosed
hemlines fell and rose
texans defeated the e.r.a.
and my oil gaskets leaked

my friend, the newest, grew tumors
my neighbor to the right was shot
cincinnati censured sin
and my dracena plant rotted

I was busy.

A MATTER OF LIFE AND DEATH

I
Curriculum Vitae

Printed Words

entombed
in tomes
in stacks

My words are there.

II
Eulogy

Recall them now?

Lundberg: So what do you want from me?

Sociologists 1 – 19: Positivist Father who now walks on earth, remind us again what sociology is!

Lundberg: (*returns to stage.*) Oh ye of little memory and less imagination: Sociology is what sociologists do.

Sociologists 1 – 19: (*silence, then, rising squawks of protest.*)

Lundberg: If a sociologist writes and publishes poems in a sociology journal, the poems are sociology.

(*The 19 preassembled sociologists hoot and crow at Lundberg. He strides off stage.*)

(*Professor Z., the discussant, enters backward from stage left, dragging a wardrobe trunk behind her. She puts on her love beads, Birkenstocks, soft-as-down lip cream, feather earrings, and hangs up her certificate to practice. She speaks breathlessly and earnestly, without notes*):

Professor Z.: How come some sociologists are so threatened by poetry? How come poetic representation poses this "great danger"? How come poetic social science makes—so to speak—birds of different feathers flock? How come they, like, go ballistic?

(*She slips into a cardinal red power suit and black pumps, small and tasteful gold hoop earrings, puts on her bird's-eye-maple framed bifocals, and retrieves her notes from her ostrich skin briefcase. Somnambulistically, she reads:*)

Professor Z.: When poetic representation is articulated, sociology's representational rules are breached, suggesting that ethnomethodological analyses of the articulation of poetic representation might be a valid method of analysis. Breaching challenges the taken-for-granted codes through which members have been socialized into role taking and "consciousness of kind" and through which communities have exerted social control over their members. As a direct result, members respond to breaches through exhibiting behaviors that indicate anger or dismissiveness—what another paradigm might refer to as "fight or flight," but our research—

(*Whipping off her bifocals, she dons a raven black cape and waves an amethyst and crystal wand*):

Professor Z.: I know why these people are so threatened. They fear that if any rule is violated, all rules might be violated. They fear lack of control not only in their professional but in their personal worlds. The subtext of the question, "But is it sociology," is their silenced fear: "If poetry is sociology and I can't do it, what happens to my identity, my prestige, my status—my place in the pecking order—ME? . . . Me, me . . ."

(*Putting her bifocals back on, dropping her cape to the floor, she slips on an oversized, bluebird-blue Nehru jacket, sprays herself with French perfume—L'Air du Tern—and reads quickly and with beguiling modernist authority*):

Professor Z.: The construction and evaluation of knowledge are situated, historically local activities; here, of course, we are situated in western colonial, patriarchal, heterosexist, racist, ageist, classist, nativist, ablest, hegemonic discourses. The speakers, here, have vested power interests and they valorize practices that advance their agendas, including their agendas for what sociology *is and will be.*

(*With nightingales and skylarks for background music, she pulls her hair into a topknot and wraps a twenty-foot feather boa around her. Perched on a high stool, she recites by heart a poem:*)

EDUCATIONAL BIRDS

(Found Poem, Raptor Barn, Felix Neck Wildlife Sanctuary)

> The Raptor Barn houses
> Various Birds of Prey
> That are being Rehabilitated
> for release. Those that
> cannot be released
> successfully
> are kept
> as Educational Birds.

(*A stirring and then a commotion in the audience. Breaching the rules, members of the audience are coming onto the stage. The day is brightening.*)

Humanities Professor: I like these poems. Submit them to a poetry journal.

Ornithologist: Who cares what sociology is?

Performance Artist: Who gives a damn anyway?

Historian: What a waste of time!

Policy Maker: What I want to know is how sociology can make the world better.

Philosopher: Or more comprehensible.

Math Major: Or maybe just more interesting!

Undergraduate: How can sociology help me get on with my life?

Senior: Or get a job?

Policy Maker: Or keep people from starvation?

Grant Giver: Or stop violence!

Graduate Student: Who is sociology for?

English Major: *Sociology for Whom?*

(*With this inadvertent mention of his famous book, Lundberg returns to the stage, beaming*):

Lundberg: Ah, so here we all are. Wonderful! (*Homing in.*) I welcome you and invite you to explore the bountiful possibilities and multiple paths that are sociology, and history, philosophy, mathematics, science, and literature. Let us learn from the great philosopher, Heraclitus, whose words (Fragment 203)—

hodós anō catō mia kai houtē

when literally translated from the Greek, are themselves a found poem:

road up
road down
one and same

Murmurs from the audience: Mmm. Poetry does help.

AFTERWORDS:

ARE YOU MY ALMA MATER?

WHEN social scientists claim their work as "science," they enact the hierarchal science/nonscience binary, legitimating their work and institutional practices as valid and true, while devaluing and marginalizing nonscience discursive practices. Scientizing social knowledge is thus inextricably linked to the suppression of other ways of knowing.

Now, when minority, queer, feminist, postcolonial, and poststructural ways of knowing break through artificial disciplinary and departmental lines, challenge the science/nonscience binary, and find voice/audience within the academy, many university administrators and disciplinary doyens are intent on shutting them up; getting them off the playing fields, permanently. The new discourses threaten not only the quaint seventeenth-century notion of a purely objective science, held by many in administrative ranks, but also the actual power (prestige/salary) of the entrenched within the university.

New mines have been set. As in real war fields, the young, inexperienced, and adventurous are the most vulnerable to detonations. Graduate students. Four examples have passed over my desk in the past two

weeks. On a feminist e-mail list came this request from a first-year graduate student:

My department has been having a series of "feminist epistemology" debates. . . . The anger/hostility/backlash/defensiveness in
some of the faculty and the increasing alienation and marginalization of feminist (and students pursuing critical race theory)
students is troublesome to me (one of the disenchanted grad
students). When I raised my concern, it was suggested that I
organize the next seminar. While I am not altogether sure this is
a responsibility I want, I am wondering if any of you have had
successful . . . forums which address hostilities within the disci-
pline/departments yet does not increase those hostilities or place
less powerful people (untenured faculty or graduate students) at
greater risk. . . . Please reply to me privately.

When I asked the student for permission to quote her e-mail, she asked
for anonymity:

It drives me crazy that I have to be afraid to even speak, but it is
realistic. Actually, even posting to [the listserve] made me nervous, but I can't think of other ways of accessing resources beyond my pathetic institution.

Another graduate student, Eric Mykhalovsky, writes about what happened to him when he used an autobiographical perspective in the
practice of sociology. Changing his "I" to "you," he writes in *Qualitative
Sociology*:

During a phone call "home" you hear that your application for
doctoral studies has been rejected. Your stomach drops. You are in
shock, disbelief. When doing your M.A. you were talked about as
a "top" student. . . . Later you receive a fax giving an "official account" of your rejection. Your disapproval, it seems, was based on
reviewers' reservations with the writing samples submitted as
part of your application. One evaluator, in particular, considered
your article, "Table Talk," to be a "self-indulgent, informal biogra-

phy—lacking in accountability to its subject matter." You feel a sense of self-betrayal. You suspected Table Talk" might have had something to do with the rejection. It was an experimental piece, not like other sociological writing—YOU SHOULD HAVE KNOWN BETTER!

Slowly self-indulgence as assessment slips over the text to name you. You begin to doubt your self—are you really self-indulgent? The committee's rejection of your autobiographical text soon feels, in a very painful way, a rejection of you. All the while you buy into the admission committee's implicit assessment of your work as not properly sociological (1996, 133–134).

In a personal letter requesting advice on whether to apply to my university, a lesbian graduate student from another university recounts:

I can't do the research I want to and stay here. The department wants to monitor how many lesbians they let in because they're afraid that gender will be taken over by lesbians. I'll be allowed to do gender here if I do it as part of the "social stratification" concentration, but not if I want to write about lesbian identity construction or work from a queer studies perspective.

And fourth, there are documents on my desk pertaining to a required graduate seminar in a "famous" department on how to teach sociology. In that seminar, according to the documents, a non-American student of color questioned the white male professor's Eurocentricism. Following a heated dispute, the professor provided a statistical count of the racial distribution of students in undergraduate classes—80 percent are white. The professor, then, putatively said that instructors cannot afford to alienate students by teaching multiculturalism; that professors are uncomfortable teaching multiculturalist "crap"; that the student raising these issues could "go to hell"; and that white heterosexual males were being discriminated against. When the student of color complained to the department administrators, they proposed he "voluntarily" withdraw from the class. The department administrators (including a new chairperson) later attended the seminar, supported the syllabus, and sidestepped discussion of the race-based issues. The professor apologized to the seminar for breaking his own code of proper behavior in the classroom, but he apparently had not grasped the import of postcolonialism. He was modeling his teaching model.

As a result, at least one graduate student has chosen to go elsewhere for the Ph.D. The student sent an e-mail to all faculty, staff, and graduate students to avert "idle speculation" regarding the reasons for departure:

> It has disgusted, saddened and enraged me that this department has chosen to ignore and avoid the serious occurrences of racism going on within it. Instead of admitting to these problems and dealing with them, the department has used its institutional power to scapegoat, marginalize and penalize individuals who dare to challenge its racist structure. Then those in power go back to their computer screens to study race as a dummy variable, not even realizing that a sociological process called *racism* is happening in their midst. . . . Students are advised to study social movements, not participate in them. . . . [H]ere racism is not considered *real* sociology, as evidenced by students having to start "extracurricular" groups to do reading on postmodernist or Afrocentric thought. Meanwhile, at national and regional meetings, presentations abound on these topics, and ASA book awards continue to be offered to scholars who use these perspectives in their work. The department seems isolated and out of touch with all but a small portion of the discipline (quantitative, positivistic thought) and becomes the laughing stock when stories get out. . . .
>
> I am leaving because, while I respect, learn and appreciate the importance of things like demography and statistics, the same appreciation and respect is not offered here to other areas of sociology which are *very* influential in the field, and institutional power is used to prevent students from learning about them. As a result students leave ill-equipped for understanding all but a limited portion of sociology.
>
> I sincerely hope that the prospect of losing more talented students, especially those who are students of color (who are *not*

leaving because they "can't handle it [statistics courses]," will compel this department to reevaluate its capacity to serve its students of diverse backgrounds and interests more effectively. My career just didn't have time to wait for all that to happen.

Feminist epistemology, autobiographical sociology, queer studies, and Afrocentric and postcolonial perspectives are apparently so dangerous that the graduate students who have been exposed to these plagues must be quarantined, invalidated, or expelled from the university nest. Graduate students are "terminated" lest they reproduce themselves. In the words of one humanities scholar:

> The rationale for this solution is that some even Higher Authority, possibly a Federal Bureaucrat . . . , will conflate the vigorous intellectual debate and exploration beyond authoritarian boundaries necessary to the greatest human endeavors (science, even) with "weakness"—and reduce sociology's funding. To counter the most dire of possibilities, we must declare total war. Beneath the night and fog of "the struggle for resources," we must cleanse speech and vision; we must discipline the Discipline (Lockridge 1995).

Like a prison warden, the university administrator struggles to construct a total institution reflective of his or her authority over who can belong, how they will be organized, and what rewards and punishments will be meted out to whom by whom. Foucault sees power congealed—tyranny—as evil, but once exposed, capable of being changed. Not so the university administrator who struggles to eliminate all obstacles to those whose will to power has met with success.

P. D. Eastman's children's book *Are You My Mother?* features a baby bird who falls out of his nest while his mother is away looking for a worm. The bird asks of everything he sees, "Are you my Mother?" The kitten, dog, cow, and hen are not his mother. The wrecked car, boat, plane, and "snort" (steam shovel) are not his mother. But the "snort" lifts him up and drops him back in his nest just as his own "real" mother is returning with a worm.

In some ways, I identify with that baby bird. I have left the nest, too. But, unlike the baby bird, I know there is no "real" mother bringing in the worms. There is no nest. There may not even be a tree. There are only the "mothers"—nurturant communities, relationships, internal dialogues—that I can (co-) construct, inside or outside the academy. The intellectual, ethical, and emotional challenge, I think, is not to find a way back to the same old nest but, for those of us who are less vulnerable—tenured professors, to rethink and restructure the university and our disciplines so that kittens, dogs, cows, hens, cars, boats, planes, and "snorts" might intercede in each other's behalf; might be nurturing, cherishing, fostering alma maters.

PART 6

ARRIVING

WHERE WE

STARTED

.
.
.
.
.
.
.
.
.

VESPERS .
.
.
.
.
.
.

Every summer until I was twelve, I went with my family to Olivet, a Presbyterian camp on Lake Geneva, Wisconsin. All the people there I called "Auntie," Uncle," or "cousin." I thought all of them were my father's relatives, since I knew he was born and raised a gentile.

Left behind in Chicago were heat, polio, Anshe Emet Synagogue where I went to Sunday school, and weekly "El" rides to visit my mother's mother, Gramma. She spoke no English, only what I called "Jewish." Each week she handed me *gelt*, which I put in my white porcelain piggy bank.

Olivet Camp was fifty or so primitive, three-room, white cottages, named for birds or flowers, set around a meadow at the top of a hill and strung alongside 179 quartz-graveled, cement-tipped steps, which led to the large wooden commons of the Camp Office, Recreation Room, Refectory, "Hotel," front porch, and then to a flight of wooden stairs, a gravel knoll, the shore path, and the expanse of the lake—a mile across, twenty-six miles around, deep and always cold. After nightfall, the grounds were dark, dark.

During the week, camp belonged to the women and children. I was the youngest child at camp. All the grown-ups and the oldest cousins called me "Baby Laurel." Aunties chatted and crocheted; children ate, swam, ate, swam, played "Sorry," and at night "Hide-and-Seek," "Packed-Like-a-Can-of-Sardines," magic shows, hypnotism, and "Post-Office." Any child could eat "by" any auntie, and any auntie could "correct" any child. Disobeying an auntie was as bad as disobeying one's mother.

Late on Friday nights, the fathers drove up from the city. My father fixed things, took me to visit my dog, Happy, at the egg lady's farm, where we got fresh corn on the cob and eggs for everybody. Father watched me swim, sailed with my brother, Barrie, "conversed" with my sister, Jessica, and "schmoozed" with the other fathers until late Sunday, when they'd all drive back to the city and—although it had not occurred to me, then—to their jobs. In my father's case, I think, he returned as well to his mistress.

This is what happened the summer I turned eight. It was late August, Tuesday night vespers in the Recreation Room at the bottom of the hill. I was sitting on a hard folding chair next to my mother. I sang out songs about "God" and "Our Lord" but sealed my lips to "Jesus" songs and prayers. Synagogue teachers had already told me what the Crusaders and Germans had done to Jews in Jesus' name. Crusaders killed them straightaway, and Germans turned little Jewish girls' skin into lamp shades. I thought the girls would look bad and feel cold without their skin. "No matter what horrors gentiles do to Jews," my teacher with the blue numbers tattooed to her arm said, "your mind is always free." My mind was free to refuse Christian words; and it did. I moved closer to Mother, felt her starched house dress against my bare legs. I felt deeply connected to her, free, courageous, and something special for which I did not yet have a label: moral.

Mrs. Auntie Baldwin brought me back to attention. She was smiling at me, calling my name, "Laurel," asking me to read a Bible verse full of Jesus. I shook my head, "No," and scrunched down closer to my mother. Mother said, "Go ahead. Read it, Laurel." Everyone was waiting. Auntie Baldwin was looking at me, talking to me. I shook my head more determinedly and whispered to Mother, "No-o-o." She nudged me and again said, "Go ahead. Read it, Laurel. Do as you are told."

Anger unlike any I had ever felt erupted from within me and washed over me. The feeling was uncontrollable. I would now call that anger "rage." I was enraged. I was a child who was sent to her room for raising her voice, a child whose father intoned, "A soft voice is becoming in a woman." Now here I was in vespers shouting in a voice I didn't recognize but knew was mine, screaming, "No! I won't!" Crying, sobbing, I ran from my seat out the back door into the dark, up the 179 steps, falling and getting up, my knees scraped, running up the hill to our cottage, Bluebird. I threw myself on my bunk bed, screamed, kicked, punched, sobbed, howled, and raged. Keened. Never had I made so much noise, felt so angry, been so frightened.

I do not remember Mother's tone of voice, but I have not forgotten the words she spoke at my bedside: "You have comported yourself very badly. When your father comes on Friday night, he will decide your punishment." This was the first I ever heard Mother defer to Father regarding my "comportment." While I waited, I experienced emotional chaos — terror, diffuse anxiety, cockiness, shame, embarrassment, sadness, and fury. Resolution would come only after judgment.

Friday night, I was in bed, but too anxious to sleep when I heard Father's Studebaker pull up behind the cottage. I listened to Mother's telling of the story. Her objective account of my behavior was accurate, but she said nothing — perhaps knew nothing — about why I had refused to obey. Then came Father's judgment. He said, "Laurel was right. There will be no punishment. She's been punished enough already."

That night I dreamed my father was going around killing everybody. As he was about to kill me, I offered to help him kill the others, including my mother and sister, if he would spare my life. He agreed. I became his accomplice but came to consciousness before I killed anyone, unsure whether it was a dream or reality. For years, I have kept this earliest dream memory a secret. When I was a child and hazy concerning the dream's "truth," I was too ashamed of myself and my father to tell anyone. Later, I thought the dream too embarrassingly Freudian to tell anyone. Now, I think differently about the meaning of the dream: It is a prophetic text, an eight-year-old's subconscious understanding of how she would shape her life.

From that Friday night in August on, I shared nothing of personal or emotional importance with my mother. I told her nothing bad that happened to me, none of my fears, misgivings, problems, failures, or longings. From that Friday night in August on, I was identified with my father and his "justness"; and I was contemptuous of my mother's hypocrisy, duplicity, and dependence on my father's judgment. My mother I now viewed as an untrustworthy household accessory. In my gut, I understood that rebellion in the face of weak authority would bring me pain, fear, and horror but ultimately win me the love, support, and respect of those worthy of my respect, people like my father.

That is what happened the summer I turned eight, the summer I "lost" a mother.

My eight-year-old vision of life has shaped much of my life. I have lived some version of this story for nearly fifty years. But late this August, my body has rebelled: It refuses to carry me through my life. My emotions and thoughts have rebelled too. My sense of self feels broken.

What is to be done? I begin by disassembling the eight-year-old's vision; I search for a new place to stand in the vespers story, a new place to stand in my life. The disassembly begins with my standing in my mother's story.

In 1908, my grandmother, Ida Foreman, escaped from a shtetl near Kiev with her life and the lives of her son, Abe, and her daughter—my mother—Rose. Had they stayed in Russia and survived the pogroms, they would have been murdered thirty-five years later at Babi Yar. But, instead, they rode Scandinavian steerage away from the pogroms to America to join Baruch, husband and father. Ida was twenty-five, Abe was ten, and Rose was eight. Rose had never seen her father.

By the time Rose was twelve, she had experienced the pogroms, immigration, her father's being kicked to death by a horse, a string of boarders, two spindly, sickly siblings, and a mother who could neither read nor write in any language and spoke only Yiddish, ending most utterances with a habitual, yet impassioned, "*Kine hora*" to ward off the evil eye. At thirteen, having finished grade school and speaking the impeccable English of the second-generation immigrant, Rose became a bookkeeper for Sears-Roebuck. Her paycheck bought piano lessons for her sister, Ceilia, books for her brother, Abe, and food for the family. She spent her weekly allowance on hosiery. She was vain about her legs.

Rose was neither a storyteller nor a complainer. She believed that if you can't say something nice, don't say anything at all. Uncle Abe told me the little I know about her childhood. Learning some Jewish history and seeing *Fiddler on the Roof* when I was myself grown, a mother, told me more—not the particulars of her experience but its general shape. There are no pictures of her as a child. How is it possible to know so little about a mother's childhood?

In college, I learned a little about the experience of the Jews in Russia. I asked my mother about her experience. She denied having had any experience. I asked her the meaning of some Yiddish expressions. She denied having any knowledge of Yiddish. Later, when I was a thoroughly expert ethnographer, two years before she would die, I pushed her hard about the pogroms. I had seen my mother express anger perhaps four or five times in my life. Her retort was as harsh and bitter as I'd ever heard in her. Her black eyes narrowed, blazed. A quarter of a century later, I can still feel her outrage at me for asking. I can still hear her exact words: "Why would you want to know about terrible things?" Subject forever closed forever.

I know somewhat more about the man my mother married, my father, Tyrrell Alexander Richardson. I even have a photograph album, annotated in white ink in his handwriting. Father's American heritage dates from the seventeenth century. Lord Tyrrell, the story goes, placed a bomb under the English Parliament House and hopped a boat to America. In every generation thereafter Scots-Irish married English married Scots-Irish. My paternal grandmother was supposedly a member of the Daughters of the American Revolution.

I know almost nothing about her—my father's mother. Supposedly, her name was "Laurel," and she had been a teacher. Mother told me that Father named me after her. My sister and brother have no explanations for their names. Why did I need an explanation? Why should my "birth story" be the only biographical story Mother ever told me? As a child, I thought it signaled the special relationship I would have with my father; as an adult, I thought Mother needed proof from Father that he would love their late-born daughter.

I don't know how I knew, but I did know that something had happened to Grandmother Laurel, something seriously awful. Too awful to talk about. Mother, if she knew, surely wouldn't have talked about it, and father surely didn't. Perhaps Grandmother Laurel died. Perhaps she ran off with another man. Maybe she was placed in a sanatorium for crazy women or alcoholics. I never knew; still don't; never will.

Something happened to Grandmother Laurel. How odd, how inappropriately familial, how inexplicably sad to call a woman for whom I have no picture, no voice, bare biographical detail "Grandmother Laurel."

It is not history that provides familial biography but willingness of families to speak their remembrances. No one spoke of Grandmother Laurel. Her absence (desertion? hospitalization? death?) from her family created four motherless children. Fatherless, too, apparently, as my mother had been. Different relatives raised my father and his two sisters, Laura and Francis, but foster parents took in baby Jack. He became a "lost" brother. Great Aunt Ruby, a well-to-do Christian Scientist, raised Father. She gave me a high-pronged diamond ring for my sixteenth birthday. I still have the ring, but the diamond is lost. Aunt Ruby came to my college graduation, the only guest besides my parents.

Father looks jaunty and handsome in the pictures from his youth at Aunt Ruby's. One shows him in a crew sweater, auburn hair slicked back, paddling a landlocked canoe. There are photos of coquettes with names—Hazel, Lois, Francie, Nera, Sedalia; others, nameless, sit on swings or fondle trees, smile at the photographer. Father's stance and demeanor prefigure the "rogue hero" he will become—an adventurer, a law unto himself, a survivor. He was, he told me, the first valedictorian at Senn High School, since his was the first graduating class, the first senior to letter in three sports, the first all-city debate champion, the first soda jerk in Chicago (or maybe the world), and the first and only guy on his block to run off at sixteen, lie about his age, and join the cavalry riding against Pancho Villa in Mexico. His division was encamped for a while in Las Cruces, New Mexico. I have photographs of him, in the encampment, on the field where I am photographed, playing, for the cover of this book.

He trained a horse, which, he said, General Pershing rode into battle. I have pictures of that horse, rearing, Father standing nonchalantly under him. I have pictures of General Pershing, surrounded by men, and Father surrounded by women. Beside the photo of an unnamed cavalry nurse, Father has pasted a typed poem, "The Chant of the Squirrel Food," which evaluates the charms of foreign women and concludes, "It's American beauties every time for me." Father was proud of his "rogue's gallery." Here are his comments written near their photos: "Elusive Elusion-Yvonne," whose "eyes see as far as the stars," and whose "thoughts reach way beyond"; "Ivy—that I were a gypsy, and she my Queen"; "They call her 'Ruby'—I wonder why"; "Beauty and the Beasts," beasts being Father and his horse. Mother hated the album so much that Father secreted it in his bureau drawer. I may have peeked at it once when I was a child rummaging through his bureau. But Father didn't show the "kids" the photos until we were adults, the year of his angina attack. The following Fourth of July, he presented each of his grown children with framed 8" x 10" copies of his "official" cavalry portrait.

While stationed in Texas, Father went to a gypsy fortune-teller who told him he had a younger brother in Chicago. The seer instructed my father to go to Seiben's Tavern and ask for "Jack Mize." When Father returned home, he followed the fortune-teller's instructions, and Jack came into his life. This is the only story my family tells about how the brothers reunited; it is a "true" family story. I even used to believe it.

It was because of Uncle Jack that we became regulars at Olivet Camp. Olivet was founded by a charismatic Presbyterian minister, Norman B. Barr, in the 1920s. He took delinquent boys off the Chicago streets into the Wisconsin air, where he put them to work building cottages. Grown to men, rehabilitated, tithing Presbyterians, many union craftsmen, they brought their wives and children, year after year, to the camp they had built as boys and lovingly tended later as skilled tradesmen.

My own father had not been a delinquent, but his "lost" baby brother, Jack, had been. Unlike the other boys, Jack retained his boyhood ways. Supposedly he was a chauffeur, but I think of him as a full-time alcoholic and part-time numbers runner and errand boy in Chicago's minor league underworld. Sometimes, at Lake Geneva, I would see Jack sleeping in the same bed as his daughter, Lilly. Lilly grew up, married, and had four sons. The day of Uncle Jack's funeral, Lilly gave birth to a fifth son. He was blind and armless, and his heart was outside his chest. She named him Jack and buried him next to her father.

Jack's wife, Aunt Gertrude, a German-American, was my mother's best friend. In Chicago, every week Mother and I would go to Aunt Gertrude's for a "Kaffeeklatsch." Mother would leave a sealed envelope by her cup. I later learned that Father supported Jack's family. I remember one odd day at Aunt Gertrude's, when I was about three years old. Uncle Jack was "asleep"—now, I would say, "passed out." Aunt Gertrude, partially submerged in their claw-footed bathtub, was crying. There was blood. Mother and another person came in and out of the bathroom, tending to her. Father came and took me home. When I was grown, I thought that I had witnessed the aftermath of a home abortion. Maybe Jack is my biological uncle. I hope, however, that he is like the others at Olivet Camp, "fictive kin."

When Father returned to Chicago from the cavalry, he not only reunited with his brother, he entered law school. Hanging around "Bughouse Square," a site of free speech on Chicago's near north side, he met my mother's older brother, Abe. Abe, a young Jewish intellectual, would eventually move to Hollywood, open a bookstore, join the Communist Party, and wife-trade with his best friend. His first wife and best friend would subsequently commit suicide, holding hands, jumping from an ocean liner on which all four had booked passage. Abe and his new wife would name their daughter after Abe's deceased ex-wife, Joanne. My cousin, Joanne, would have plastic surgery, contact lenses, and years of dance lessons. She would dance naked for her father. When she was twenty-two, she would leave for New York and not see her parents again, except once. She and I were the same age and were pen pals. When she was eight, she renamed herself, Laura, a self-consciously chosen variant of my name. She still goes by "my" name.

But before all that happened, Abe brought Tyrrell home to Ida and Rose. Charmed by him, the first goy ever to set foot in her home, Gramma agreed to take him in as a boarder. Before long, Tyrrell fell in love with Rose. Once when I asked him why he had fallen for my mother, he said, "I'm always on the side of the underdog."

The story goes that Gramma objected to Tyrrell's desire to marry Rose. But Father learned Yiddish and promised on his word of honor that the children would have a Jewish education. Supposedly, this promise sufficed. When I was an adult, I learned that Gramma did not attend their wedding; she was in the hospital having shock treatments for a nervous breakdown. Perhaps it was not until after the shock treatments, after the breakdown, that father made his solemn promise to raise his children Jewish. I don't know the true order of events. But, in each casting of the story, Father engages in an "oral contract," makes the promise to raise the children Jewish—as if they were "his" to promise.

Mother did not want "her" children to be raised Jewish. Being Jewish was being in the pogroms and Chicago ghettos, poor and persecuted. Being married to "Mr. Richardson"—*not* "Mr. Rich," as Gramma insisted on calling him because it sounded Jewish—gave Mother a ticket into safe, mainstream America. What immigrant child didn't long for that ride?

But, because of Father's vow, we were raised Jewish—sort of. We went to Anshe Emet, a Reconstructionist synagogue (similar to conservative Judaism but more intellectual). Rabbi M. said that there was no such thing as looking Jewish, only stereotypes about how Jews looked. He pointed at me to prove his point and spoke my Jewish name, "Leah." I responded, "My father isn't Jewish. I look like him." I was not invited to boy-girl parties after that.

The year I turned thirteen, I was in temple six days a week, preparing for confirmation. On Confirmation Day, I walked down the aisle, muttering under my breath, "I have fulfilled my obligation to my grandmother; I'll never have to go to a synagogue again." I can count on my hands how often I have been back. Yet my confirmation workbook, *Little Lower than the Angels*, and my confirmation giftbook, *In the Beginning: Human Destiny 2*, written and signed by our then blind rabbi, Rabbi Solomon Goldman, are in my upstairs "best books" shelves, next to poetry and my husband's novels.

"Father's children" were sent to *shul* (synagogue school), but "Mother's children" did not experience a Jewish home. Mother didn't know what "the Jews" believed. She never went to temple. She said that there might be a heavenly afterlife, which sounded suspiciously Christian-like to me. No Sabbath candles for us, no Seders, challah, gefilte fish, chicken soup, lox. We ate American: meats dipped in milk, like breaded veal; macaroni and cheese with hot dogs; bacon and eggs. When Gramma came to our house, she muttered about the *traife* (nonkosher food). Bringing her own table cloth, dishes, and food, she ate her dinner on "her" card table.

My home felt Jewish only at Passover, the celebration of the liberation story of the Jewish people, but which I understood only as a holy week with ritual observances to protect first-born Jewish sons from God's wrath. We changed dishes and ate matzos. Mother fasted. Father called her "his Jewess" and told us to be kind to her because she was hungry. My brother must have felt important, since all this Jewish activity was on his behalf. Being a Jewish girl, I never felt in danger from God's vengeance, only vulnerable to God's voyeurism. God was an old man who could see me dress and undress, even when I hid in the closet or under the sheets; I learned to change clothes without ever being naked.

We didn't have a Christmas tree or even a "Hannukah Bush," although we were feted with Christmas presents. One year, Father surprised Mother with a table-top artificial tree, electrified, shining with miniature colored lights. It was easily unplugged and hidden from Gramma. Mother loved it. After Gramma died, the miniature faux tree was replaced with overdecorated, angel-topped, live Christmas trees. Mother loved them. I feel nostalgic for the faux tree. I look for replicas now and then, but none seems right.

Mother was fond of saying, "You don't marry a man, you marry a life." What kind of a man—what kind of a life—did my mother marry? Father began his career as a Chicago criminal lawyer; later, he became a prosecutor and state's attorney. During World War II, he created immigration papers for German "fictive kin" who feared extradition. He "produced" birth certificates, death certificates, naturalization papers as needed. Father's motto was to never owe any one a favor but to have many in his debt. He claimed that Saul Bellow had based the character Augie March on him.

Mother's role was to be a good mother and wife. Father decreed Sunday a "day of rest for Mother." The children went to Anshe Emet Sunday school and then to the movies — double features, newsreels, previews, selected shorts, and serials. By 6:00, my family was at Edward's, wolfing down "all you can eat" barbecued spareribs. Father would order a double Scotch, with water on the side, and mix them together himself.

Mother's typical day was quite different. She would get up, get dressed in a clean, starched house dress; wake the children; make breakfast for the children; get the children off to school before Father got up (or we noticed he wasn't home?); make beds (clean sheets every day), clean up kitchen, clean house; prepare hot lunch for children (breaded veal, bacon, lettuce, and tomato sandwiches, Campbell's soup); eat lunch with children while listening to "Ma Perkins" on the radio; help Barrie with his schoolwork; clean up lunch dishes; make pies; read; start dinner; get laundry ready for pickup; put away clean laundry; sit on porch, crochet until children home from school; serve children's after-school snacks; crochet, listen to radio, read, be available for children; make children's dinner; serve children's dinners at 5:00 sharp; clean up kitchen; supervise children's baths; get children ready for bed and into bedrooms by 7:00; take bath, dress up, fix hair, rouge cheeks; greet husband; serve parents' dinner; serve children's evening snacks in their bedrooms or have husband do so — when he does so, he sings old cavalry songs to Laurel; children's lights out. Mother believed that you should "always stay ahead of what was next."

I was not fatherless. Father thought me bright and took the development of my mind as his moral obligation. He told me I had a moral obligation, as well, to use my intelligence for the betterment of others. By "others," I think he meant "underdogs." I longed for the academic challenges that I saw my Sunday school peers getting at Girl's Latin. When I was twelve, I phoned Girl's

Latin hoping they would scholarship me. Father said, "No. You belong in public schools."

From about age four on, I was responsible for remembering the Saturday grocery shopping list. If something was forgotten, it was my fault—not Mother's. When I was seven, I remember organizing the list in my mind alphabetically and feeling grateful for a memory crutch ("A" is for applesauce, "B" is for baking soda . . .). At Olivet Camp, I kept track of which auntie wanted how much corn on the cob and how many dozens of eggs from the egg lady's farm. But I was to "forget" Father's telephone conversations. He talked to clients on our home phone. I was a trustworthy secret-keeper. I still am.

Father must have taught me to read, but I don't remember *being* taught— only being able to read. I can see the two of us with the newspaper, reading. Father had strong ideas about what writers were worthwhile, and so did I. I hated his favorite male adventure story writers, like Fenimore Cooper and Daniel Defoe, but I loved the animal adventure stories by Jack London and Alfred Payson Terhune. We argued a lot about books and authors. I knew I had "won" a literary point when his retort was, "Someday you'll grow up."

We had philosophical conversations, too, which I enjoyed much more. He said he used to be a Druid but that now he was a Deist. He believed an Almighty Force put the whole universe into motion, then bowed out. I suspect that rogue heroes everywhere are attracted to deistic cosmology because they can have a sense of purpose without having to deal with a living, meddlesome God. He believed that suicide was not a sin but often a moral choice. "Three score and ten years," he said, "was one's allotted time." He would not want extreme measures taken to preserve his life. He was confident that he would die before Mother. I should take care of her after he was gone, he said. Mother died three years before Father.

Every other month or so, Father would take me downtown. We wouldn't ride on the El, as Mother and I did when we went places; rather, Father would drive down Lake Shore Drive with me in the front passenger seat, not crowded in the back with my siblings. He'd hand the car keys to the black parking attendant in "his" garage, reach into his pocket and hand him some bills, always saying, "Take your kids out, Partner." "Thank you, Mr. Richardson, sir," the attendant always replied. We'd eat lunch at Berghoff's, where the white maître d' greeted Father by name. Father handed him some bills, too, but he didn't tell the maître d' to take his kids out or call him "Partner." I thought everyone in Chicago knew my father.

After lunch, we spent the afternoons at the legitimate theater, ballet, movies, or the downtown library. I must have seen every musical comedy that ever came through Chicago when I was a child. I loved the feel underfoot of the library's worn marble steps. I imagined myself connected to a historical procession of book lovers; I thought of myself as a reader, then, not a writer. My favorite outing was when Father took me to the Chicago Symphony Hall to see the movie *The Red Shoes*. We sat in the loge, and I was wearing red shoes and a red velvet dress. I was mesmerized by the movie's beauty, intensity, and message: The woman who tries to have both love and a career will die a horrible, uncontrollable death.

The year the Cubs played in the World Series — the fall following my vespers experience — my father had box seats on the first base line. We lived a half mile from Wrigley Field. I was immersed in baseball and thought I knew everything about the game and the players. One fall day, I was taken to the ballpark with my Father and a bunch of his "cronies." I happily filled in the scorecards, figured statistics, coached, and ate hotdogs without mustard. I felt simultaneously very small and very grown-up. As we climbed the cement stairs, I heard my father and his friends laughing, and Father saying about me, "She's a Yiddisha."

I felt like I had been jabbed in my stomach. Was that what I was to him — "a Yiddisha"? I felt betrayed, belittled, deeply confused, and angry. Today, I would label it "shame." At that moment, I felt my father was an anti-Semite. I talked to no one about this. Who could I have talked to? Even now, I feel the tension in my body as I write about what has been for me an "unspeakable experience." A deep wound.

In the Hebrew Sunday school that Father sent us to, I was learning that no matter how kind and generous the goyem made themselves out to be, they could not be trusted. They killed Jews — big time, like the Holocaust, and small time, through castigations and stereotyping. Sunday school teachers had taught me how Jews, like witches and cats, were burned on pyres during the Inquisition; skewered, stabbed, and deboweled during the Crusades. Teachers told me about Nazi medical experimentation, surgeries without anesthesia, bacterial injections, animal fetuses implanted in young Jewish women's wombs. I heard about the "Nazi showers"; Jews, thinking they were to be cleansed, were gassed en masse. Speakers from the Anti-Defamation League told me the names of hatred—*hymie, kike, jewboy, quotas.* Was my father just like the rest of the goyem?

As I write this, now, though, I am surprised at how tenaciously I have held on to the "anti-Semitic" interpretation of this childhood experience. The "cronies" I see in my memory might themselves have been Jewish. Father may have been deploying his "Jewish credentials." He may have been explaining to them why I was so smart. Or maybe the men were about to engage in anti-Semitic remarks, and Father was protecting me from them. That's how I deal today with anti-Semitic comments; I come out as a Jew. Maybe none of these alternatives is "true," but I like giving Father a chance at redemption, myself a chance to be unashamed.

Mother strongly believed families should be kept together. The wife was wholly responsible if her marriage failed. Father never handled divorce cases. "Nothing was worse," he said, "than breaking up a family." I stayed in a dreadful marriage for twelve years, waiting until Father died before I filed for divorce.

Before my wedding ceremony, Mother asked for a few minutes alone with me. I felt awkward, as though she were casting us into a Hollywood movie scene unsuited to us or our relationship. We sat on a maroon couch in an anteroom in the Edgewater Beach Hotel. I was dressed in ice-blue taffeta, not wanting to pass myself off as a virgin, enjoying the embarrassment it created for my parents, and thinking I could wear the blue dress again, which I never did. I was glad to have found a man who would "let" me have both children and a career. Mother was nervous. She said, "You will experience great pain and sorrow in marriage. All women do. But you put up with it, for the sake of the children." This was the first I'd heard her allude to anything bad in her world. I thought then that she was referring to sex. Later, I thought she foresaw the bad time I'd have in my first marriage. Much later, I thought she was probably speaking about Father's extramarital liaisons, one perhaps resulting in a son.

When I was fourteen, I was working after school on Monday and Thursday nights in the optometry department of Goldblatt's Department Store on Lincoln Avenue. I would leave my house on Hermitage at 6:00 A.M., walk to the streetcar, take it to Senn High School; practice with the synchronized swim team, go to my classes; take the streetcar to Goldblatt's, work until 9:00 selling frames, fitting glasses, and ignoring the lecherous optometrist; and arrive back home, by streetcar and foot, around 10:00 P.M., which allowed almost an hour for homework before the 11:00 lights out.

On a Sunday in April, Mother lost a pin in her reading glasses. Father taped the temple to the frame and asked me to get a replacement pin from the optometry department. On Monday night, as I came up the stairs, I remembered I had forgotten Mother's pin. "Hi," I yelled up from the staircase, "I'm sorry, I forgot the pin." Father stormed out of my parents' bedroom calling me all manner of bad names: spoiled; inconsiderate; selfish; slothful; like my Aunt Ceilia; indolent. We went into the living room. I tried to defend myself, but I don't remember a word I said. Father called me "insolent" and "disrespectful." The name-calling escalated. He said I was "incorrigible" and that I belonged in juvenile detention, whereupon he phoned someone and told them to come pick me up. My mind focused on how I would sneak the Pall Mall cigarettes, hidden in my coat pocket, into the juvenile center. Mother was crying and arguing with him. I had never heard them argue before. Then she stopped crying, took a determined breath, and said words I still remember, "Tyrrell, if you send her away, I will leave you."

Whether Father called someone or was merely bluffing, I wasn't sent to juvenile detention. Mother's words had shocked and cradled me: She was choosing me over my father. She was willing to break up a family on my behalf. I refused to even talk to Father after that night for a long time thereafter. Mother implored me to apologize, but I stonewalled him. One day, he said to me, "This is breaking your mother's heart." After that, I talked to him, although I never did apologize; nor did he. This story I kept hidden for years.

After Father's death, a woman came to his condominium, claiming she had been Father's long-term mistress. She said she had caught glimpses of me as a child downtown with Father. She remembered how thrilled I was with *The Red Shoes* and showed us a photograph of a young man named Richard, who looked like my father. She said Richard was her son by my father and that Father had provided for them throughout the years. Richard was born the April I was fourteen, the April Father called me incorrigible.

The year after experiencing my father's explosive wrath, I asked my parents if I could apply for early entrance to the University of Chicago. If I passed the test and received a Ford Fellowship, they promised I could matriculate and live in a dorm. My parents never broke their promises to me. Mother told me later that she didn't think I would pass; she was furious at Father, she said, because he *knew* I would pass *and* let me apply. Her heart was breaking. I was jubilant.

After I left for college, Mother gave away to a "deserving little girl" my prized possessions — a pristine (new-in-box) Storybook Doll collection and all my books, save my confirmation ones. She told me she didn't think I would miss my childhood toys, since I was in college now. I've tried to re-create my old Storybook Doll collection, but the available dolls are not the same. They have been played with.

When my younger son, Josh, left home at much too young an age, my grief was intense. I did not rest until I had purged his room — boxed away his possessions, removed his blue rug, and stripped away the red bandanna wallpaper. I redecorated the room with a rosy-pink rug, rose-scattered wallpaper, and pristine white shelves to hold my "best books." I call it the "Rose room."

In my earliest visual memories, I see Mother dressed in long, flowing burgundy satin, her black hair in French braids, and Father in a tuxedo. He was Joe Generous to everyone — busboys, waiters, gas-station attendants, poor relations. But once while hiding under the dining room table, I overheard Mother plead, "Please, Tyrrell. I need money." Father reached in his pants pocket and handed her some bills. I felt disgusted with and humiliated for her. I vowed at that moment never to be financially dependent on a man, never to have to ask a man for money. Like other childhood vows, this one has been kept, too.

My college sophomore grades were less than perfect. But I was proud of them, given I was young, my courses difficult, and my fellow students brilliant. Father took me on a walk to "converse" about my "performance" and whether he would continue to support me financially. I was taken off guard, defensive and angry. Haughtily, I said, "Then, don't! And we'll never have to discuss my 'performance' again." From age seventeen I have supported myself through fellowships, scholarships, and employment. One of my college jobs was lifeguard for Bruno Bettleheim's Orthogenic School, a school for severely emotionally disturbed children. I was paid five dollars an hour; earned every penny. I graduated with two hundred in the bank. Father and I never again discussed my grades.

Father was active in public life. Paul Douglas, the reigning Democratic senator from Illinois, was a friend from law school; Everett Dirksen, the reigning Republican senator from Illinois, was Father's colleague. Father ran Dirksen's Illinois campaigns. When I was a graduate student, I mentioned to Father that my National Science Foundation Pre-Dissertation Fellowship money was slow arriving. The next day, the director of the foundation phoned, apologized for the delay, and said he had dispatched a courier with my stipend. In all his years of government service, the director said, this was the first time he had been contacted by both the leading Republican and leading Democratic senators. "You must be someone important," he said.

I do not know what Mother thought of Father's work, but I know that his career and my "moral development" were at odds. When I was in elementary school, I was ashamed and morally outraged that he defended criminals. When I asked him why, he said, "Everyone must be presumed innocent—and therefore defended—until proven guilty." When I was an undergraduate at the University of Chicago in the 1950s, I was ashamed and morally outraged that Father prosecuted people. When I confronted him, he said, "I never ask for the death penalty. I always ask for mercy." When he decided to retire to Miami Beach, I thought it wrong for Mother, but I said nothing.

Father loved swaying juries. He never lost a defense trial; I don't know how he scored as a prosecutor. Once, early in his career, hampered with a weak defense, he brought a visibly pregnant Rose to meet the defendant, an accused murderer. He told the jury how much he loved his wife and how he would never endanger her. That was the summation. Mother cried; the jury voted to acquit.

Early in his career, Father became one of Al Capone's lawyers. Recently, my brother-in-law, John Phillips, told me this story. John began dating my sister when they were Lakeview High School freshmen. Upon meeting John, Father asked, "Were you any relation to Big John Phillips?" Big John Phillips had been a crooked cop with loyalties to the Moran Gang. "Yes," John answered. "He was my uncle—my father's twin brother. I'm named for him." Father, chuckling, said, "Well, let me tell you how I got your uncle's murderer off." The murderer had come to Father and told him he'd just murdered Big John Phillips. Father immediately brought the murderer to the police station and introduced him to Father's friends on the force. Father and the murderer hung out and "shot the breeze" with the cops. Because the time of death could never be fixed with certainty, the alibi was perfect.

My father told a story of how his alliance with Capone ended. One day my father told "Al" that he had to pay his taxes. Al didn't like that advice. That night while my parents and "baby Jessica" were at a Capone party, their house was robbed, but only of Al's gifts for Father's legal services. Father immediately packed up his family and took a night train to Hollywood, where he invested in silent movies, just as talkies were coming in, lost all his money, noted that Capone was incarcerated on tax evasion, and drove Rose and Jessica back to Chicago. The car, so the story goes, died in front of Gramma's house. He had brought Rose home. All this happened before I was born. I have Capone gifts — the "gold" silverware, chinoiserie desk, and my sister's silk baby clothes.

Father told me he was the only lawyer leaving Capone's service who wasn't subsequently murdered. He may have been too sanguine. Although he worked in Republican politics, he refused to participate in Richard Nixon's presidential campaign, claiming that if Nixon was elected, organized crime would run America. He professed to have materials documenting this claim. At the end of his life, widowed in Nixon territory, Key Biscayne, Father was writing his memoirs. It was July 4, 1970. On his couch, the *Miami Herald* was opened to an article, "One of Villa's Guards Buried: 'Not Many Are Left Now.'" The homicide police told us Father died of a stroke. I never saw the body. There were no memoirs in his condominium — no typing paper, no carbons, no Father's Day cards, no letters, nothing written to or by him. I asked a Chicago lawyer to check out the circumstances of Father's death. The lawyer did. He said, "You have a life and children in Columbus. Let it be."

The last time I saw my father was two years after Mother's death. He had come to Columbus to see his grandsons — my sons, Ben and Josh. He charmed my friends with the stories of his life. He patched the cement on the front steps. He discussed Daniel Defoe and General Pershing with Ben. He walked in "baby steps" in the Park of Roses with Josh. I could see Father's fingers and Josh's fingers in motion, mimicking butterfly wings, and imagined Father was telling Josh, as he had told me when I was Josh's age, not to step on ants or crush caterpillars, for all things had a right to live. Near the end of his visit, Father and I talked about the possibility of his moving to Columbus, but we both knew it wouldn't work. We cried together. It was the only time, other than around Mother's death, that I had seen him cry.

In May 1968, Mother was determined to take a bus trip north to see her three children, grandchildren, and sister. She'd be traveling alone, without Father, to Ohio, West Virginia, Chicago, and Iowa. She would visit me first. I came to the Greyhound Bus Depot. I looked around. I didn't recognize her. She had to call my name, "Laurel, here I am." She was so thin and wasted but so pretty. She was so tired. My heart nearly broke. What we did during her visit is vague in my memory. My brother was to drive her to West Virginia, but that didn't work out, so at her insistence, I put her on an airplane to Chicago. She collapsed at her sister's house, the house in which Gramma had died. My sister flew in from Des Moines and then flew with Mother back to Miami Beach.

Mother rested for a while at home. Then, the pain must have become unbearable. Father brought her to a doctor, who hospitalized her immediately. I flew down. I asked the doctor to do something—surgery, something, anything. He thought I was crazed. "Your mother," he said, "is in the final stages of breast cancer." It was the first I knew. It was the first any of the family knew. Mother was never told. That night the cancer reached her brain. She screamed, raged, shouted, yelled. Keened. "Remember, Tyrrell," she said, "there are *four* children. Love all *four* children." And then, the crazedness passed.

Mother came home. The doctor stopped by almost daily, as did a visiting nurse. I took care of her bodily needs, bathed and soothed her, and I read to her. But we never spoke about anything bad, from the past, present, or imminent future. We never spoke about vespers at Lake Geneva or how we had never spoken about ourselves since that night in August. We never mentioned that we had lost each other twenty-two years earlier. Yet I was finding my mother not through words or stories, recriminations or apologies, not through the mind or through family history, but through the heart, through simple acts of tending to her body, as she had tended to mine, when I was very young and as vulnerable as she was now. I felt graced by my love for her.

On June 8, I woke up determined to drive to Key West for the day. I sponge-bathed Mother, greeted the nurse, kissed my parents good-bye, and drove off in Father's Dodge Dart. When I got to Long Key, I was overwhelmed with the need to phone my parents. Mother had just died—less than a minute ago —Father said. I was grateful to have not witnessed her passing-on. I was thirty years old — too young to lose a mother, again.

Ten years after her death I wrote this poem:

LAST CONVERSATION

We tacitly agree
there are only vitamins
in the shot the doctor
gives you, but there is
morphine dancing in your eyes.

You say, "I feel like a schoolgirl."
The room shines with suitors
wanting you to dance. You flirt.
Oh, how you flirt. We laugh.

I clip your toenails and soothe
lemon lotion on your legs. Still
beautiful. We do not mention
that the cancer has stopped
at your hips. We do not mention
cancer.

I want to hold your
weightless body to my
breasts, cradle you,
rock you to sleep,
mother grown little.
You want to be held,
mother, tired of the
dance.

We tacitly agree
cancer might be catching.
I brush your hair and
talk about the last picture

show. We do not mention
we are afraid. We kiss
each other's cheeks.
I leave your room.
That afternoon, we do not
mention dances or your
having died.

For a long while, I was angry at my father. How could he not have noticed
the physical changes in my mother? How could he have ignored her black-
ened, hardened breasts? But he was who he was—raised by a Christian Scientist and steeped in a family of secrets and denials. Would Mother have been
any happier if she had been diagnosed? No. Would she have lived any longer?
Probably not. In 1968, cancer was a dirty word; Mother would have hated that
word attached to her. Breast cancer was then almost always fatal and its treat-
ment brutal. Living out denial proved merciful.

I tried to track down the "fourth child" who haunted Mother so near her
death. Father, the fictive kin, and real kin all denied the existence of a fourth
child. But I have two theories. One is that the fourth child is Richard, my father's illegitimate son, born in the month that my father labeled me "incorrigible," when my mother nearly left him. The second theory is that Mother
had an abortion between my brother's birth and mine. These were depression
years; I am a late-born child, and I have no "cousins" near my age. I can imagine Mother telling Father she would not have another abortion. This would explain the need for a story that proves Father wanted me, a story a mother who
told me no other stories told me: the story of my name.

I feel exhausted, emptied out.

As I write this, my sister phones. She will send me materials, retrieved from
her attic, about Father's family. There are no materials about Mother's family.
Father's mother's name, she says, is Matilda—not Laurel. I never had a Grandmother Laurel, after all. I feel the loss more deeply now. The Laurel Story, the
story of my name—an untrue story. Even it—untrue.

The packet from my sister arrives, regular mail. I open it. Notes are in
Father's handwriting, and I am crying. There are ancestral *names* and some

history. Here are family names, wonderful, wonderful names: Kansas home-steaders James McCanna, Laura McCanna and the never-married twins, Jenny and Jess McCanna; Salem, Illinois, homesteader, James Richardson and his wife, "somewoman" Pitts, parents of four sons—all of whom comported themselves well in the Civil War; Scott Richardson, "one of the famous es-capees from Libby Prison." Great-Grandfather Scott! And Bridget Kelly! What a name!

And Matilda. She is a Tyrrell—"Thor's Woods"! My auburn-haired father, nicknamed "Red" in high school, descends from *the* Tyrrell the Red, a Viking who mercilessly hacked a kingdom for himself in the Irish midlands. Having been told about the Tyrrell connection by my father, when I was a child, I had already visited Tyrrellspass, a midlands town. Lord Tyrrell's castle just hap-pened to be for sale. I knocked on the door and introduced myself as "Laurel Tyrrell." "Well, it wouldn't be smart to deny a Tyrrell a tour of their castle, now would it," the owner said, inviting us in. The Tyrrell family motto is "Truth Is the Way of Life."

More notes from Father. Early American Tyrrells were law enforcers. One was the first marshal elected in Chicago. Another was in the "secret service during the Civil War and later exposed and prevented the plot to kidnap and hold for ransom Lincoln's body from the tomb in Springfield, for which a letter of appreciation was sent by Lincoln's son." These names, activities, thrill me. Forever the Tyrrells have been involved in crime and punishment. Forever.

I imagine now that Father invented my name. I like to think that he mated his grandmother's name, "Laura," with his mother's maiden name, "Tyrrell," making me a "Laur-el." See, I tell myself, I am truly named for Matilda Tyrrell. Jewish tradition would prevent the naming of children after living people ("What you wish them dead? *kine hora*"). So, I could not be named "Laura," like his older sister, or Tyrrell, like himself. Besides Laurel is a wonderful, mythically resonant name. Sometimes Father called me "Daphne." I do love the forest.

After an absence of forty-two years, I returned to Olivet Camp on Lake Geneva. I walked along the shore path, crossed the gravel knoll, climbed up the wooden stairs, crossed the porch, looked at the Recreation Room where I had attended vespers, which was now sanctified with a permanent altar and cross, climbed the 179 gravel steps, counting each under my breath, surprised at how wide they still felt and what a stretch they would have been for a child's legs — how easy it would be to trip, fall, scrape bare shins — and then walked up the hill to Bluebird cottage. I looked inside. The sleeping room and porch seemed unchanged. I took pictures. Four decades were like a fortnight, only now the "cousins" were the "aunties." I was welcomed as "Auntie Laurel," but I had not been missed. I declined the invitation for church and potluck.

I was eight years old again, and I began to write.

REFERENCES

Agger, Ben. n.d. "Marxism, Feminism, Deconstructionism: Reading Sociology." Manuscript, Department of Sociology, State University of New York–Buffalo.

———. 1989a. "Do Books Write Authors?: A Study of Disciplinary Hegemony." *Teaching Sociology* 17:365–369.

———. 1989b. *Reading Science: A Literary, Political, and Sociological Analysis.* Dix Hills, N.Y.: General Hall.

———. 1989c. *Socio(onto)logy: A Disciplinary Reading.* Urbana: University of Illinois.

Alexander, Jeffrey C., and Paul Colomy. 1989. "Neofunctionalism Today: Reconstructing a Theoretical Tradition." Presented to the North Central Sociological Association Meetings, Akron, Ohio.

Balzac, Honoré de. [1842] 1965. Preface to *The Human Comedy,* from *At the Sign of the Cat and Racket,* translated by Clara Bell (1897). In *The Modern Tradition: Backgrounds of Modern Literature,* edited by Richard Ellman and Charles Feidelson Jr., 246–254. New York: Oxford University Press.

Barthes, Roland. 1966. "Introduction to the Structural Analysis of the Narrative." Occasional paper, Centre for Contemporary Cultural Studies, University of Birmingham.

Baudrillard, Jean Paul. 1989. *America.* Translated by C. Turner. London: Verso.

Bazerman, Charles. 1987. "Codifying the Social Scientific Style: The APA Publication Manual as a Behaviorist Rhetoric." In *The Rhetoric of the Human Sciences: Language and Argument in Scholarship and Human Affairs,* edited by John S. Nelson, Allan Megill, and Donald N. McCloskey, 125–144. Madison: University of Wisconsin Press.

———. 1988. *Shaping Written Knowledge: The Genre and Activity of the Experimental Article in Science.* Madison: University of Wisconsin Press.

Becker, Howard S. 1986. "Telling about Society." In *Doing Things Together,* 121–136. Evanston: Northwestern University Press.

Bertaux-Wieme, Isabelle. 1981. "The Life History Approach to the Study of Internal Migration." In *Biography and Society: The Life History Approach in the Social Sciences,* edited by Daniel Bertaux. Thousand Oaks, Calif.: Sage Press.

Boelen, W. A. Marianne. 1992. "Street Corner Society: Cornerville Revisited." *Journal of Contemporary Ethnography* 21:11–51.

Bogard, William. 1992. "Postmodernism One Last Time." *Sociological Theory* 21:231–243.

Borroff, M. 1993. "Cluster on the Poetic: From Euripides to Rich." *Publications of the Modern Language Association of America* 108:1032–1035.

Brady, Ivan, ed. 1991. *Anthropological Poetics*. Savage, Md.: Rowman and Littlefield.

Brodkey, Linda. 1987. *Academic Writing as Social Practice*. Philadelphia: Temple University Press.

Brown, Richard H. 1977. *A Poetic for Sociology*. Cambridge: Cambridge University Press.

Bruner, Edward M. 1986. "Ethnography as Narrative." In *The Anthropology of Experience*, edited by Victor Turner and Edward M. Bruner, 137–155. Champagne: University of Illinois Press.

Bruner, Jerome. 1986. *Actual Minds, Possible Worlds*. Cambridge: Harvard University Press.

Butler, Sandra, and Barbara Rosenblum. 1991. *Cancer in Two Voices*. San Francisco: Spinsters Book Company.

Campbell, John Angus. 1987. "Charles Darwin: Rhetorician of Science." In *The Rhetoric of the Human Sciences: Language and Argument in Scholarship and Public Affairs*, edited by John S. Nelson, Allan Megill, and Donald N. McCloskey, 69–86. Madison: University of Wisconsin Press.

Carey, James W. 1989. *Communication as Culture: Essays on Media and Society*. Boston: Unwin Hyman.

Cheal, David. 1989. "Family Theory after the Big Bang: Postmodern Knowledge and the Sociology of the Family." Presented to the American Sociological Association Meetings, San Francisco.

Clifford, James. 1986. "Introduction: Partial Truths." In *Writing Culture: The Poetics and Politics of Ethnography*, edited by James Clifford and George E. Marcus, 1–26. Berkeley and Los Angeles: University of California Press.

Clifford, James, and George E. Marcus, eds. 1986. *Writing Culture: The Poetics and Politics of Ethnography*. Berkeley and Los Angeles: University of California Press.

Clough, Patricia Ticento. 1987. "Feminist Theory and Social Psychology." *Studies in Symbolic Interaction* 8:3–22.

———. 1992. *The End(s) of Ethnography: From Realism to Social Criticism*. Thousand Oaks, Calif.: Sage.

Coleman, James S. 1990. *Foundations of Social Theory*. Cambridge: Harvard University Press.

Cook, Judith A., and Mary Margaret Fonow. 1986. "Knowledge in Women's Interests: Issues in Epistemology and Methodology in Feminist Sociological Research." *Sociological Inquiry* 56:2–29.

Crawford, Marion Ayton. 1951. Introduction to *Old Goriot*. New York: Penguin Books.

Davies, Bronwyn. 1989. *Frogs and Snails and Feminist Tales: Preschool Children*. St Leonards, Australia: Allen & Unwin.

De Certeau, Michel. 1983. "History: Ethics, Science, and Fiction." In *Social Science as Moral Inquiry*, edited by Norma Hahn, Robert Bellah, Paul Rabinow, and William Sullivan, 173–209. New York: Columbia University Press.

Deegan, Mary J. 1988. *Jane Addams and the Men of the Chicago School, 1892–1918*. New Brunswick, N.J.: Transaction.

De Man, Paul. 1979. *Allegories of Reading*. New Haven: Yale University Press.

Denzin, Norman K. 1986. "'Postmodern Social Theory.'" *Sociological Theory* 4:194–204.

————. 1987. *The Alcoholic Self.* Thousand Oaks, Calif.: Sage.

————. 1989a. *Interpretive Biography.* Thousand Oaks, Calif.: Sage.

————. 1989b. *Interpretive Interactionism.* Thousand Oaks, Calif.: Sage.

————. 1990. "Writing the Interpretive Postmodern Essay." *Journal of Contemporary Ethnography* 19 (2): 235–251.

————, ed. 1990–1996. *Studies in Symbolic Interaction.* Vols. 11–17.

Denzin, Norman K., and Yvonna S. Lincoln. 1994. *Handbook of Qualitative Research.* Thousand Oaks, Calif.: Sage.

Derrida, Jacques. 1982. *Margins of Philosophy.* Translated by Alan Bass. Chicago: University of Chicago Press.

DeShazer, Mary K. 1986. *Inspiring Women: Reimagining the Muse.* New York: Pergamon.

DeVault, Marjorie L. 1990. "Talking and Listening from Women's Standpoint: Feminist Strategies for Interviewing and Analysis." *Social Problems* 37 (1): 96–116.

Diamond, Stanley. 1985. *Totems.* New York: Open Book/Station Hill.

Diamond, Timothy. 1992. *Making Gray Gold: The Everyday Production of Nursing Home Life.* Chicago: University of Chicago Press.

DiIorio, Judi. 1989. "Sex Glorious Sex." In *Feminist Frontiers: Rethinking Sex, Gender, and Society*, 2d rev. ed., edited by Laurel Richardson and Verta Taylor, 261–267. New York: Random House.

Dorst, John D. 1989. *The Written Suburb: An American Site, an Ethnographic Dilemma.* Philadelphia: University of Pennsylvania Press.

Eagleton, Terry. 1983. *Literary Theory: An Introduction.* Minneapolis: University of Minnesota Press.

Edmondson, Ricca. 1984. *Rhetoric in Sociology.* London: Macmillan.

Ellis, Carolyn. 1991a. "Emotional Sociology." *Studies in Symbolic Interaction*, 12. Greenwich, Conn.: JAI.

————. 1991b. "Sociological Introspection and Emotional Experience." *Symbolic Interaction* 14: 23–50.

————. 1995a. *Final Negotiations.* Philadelphia: Temple University Press.

————. 1995b. "The Other Side of the Fence: Seeing Black and White in a Small, Southern Town." *Qualitative Inquiry* 1: 147–167.

————. 1995c. "Speaking of Dying: An Ethnographic Short Story." *Symbolic Interaction* 18: 73–81.

Ellis, Carolyn, and Arthur P. Bochner. 1991. "Telling and Performing Personal Stories: The Constraints of Choice in Abortion." In *Investigating Subjectivity: Research on Lived Experience*, edited by Carolyn Ellis and Michael G. Flaherty, 79–101. Thousand Oaks, Calif.: Sage.

————, eds. 1996a. "Taking Ethnography into the Twenty-first Century." Special issue of *Journal of Contemporary Ethnography*.

————, eds. 1996b. *Composing Ethnography: Alternative Representation for Qualitative Research.* Thousand Oaks, Calif.: AltaMira.

Ellis, Carolyn, and Michael G. Flaherty, eds. 1992. *Investigating Subjectivity: Research on Lived Experience.* Thousand Oaks, Calif.: Sage.

Epstein, Jon. 1996. "Americans Have No Identity but They Do Have Wonderful Teeth." CTHEORY Website. http://www.ctheory.com. a-americans-have.html.

Erikson, Erik H. 1975. "On the Nature of 'Psycho-Historical' Evidence." In *Life Span Development and Behavior*, edited by Paul Baltes. New York: Norton Press.

Erikson, Kai T. 1976. *Everything in Its Path: Destruction of the Community in the Buffalo Creek Flood*. New York: Simon & Schuster.

Ferraro, Kathleen, and John M. Johnson. 1983. "How Women Experience Battering: The Process of Victimization." *Social Problems* 30:325–339.

Fine, Michelle. 1992. *Disruptive Voices: The Possibility of Feminist Research*. Ann Arbor: University of Michigan Press.

Fisher, W. R. 1987. *Human Communication as Narration: Toward a Philosophy of Reason, Value, and Action*. Columbia: University of South Carolina Press.

Fiske, Donald W., and Richard A. Shweder, eds. 1986. *Metatheory in Social Science: Pluralisms and Subjectivities*. Chicago: University of Chicago Press.

Flax, Jane. 1987. "Postmodernism and Gender Relations in Feminist Theory." *Signs* 12: 621–643.

Fonow, Mary Margaret, and Judith A. Cook, eds. 1991. *Beyond Methodology: Feminist Scholarship as Lived Research*. Bloomington: University of Indiana Press.

Forster, E. M. 1954. *Aspects of the Novel*. New York: Harcourt, Brace.

Foucault, Michel. 1978. *The History of Sexuality: An Introduction*. New York: Pantheon.

Franklin, Clyde W., and Laurel Richardson. 1972. "Sex and Race: A Substructural Paradigm." *Phylon* 2:242–253.

Fraser, Nancy, and Linda Nicholson. 1988. "Social Criticism without Philosophy: An Encounter between Feminism and Postmodernism." In *Universal Abandon: The Politics of Postmodernism*, edited by A. Ross, 83–104. Minneapolis: University of Minnesota Press.

Frohock, Fred. 1992. *Healing Powers*. Chicago: University of Chicago Press.

Frye, Northrop. 1957. *Anatomy of Criticism*. Princeton: Princeton University Press.

Gammell, Linda, Michael McCall, and Sandra Menefee Taylor. 1995. "The One about the Farmer's Daughter: Stereotypes and Self Portraits." (An exhibition and postcards.) Minneapolis, Minn.: pARTs Gallery.

Geertz, Clifford. 1980. "Blurred Genres." *American Scholar* 49:165–179.

———. 1988. *Works and Lives: The Anthropologist as Author*. Stanford: Stanford University Press.

Glassner, Barry. 1991. "The Medium Must Not Deconstruct: A Postmodern Ethnography of USA Today Television Show." *Media Culture and Society* 13: 53–70.

Gleick, James. 1984. "Solving the Mathematical Riddle of Chaos." *New York Times Magazine*, June 10, 30–32.

Grosz, Elizabeth. 1989. *Sexual Subversions: Three French Feminists*. Boston: Allen & Unwin.

Gusfield, Joseph. 1976. "The Literary Rhetoric of Science: Comedy and Pathos in Drinking Driver Research." *American Sociological Review* 4:16–34.

Haraway, Donna. 1988. "Situated Knowledges: The Science Question in Feminism and the Privilege of Partial Perspective." *Feminist Studies* 14:575–599.

Harding, Sandra. 1986. *The Science Question in Feminism*. Ithaca, N.Y.: Cornell University Press.

Harper, Douglas. 1987. *Working Knowledge: Skill and Community in a Small Shop*. Chicago: University of Chicago Press.

Hassan, Ihab. 1987. *The Postmodern Turn: Essays in Postmodern Theory and Culture*. Columbus: Ohio State University Press.

Heilbrun, Carolyn G. 1988. *Writing a Woman's Life*. New York: W. W. Norton.

Heisenberg, Werner. 1965. "Non-Objective Science and Uncertainty." In *The Modern Tradition: Backgrounds of Modern Language*, edited by Richard Ellman and Charles Feidelson Jr. New York: Oxford University Press.

Herman, Andrew. 1995. "Soctribe." Website. http://www.drake/artsci/soc/tribe/tribehomepage.hmtl.com.

Hooks, Bell. 1990. *Yearning: Race, Gender, and Cultural Politics*. Boston: South End Press.

Husserl, Edmund. 1964. *The Phenomenology of Internal Time Consciousness*. Translated by James S. Churchill. Bloomington: Indiana University Press.

Hutcheon, Linda. 1988. *A Poetics of Postmodernism: History, Theory, Fiction*. New York: Routledge.

Irigaray, Luce. 1985. *This Sex Which Is Not One*. Ithaca, N.Y.: Cornell University Press.

Jakobson, Roman. 1960. "Linguistics and Poetry." In *Style and Language*, edited by T. A. Sebock, 350 –377. Cambridge: MIT Press.

Jameson, Fredric. 1981. *The Political Unconscious*. Ithaca, N.Y.: Cornell University Press.

Kaufman, Sharon. 1986. *The Ageless Self: Sources of Meaning in Later Life*. Madison: University of Wisconsin Press.

Kirschner, Betty Frankle, and Laurel Richardson [Walum]. 1978. "Dual Location Families: Married Singles." *Alternative Life Styles* 1:513 –525.

Kohli, Martin. 1981. "Biography: Account, Text, Method." In *Biography and Society: The Life History Approach in the Social Sciences*, edited by Daniel Bertaux. Thousand Oaks, Calif.: Sage Press.

Kondo, Dorinne. 1990. *Crafting Selves*. Chicago: University of Chicago Press.

Krieger, Susan. 1983. *The Mirror Dance: Identity in a Woman's Community*. Philadelphia: Temple University Press.

———. 1991. *Social Science and the Self: Personal Essays on an Art Form*. New Brunswick, N.J.: Rutgers University Press.

Lakoff, George, and Mark Johnson. 1980. *Metaphors We Live By*. Chicago: University of Chicago Press.

Lather, Patti. 1986. "Research as Praxis." *Harvard Educational Review* 56:257–277.

———. 1991. *Getting Smart: Feminist Research and Pedagogy with/in the Postmodern*. New York: Routledge.

Lather, Patti, and Christine Smithies. 1996. *Troubling Angels: Women Living with HIV/AIDS*. Columbus, Ohio: Greyden Press.

Lawrence-Lightfoot, Sara. 1995. *I've Known Rivers: Lives of Loss and Liberation*. Reading, Mass.: Addison-Wesley.

Lehman, David. 1991. *Signs of the Times: Deconstruction and the Fall of Paul De Man*. New York: Poseidon Press.

Levine, Donald N. 1985. *The Flight from Ambiguity: Essays in Social and Cultural Theory*. Chicago: University of Chicago Press.

Liebow, Elliot. 1967. *Tally's Corner: A Study of Negro Streetcorner Men.* Boston: Little, Brown.

Lincoln, Yvonna S., and Norman K. Denzin. 1994. "The Fifth Moment: Out of the Past." In *Handbook of Qualitative Research,* edited by Norman K. Denzin and Yvonna S. Lincoln, 575 – 586. Thousand Oaks, Calif.: Sage.

Linden, R. Ruth. 1992. *Making Stories, Making Selves: Feminist Reflections on the Holocaust.* Columbus: Ohio State University.

Livingston, Debra. 1982. " 'Round and 'Round the Bramble Bush: From Legal Realism to Critical Legal Scholarship." *Harvard Law Review* 95 : 1650 – 1676.

Lockridge, Ernest. 1988. "Faithful in Her Fashion: Catherine Barkley, the Invisible Hemingway Heroine." *Journal of Narrative Technique* 18 : 170 – 178.

————. 1995. Unpublished letter to the *American Journal of Sociology.*

Long, Judy. 1987. "Telling Women's Lives: The New Sociobiography." Presented at the American Sociological Association Meetings, Chicago.

Lugones, Maria. 1987. "Playfulness, 'World'-Travelling, and Loving Perception." *Hypatia* 2:3 – 19.

Lyotard, Jean Paul. 1979. *The Postmodern Condition: A Report on Knowledge.* Translated by G. Bennington and B. Massumi. Minneapolis: University of Minnesota Press.

McCall, Michael, and Howard Becker. 1990. "Performance Science." *Social Problems* 37 (1): 117 – 132.

McClelland, D. C. 1961. *The Achieving Society.* New York: Free Press.

McCloskey, Donald N. 1985. *The Rhetoric of Economics.* Madison: University of Wisconsin Press.

Maines, David. 1989. "The Storied Nature of Diabetic Self-Help Groups." Presented to the Stone Symbolic Interaction Symposium, Arizona State University, Tempe.

Manning, Peter. 1991. "Strands in the Postmodernist Rope: Ethnographic Themes." *Studies in Symbolic Interaction* 12 : 3 – 28.

Marcus, George E., and Michael M. J. Fisher. 1986. *Anthropology as Cultural Critique: An Experimental Moment in the Human Sciences.* Chicago: University of Chicago Press.

Mills, C. Wright. 1959. *The Sociological Imagination.* New York: Oxford University Press.

Mischler, Elliot G. 1986. *Research Interviewing.* Cambridge: Harvard University Press.

Morris, Meaghan. 1988. *The Pirate's Fiancée: Feminism, Reading, and Postmodernism.* London: Verso.

Musolf, Gil. 1989. "The Negotiated Order: Bringing in Social Power, Social Structure, and Social Organization." Presented to the North Central Sociological Meetings, Akron, Ohio.

Mykhalovsky, Eric. 1996. "Reconsidering Table Talk: Critical Thoughts on the Relationship between Sociology, Autobiography, and Self-Indulgence." *Qualitative Sociology* 19 (1): 131 – 151.

Nelson, John S. 1987. "Stories of Science and Politics: Some Rhetorics of Political Research." In *The Rhetoric of the Human Sciences: Language and Argument in Scholarship and Human Affairs,* edited by John S. Nelson, Allan Megill, and Donald N. McCloskey, 198 – 219. Madison: University of Wisconsin Press.

NeSmith, G. 1989. "Women on the Edge of Time: Feminist Theory and the Horizons of

History." Presented to the Discourse, Rhetoric, and Culture Conference, University of Iowa, Iowa City, March.

Noyes, Russell. 1956. *English Romantic Poetry and Prose*. New York: Oxford University Press.

Orlandello, Angelo Ralph. 1992. "Boelen May Know Holland, Boelen May Know Barzini, but Boelen 'Doesn't Know Diddle' about the North End." *Journal of Contemporary Ethnography* 21:69–79.

Paget, Marianne. 1990. "Performing the Text." *Journal of Contemporary Ethnography* 19:136–153.

Patai, Daphne. 1988. "Constructing a Self: A Brazilian Life Story." *Feminist Studies* 14:143–660.

Pfohl, Stephen. 1992. *Death at the Parasite Cafe: Social Science (Fictions) and the Postmodern.* New York: St. Martin's Press.

Polkinghorne, Donald E. 1988. *Narrative Knowing and the Human Sciences*. Albany: State University of New York.

Pratt, Mary Louise. 1986. "Fieldwork in Common Places." In *Writing Culture: The Poetics and Politics of Ethnography*, edited by James Clifford and George E. Marcus. Berkeley: University of California Press.

Prattis, I., ed. 1985. *Reflections: The Anthropological Muse*. Washington: American Anthropological Association.

Quinney, Richard. 1991. *Journey to a Far Place*. Philadelphia: Temple University Press.

Reinharz, Shulamit. 1979. *On Becoming a Social Scientist*. San Francisco: Jossey-Bass.

Richardson, Laurel [Walum]. 1965. "Pure Mathematics Publications: 1939–1958." *American Mathematics Monthly* 73:192–195.

———. 1968. "Group Perception of Threat of Non-Members." *Sociometry* (now *Social Psychology*) 3:278–284.

———. 1970. "Sociologists as Signers: Some Characteristics of Protesters of Vietnam War Policy." *American Sociologist* 5:161–165.

———. 1974. "The Changing Door Ceremony: Some Notes on the Operation of Sex-Roles in Everyday Life." *Urban Life and Culture* [now *Journal of Contemporary Ethnography*] 2:506–515.

———. 1975. "The Art of Domination: An Analysis of Power in Paradise Lost." *Social Forces* 53:573–580.

———. 1977. *The Dynamics of Sex and Gender: A Sociological Perspective*. Chicago: Rand McNally.

———. 1981. *The Dynamics of Sex and Gender: A Sociological Perspective*. 2d ed. Boston: Houghton Mifflin.

———. 1985. *The New Other Woman: Contemporary Single Women in Affairs with Married Men*. New York: Free Press [Macmillan].

———. 1987. "Disseminating Research to Popular Audiences: The Book Tour." *Qualitative Sociology* 10:164–176.

———. 1988a. "The Collective Story: Postmodernism and the Writing of Sociology." Presidential address presented to the North Central Sociological Association. *Sociological Focus* 21:199–208.

———. 1988b. *The Dynamics of Sex and Gender: A Sociological Perspective*. 3d rev. ed. New York: Harper & Row.

———. 1988c. "Secrecy and Status: The Social Construction of Forbidden Relationships." *American Sociological Review* 53:209–219.

———. 1988d. "Sexual Freedom and Sexual Constraint: The Paradox of Single Woman and Married Man Liaisons." *Gender & Society* 2:368–384.

———. 1990a. "Narrative and Sociology." *Journal of Contemporary Ethnography* 20:126–135.

———. 1990b. *Writing Strategies: Reaching Diverse Audiences*. Thousand Oaks, Calif.: Sage.

———. 1991. "Speakers Whose Voices Matter: Toward a Feminist Postmodernist Sociological Praxis." *Studies in Symbolic Interaction* 12:29–38.

———. 1992a. "The Consequences of Poetic Representation: Writing the Other, Rewriting the Self." In *Investigating Subjectivity: Research on Lived Experience*, edited by Carolyn Ellis and Michael G. Flaherty, 125–140. Thousand Oaks, Calif.: Sage.

———. 1992b. "The Poetic Representation of Lives: Writing a Postmodern Sociology." *Studies in Symbolic Interaction* 13:19–29.

———. 1992c. "Resisting Resistance Narratives: A Representation for Communication." *Studies in Symbolic Interaction* 13:77–82.

———. 1992d. "Trash on the Corner: Ethics and Ethnography." *Journal of Contemporary Ethnography* 21:103–119.

———. 1992e. "Hide-and-Seek." *Sociological Theory* 10 (2): 252–257.

———. 1993a. "Interrupting Discursive Spaces." *Studies in Symbolic Interaction* 14:77–83.

———. 1993b. "Poetics, Dramatics, and Transgressive Validity: The Case of the Skipped Line." *Sociological Quarterly* 35:695–710.

———. 1994. "Glossing *The Werald*." *Studies in Symbolic Interaction* 14:63–69.

Richardson, Laurel, and Ernest Lockridge. 1991. "The Sea Monster: An Ethnographic Drama and Comment on Ethnographic Fiction." *Symbolic Interaction*: 335–341.

Richardson, Laurel, and Verta Taylor. 1993. 3d ed. *Feminist Frontiers: Rethinking Sex, Gender, and Society*. New York: McGraw-Hill.

Richardson, Laurel, Verta Taylor, and Nancy Whittier. 1997. 4th ed. *Feminist Frontiers*. New York: McGraw Hill.

Ricoeur, Paul. 1984–1986. *Time and Narrative*, 2 vols. Translated by K. MacLaughlin and D. Pellauer. Chicago: University of Chicago Press.

Riley, Denise. 1988. *"Am I That Name?": Feminism and the Category of "Women" in History*. Minneapolis: University of Minnesota Press.

Rogers, Mary F. 1992. "Teaching, Theorizing, Storytelling: Postmodern Rhetoric and Modern Dreams." *Sociological Theory* 10:231–240.

Ronai, Carol Rambo. 1992. "The Reflexive Self through Narrative: A Night in the Life of an Erotic Dancer/Researcher." In *Investigating Subjectivity: Research on Lived Experience*, edited by Carolyn Ellis and Michael G. Flaherty, 102–124. Thousand Oaks, Calif.: Sage.

Rorty, Richard. 1979. *Philosophy and the Mirror of Nature*. Princeton: Princeton University Press.

———. 1987. "Science as Solidarity." In *The Rhetoric of the Human Sciences: Language and*

Argument in Scholarship and Human Affairs, edited by John S. Nelson, Alan Megill, and Donald S. McCloskey. Madison: University of Wisconsin Press.

Rose, Edward. 1992. *The Werald.* Boulder, Colo.: Waiting Room Press.

Roth, Peter. 1989. "How Narratives Explain." Presented to the University of Iowa Faculty Rhetoric Seminar, Iowa City.

Rubin, Lillian B. 1976. *Worlds of Pain: Life in the Working-Class Family.* New York: Basic Books.

St. Pierre, Elizabeth Adams. 1995. "Arts of Existence: The Construction of Subjectivity in Older White Southern Women." Ph.D. diss., Ohio State University.

Schneider, Joseph. 1991. "Troubles with Textual Authority in Sociology." *Symbolic Interaction* 14:295–320.

Schutz, Alfred. 1962. *Collected Papers.* The Hague: Nijhoff.

Schwalbe, Michael. 1995. "The Responsibilities of Sociological Poets." *Qualitative Sociology* 18:393–412.

Scott, Joan. 1988. "Deconstructing Equality-versus-Difference: Or, the Uses of Poststructuralist Theory for Feminism." *Feminist Studies* 14:33–50.

Seidman, Stephen. 1991. "The End of Sociological Theory." *Sociological Theory* 9:131–146.

Shapiro, Michael. 1985–1986. "Metaphor in the Philosophy of the Social Sciences." *Cultural Critique* 2 (Winter): 191–214.

Shelten, Allen. 1995. "The Man at the End of the Machine." *Symbolic Interaction* 18:505–518.

Simons, Herbert W. 1990. *Rhetoric in the Human Sciences.* London: Sage.

Slobin, Kathleen. 1995. "Fieldwork and Subjectivity: On the Ritualization of Seeing a Burned Child." *Symbolic Interaction* 18:487–504.

Stack, Carol B. 1974. *All Our Kin: Strategies for Survival in a Black Community.* New York: Harper & Row.

Statham, Anne, Laurel Richardson, and Judith A. Cook. 1991. *Gender and University Teaching: A Negotiated Difference.* Albany: State University of New York Press.

Steedman, Kay. 1986. *Landscape for a Good Woman: A Story of Two Lives.* New Brunswick, N.J.: Rutgers University Press.

Stewart, John O. 1989. *Drinkers, Drummers, and Decent Folk: Ethnographic Narratives of Village Trinidad.* Albany: State University of New York Press.

Strathern, Marilyn. 1987. "Out of Context: The Persuasive Fictions of Anthropology." *Current Anthropology* 28:251–270.

Targ, Dena B. 1989. "Feminist Family Sociology: Some Reflections." Presidential address presented to the North Central Sociological Association Meetings, Akron, Ohio.

Tedlock, Dennis. 1983. *The Spoken Word and the Work of Interpretation.* Philadelphia: University of Pennsylvania Press.

Trinh, T. Minh-ha. 1989. *Woman, Native, Other: Writing Postcoloniality and Feminism.* Bloomington: Indiana University Press.

Turner, Victor, and Edward M. Bruner, eds. 1986. *The Anthropology of Experience.* Champagne: University of Illinois Press.

Ueland, Brenda. [1938] 1987. *If You Want to Write.* St. Paul: Graywolf Press.

Ulmer, Gregory. 1989. *Teletheory: Grammatology in the Age of Video*. New York: Routledge.

Van Maanen, John. 1988. *Tales of the Field: On Writing Ethnography*. Chicago: University of Chicago Press.

———, ed. 1995. *Representation in Ethnography*. Thousand Oaks, Calif.: Sage.

Visweswaran, Kamala. 1994. *Fictions of Feminist Ethnography*. Minneapolis: University of Minnesota Press.

Walkerdine, Valerie. 1990. *Schoolgirl Fictions*. London: Verso.

Weedon, Chris. 1987. *Feminist Practice and Poststructuralist Theory*. Oxford, England: Basil Blackwell.

Whyte, William Foote. [1943] 1981. *Street Corner Society: The Social Structure of an Italian Slum*. Chicago: University of Chicago Press.

———. 1992. "In Defense of *Street Corner Society*." *Journal of Contemporary Ethnography* 21:52–68.

———. 1996. "Qualitative Sociology and Deconstructionism." *Qualitative Inquiry* 2 (2): 220–226.

Williams, Patricia J. 1991. *The Alchemy of Race and Rights: Diary of a Law Professor*. Cambridge: Harvard University Press.

Wolf, Margery. 1992. *A Thrice-Told Tale: Feminism, Postmodernism, and Ethnographic Responsibility*. Stanford: Stanford University Press.

Wordsworth, William. 1956. "Preface to the Lyrical Ballads." In *English Romantic Poetry and Prose*, edited by Russell Noyes, 357–367. New York: Oxford University Press.

Young, T. R. 1989. "Postmodern Sociology." Presented to the Midwest Sociological Society, Chicago. (Unpublished manuscripts 138a and 138b, Red Feather Institute.)

Zola, Emile. [1880] 1965. "The Novel as Social Science." In *The Modern Tradition: Backgrounds of Modern Literature*, edited by Richard Ellman and Charles Feidelson Jr., 270–289. New York: Oxford University Press.

INDEXES

crystallizing, 92, 135–136
cultural story, 2, 32. *See also* story line

deconstructionism, 46, 52–53, 103, 112
Department of Sociology, *see* sociology:
  department of
discourse analysis, 46, 78, 181; civic,
  33–34; scientific, 37–43; sociological,
  185–186. *See also* literary writing; science: writing of; text
divorce: author's, 229; and Louisa May,
  131–135

education: author's, 21, 188–189, 226–
  227, 230–231, 232; College of, symposium, 126–127; graduate, 99–101,
  126, 199, 208–213; and life writing,
  119, 123; and performance, 196; as
  safe space, 186
emotion work, in research, 165, 167
ethics: and family, 226; and feminism,
  56–58, 124–125; and field research,
  102–116, 157, 166; and poetic representation, 146; and writing, 21, 68,
  116–118, 166
ethnographic drama, 63–68, 70–72,
  75–80, 154–168, 197–208; fact/
  fiction, 64–67, 108–110. *See also* fiction writing; science: writing of
ethnography: authority in, 18, 46, 108;
  ethics in, 102–115; spiritually metaphored, 185–186; writing practices of,
  52, 90–91, 108–109. *See also* alternative representation
experimental writing, 3, 18, 91–93. *See
  also* alternative representation; ethnographic drama; Index to Poems

family, author's, ix, 50, 82, 85, 168–169;
  history of, 236–237; relationships
  within, 217–238; roles in drama, 157.
  See also Phillips; Richardson; Walum in
  Index of Names
father (author's), *see* Richardson, Tyrrell
  Alexander in Index of Names

feminism: failure of, 106; metanarrative
  of, 55–57; movement, 55–59, 122;
  practices of, 48–49, 164–166. *See also*
  Feminist-Postmodernism Study Group;
  feminist-poststructuralism
Feminist-Postmodernism Study Group
  (PMS): community building through,
  56, 81, 153; formation of, 36–37;
  members, x; readings, 69
feminist-poststructuralism, 37, 48–49,
  52–59, 154–168
fiction writing: and fact/fiction debates,
  64–67, 108–110; history of, 64, 90;
  techniques, 70–71, 109–110
Florida, 232, 234–235
formats, 42–43
found poems, examples of, 78, 206
Freudianism, 76, 159, 219

gender studies, 11, 94–95
genre bending, *see* alternative representation
graduate education, *see* education:
  graduate

Holocaust, *see* Judaism

identity, *see* subjectivity
illegitimacy, 136–137, 194–195. *See also*
  unwed mothers
interview, *see* qualitative methods

Judaism, 217–218, 220–221, 224–225,
  228–229

Lacanian father, 166
Lake Geneva, Wis., 189, 217–219, 223,
  227, 237–238
language, 39–49, 89
Las Cruces, N.M., cover illustration, 222
life-story, *see* autobiography; story line;
  writing-stories
literary writing, 14–16, 89–90, 155. *See
  also* fiction writing
logic of inquiry, 41

"Lundberg," 201, 204–207
lyric poetry, examples of, 175–183,
202–204

Marxism, 76, 81, 199
metanarrative, 28, 55–59, 76
metaphor: guiding, 17; in social science,
43–46; voice as, 122
methods, *see* ethnography; qualitative
methods
mother, author's, *see* Richardson, Rose
Foreman in Index of Names
mother, unwed, *see* illegitimacy; unwed
mother
multiculturalism, 126, 127, 152, 210–212

narrative: defined, 27–29; mode of reasoning, 28; resistance, 75–80; poems,
examples of, 131–135, 235–236; poetry, discussion of, 181–182; and social change, 17, 120–121; in sociology,
26–37; and time, 29–33; voice in, 18,
37, 58–59. *See also* autobiography;
metanarrative; writing-stories

Olivet Camp, *see* Lake Geneva
oral/written texts, dispute, 158–163. *See
also* text
"Other Woman, the," 18–21, 229–230,
236

Park of Roses, xii, 65, 117, 232
participant-observation, *see* qualitative
methods
pedagogy, *see* education
performance: attendance at, 228; discussion of, 82, 169–170, 188, 196, 231;
pieces, 75–80, 157–163, 175–179,
197–207
plot, *see* story line
PMS, *see* Feminist-Postmodernism Study
Group
poetic representation: examples of, 78,
131–135, 175–179, 202–204, 208,
235–236; as method, 139–145, 199,

202, 205–208; responses to, 150–151,
154–168. *See also* Index to Poems
point of view, 18, 73
postmodernism: and the crisis of representation, 13–14; and qualitative writing, 2, 87–88, 119; and social theory,
120–123; and sociology, 52–59. *See
also* feminist-poststructuralism
positioning: as feminist speaker, 119,
120–123, 125–126; as method,
136–157
power, *see* authority; writing
pragmatism, 120–121
prose, as trope, 139–145, 155

qualitative methods, 87–88; crystallization, 92, 135–136; data collection, 26;
emotion work in, 165; ethics in, 111–
115; field work, 102–118, 156–158;
interviews, 140–141, 149–150, 152;
member checks, 181; poststructuralist,
136, 146; reliability of, 159; transcripts,
140–141; triangulation, 92; validity
of, 150, 156–158, 167–168, 181–183;
writing of, 26, 66–67, 165–166. *See
also* ethnography; voice

realism, 90
reasoning, modes of, 28
reflexivity, 2, 46, 67, 107–108; and
Derrida, 143, 166
representation, 2, 13–14, 39–49, 57–58.
See also alternative representation;
writing
resistance: and alternative sites, 153; and
community building, 36–37, 56, 81;
narratives, 75–80; poem, 78
responsive reading, 75–80
rhetoric of inquiry, 39–43, 47

St. Petersburg Beach, 63, 67, 70
science: conventions of, 23, 147, 208; and
validity, 18, 165–166; writing of,
14–16, 39–49, 89–90

self, *see* autobiography; subjectivity; writing-stories

Shenandoah, 151–152, 170, 186

Society for the Study of Symbolic Interaction (SSSI), conferences, 23, 24, 68, 75, 80, 138, 154, 156, 184, 199–200

space: alternative sites, 36–37, 56, 81, 153; safe, 100, 117–118; sacred, 185–187

sociobiography, *see* autobiography

sociological imagination, 1, 5, 14, 122

sociology: department of, 9–12, 37–38, 126, 169; discipline of, 1–3; discourses in, 200–201, 205–207; future of, 52–59; and postmodernism, 52–59; meta-narrative of, 58–59; of science, writing practices of, 1–6, 12, 20, 39–49, 165–166

speaking position, *see* positioning; subjectivity

spirituality, 83, 85, 169, 184–187, 218; enacted, 65–80; parents', 225–227

SSSI, *see* Society for the Study of Symbolic Interaction

Stone Symposia, 23–24, 63, 68, 168

stories, *see* narrative

story line: academic, 2, 136–137, 169; as literary technique, 17, 58, 109–110; Louisa May's, 136; Whyte's, 106–107, 115. *See also* writing-stories

Street Corner Society (Whyte), 101, 102–118

subjectivity, 2, 48–49, 145, 190; and language, 89, 182; and Louisa May, 147–149, 151–153, 164; and writing, 67, 147–148, 151–153, 166; reconstruction of, 222–238. *See also* writing-stories

teaching, *see* education

temporality, 29–33

text: authority of, 68, 72, 106–107, 155; oral/written, 157

theater: Compass Players, 195; downtown Chicago, 227; Goodman Theater,

189–190; University Theater, 193–196. *See also* performance

theory: grand, loss of, 13; social, deconstructed, 121–122

transcript, *see* poetic representation; qualitative methods

triangulation, 92

university, *see* academia; community building; sociology: department of

University of Chicago, *see* Chicago: University of

University of Colorado, *see* Colorado, University of

unwed mothers: in family, 230; in "Lord Byron's Love Letter," 194; in "Louisa May's Story of Her Life," 131–135; and phallocentrism, 164–166

validity: oral/written, 156, 157–158; in poetic representation, 150, 181–183; transgressive, 167–168

voice: co-authored, 80; control, as trope, 110; feminist speaking, 52–59, 193; masculine, 72–73, 164–166; "others" in text, 209–213; postmodernist, 89, 93

woman's movement, *see* feminism

writing: ethics in, 101, 102–115, 186; formats, 84–95; history of, 89–90; method of discovery, 84–95

writing-stories: defined, 3, 5, 74; examples of, 9–12, 23–26, 36–39, 50–52, 68–75, 80–86, 99–102, 116–120, 123–127, 138–139, 145–147, 168–170, 173–174, 183–187, 188–197, 208–213

INDEX OF NAMES

Adler, Patti and Peter, xi, 104, 179

Agger, Ben, xi, 119; and social science writing, 39, 58, 90, 93, 139

Alexander, Jeffrey C., 54, 117

Altheide, David, 25, 80
Ault, Amber, x, 100

Balzac, Honoré de, 90
Barthes, Roland, 27
Baudrillard, Jean Paul, 52
Bazerman, Charles, 42
Becker, Howard S., 14, 92
Bentham, Jeremy, 15
Bertaux-Wieme, Isabelle, 30
Bochner, Arthur P., xi, 92, 94
Boelen, W. A. Marianne, 101, 103–106,
    116, 125
Bogard, William, 123–124
Borroff, M., 180
Brady, Ivan, 92
Brodkey, Linda, 90
Brown, Richard H., xi, 26, 58, 139, 148
Bruner, Edward M., 17
Bruner, Jerome, 28
Brydges, Edgerton, 75
Butler, Sandra, 92

Campbell, John Angus, 42
Capone, Al, 232–233
Carey, James W., 75, 79–80, 81, 139
Cheal, David, 54
Clifford, James, 14, 15, 16, 18
Clough, Patricia Ticento, xi, 80, 90,
    156–163, 169
Colomy, Paul, 54
Cook, Judith A., x, 14, 22, 92, 192
Condorcet, Marquis de, 16
Corroto, Carla, x, 100
Crawford, Marion Ayton, 90

Darwin, Charles, 42
Davies, Bronwyn, xi, 53
De Certeau, Michel, 15
Deegan, Mary Jo, 32
Denzin, Norman K., ix, 140, 143, 169; as
    character in ethnographic drama,
    158–163, 199; as editor, 84, 85, 94; as
    ethnographer, 33, 92, 94, 181; as sym-

posium organizer, 24, 50, 80, 81, 138,
    139, 156
Derrida, Jacques, 44, 53, 140, 143, 199
Defoe, Daniel, 182, 227, 233
DeVault, Marjorie L., 139
Diamond, Stanley, 92
Diamond, Timothy, 53, 100
DiIorio, Judi, 14, 53, 100
"Doc" (in *Street Corner Society*), 110–115,
    116
Dorst, John D., 92
Durkheim, Emile, 16

Eagleton, Terry, 124
Eastman, P. D., 212–213
Edmondson, Ricca, 26, 45
Eliot, T. S., 1
Ellis, Carolyn, ix; as ethnographer, 31, 53,
    92, 165, 181; and service to the disci-
    pline, 80, 94, 145, 165
Epstein, Jon, 92
Erikson, Erik H., 15
Erikson, Kai T., 91, 182

Fenner, Gloria, 23
Ferraro, Kathleen, 33
Fine, Michelle, 92
Fisher, Michael M. J., 13, 18
Fisher, W. R., 26
Fiske, Donald W., 13, 14
Flaherty, Michael G., xi, 145, 165, 181
Flax, Jane, 53
Fonow, Mary Margaret, x, 14, 100
Fontana, Andrea, xi, 80, 94
Forster, E. M., 28, 109
Foucault, Michel, 58, 212
Franco, Sam, *see* Orlandello, Angelo
    Ralph
Franklin, Clyde W., 21
Fraser, Nancy, 55, 56, 57
Frye, Northrop, 40

Gammell, Linda, 92
Ganson, Harriet, 100
Geertz, Clifford, 13, 92

INDEX TO POEMS

Laurel Richardson is professor of sociology, visiting professor of cultural studies in the School of Educational Policy and Leadership, and graduate faculty of women's studies at The Ohio State University. She is the author of five previous books, including *Writing Strategies* (Sage), *Gender and University Teaching* (SUNY), *The New Other Woman* (Free Press), and *Feminist Frontiers* (McGraw-Hill), and many articles. She is the mother of two grown sons and lives in Worthington, Ohio, with her husband, Ernest Lockridge.

Printed in the United States
133587LV00005B/70/A

9 780813 523798